THE POLITICAL ECONOMY OF ECONOMIC POLICIES

The Political Economy of Economic Policies

Edited by

Philip Arestis
Professor of Economics
University of East London

and

Malcolm Sawyer
Professor of Economics
University of Leeds

338.9
P7697

First published in Great Britain 1998 by
MACMILLAN PRESS LTD
Houndmills, Basingstoke, Hampshire RG21 6XS and London
Companies and representatives throughout the world

A catalogue record for this book is available from the British Library.

ISBN 0–333–71676–0

First published in the United States of America 1998 by
ST. MARTIN'S PRESS, INC.,
Scholarly and Reference Division,
175 Fifth Avenue, New York, N.Y. 10010

ISBN 0–312–21434–0

Library of Congress Cataloging-in-Publication Data
The political economy of economic policies / edited by Philip Arestis
and Malcolm Sawyer.
p. cm.
Includes bibliographical references and index.
ISBN 0–312–21434–0
1. Economic policy.   I. Arestis, Philip, 1941–   . II. Sawyer,
Malcolm C.
HD87.P639   1998
338.9—DC21   98–5589
                                                          CIP

© International Papers in Political Economy 1998

Chapters 1–5 of this volume previously appeared as papers in *International Papers in Political Economy*: Chapter 1 in vol. 3 (1996) no. 2; Chapter 2 in vol. 2 (1995) no. 1; Chapter 3 in vol. 1 (1996) no. 3; Chapter 4 in vol. 2 (1995) no. 3; Chapter 5 in vol. 3 (1996) no. 1.

This book is printed on paper suitable for recycling and made from fully managed and sustained forest sources.

10   9   8   7   6   5   4   3   2   1
07   06   05   04   03   02   01   00   99   98

Printed in Great Britain by
The Ipswich Book Company Ltd
Ipswich, Suffolk

JK

Contents

v

Notes on the Contributors

Philip Arestis is Professor of Economics at the University of East London. He has also taught at the Universities of Surrey and Cambridge (Department of Extra-Mural Studies) and Greenwich University (where he was Head of Economics Division). He was editor of the *British Review of Economic Issues* and joint editor of the *Thames Papers in Political Economy*, and is joint editor of the *International Papers in Political Economy*. He has been on the editorial board of a number of journals and an elected member of the Council of the Royal Economic Society. His publications include: his co-authored *Introducing Macroeconomic Modelling: an Econometric Study of the United Kingdom* (1982); his edited *Post-Keynesian Monetary Economics: New Approaches to Financial Modelling* (1988); his co-edited *Post-Keynesian Economic Theory: A Challenge to Neo-Classical Economics* (1984), *The Biographical Dictionary of Dissenting Economists* (1992), *The Elgar Companion to Radical Political Economy* (1994), *Keynes, Money and the Open Economy: Essays in Honour of Paul Davidson, Volume One* (1996), *Employment, Economic Growth and the Tyranny of the Market: Essays in Honour of Paul Davidson, Volume Two* (1996), *Method, Theory and Policy in Keynes: Essays in Honour of Paul Davidson, Volume Three* (1998), *Capital Controversy, Post-Keynesian Economics and the History of Economics: Essays in Honour of Geoff Harcourt, Volume One* (1997), *Markets, Unemployment and Economic Policy: Essays in Honour of Geoff Harcourt, Volume Two* (1997); also his two books *The Post-Keynesian Approach to Economics: An Alternative Analysis of Economic Theory and Policy* (1992), and *Money, Pricing, Distribution and Economic Integration* (1997). He has published widely in journals and books in post Keynesian economics, macroeconomics, monetary economics and applied econometrics.

George DeMartino is Assistant Professor of Economics at the Graduate School of International Studies, University of Denver. He has also taught at Dickinson College. He has served as a member of the editorial board of *Rethinking Marxism*. He has published extensively in the area of Political Economy in books and journals which include *International Papers in Political Economy*, *International Review* *of Applied Economics, Social Text, New Political Science, Review of Radical Political Economics, Journal of Economic Issues, Politics and Society, Rethinking Marxism.*

Ilene Grabel is Assistant Professor of International Finance at the Graduate School of International Studies, University of Denver. She has also taught at Smith College. She has published essays in books and in the journals *International Review of Applied Economics, World Development, International Papers in Political Economy, Journal of Development Studies, Journal of Economic Issues,* and the *Review of Political Economics*.

Robert Pollin is Professor of Economics at the University of California-Riverside, specializing in macroeconomics, money and finance and political economy. His publications include the monograph, *Deeper in Debt: The Changing Financial Conditions of U.S. Households* (Economic Policy Institute) and the edited-volumes *Transforming the U.S. Financial System: Equity and Efficiency for the 21st Century, New Perspectives in Monetary Macroeconomics: Explorations in the Tradition of Hyman P. Minsky* and *The Macroeconomics of Saving, Finance and Investment.* He has also written widely for many academic and non-academic publications. He has worked with the Joint Economic Committee of the US Congress, the United Nations Development Program and the Competitiveness Policy Council of the US government and was the Economic Spokesperson for the 1992 Presidential Campaign of Governor Jerry Brown. He was on the National Steering Committee of the Union for Radical Political Economics and is currently on the editorial boards of *International Review of Applied Economics* and *Dollars and Sense Magazine.*

Malcolm Sawyer is Professor of Economics at the University of Leeds and formerly Professor of Economics at the University of York. He is the author of several books including *Macroeconomics in Question* (1982), *The Economics of Michał Kalecki* (1982, 1985), *The Challenge of Radical Political Economy* (1989) and *Unemployment, Imperfect Competition and Macroeconomics* (1995). He is the managing editor of *International Review of Applied Economics,* joint editor of the recently launched *International Papers in Political Economy,* and editor of the series *New Directions in Modern Economics,* published by Edward Elgar. He has recently co-edited *The Biographical Dictionary of Dissenting Economists* and *The Elgar*

Companion to Radical Political Economy. He has published widely in journals and books in the areas of industrial economics, macroeconomics and political economy. His current research interests include the theory of industrial policy and the conceptualization of competition and markets in economic theory, the causes and cures for unemployment, as well as continuing to work on Post-Keynesian macroeconomics.

Ajit Singh graduated from Punjab University and obtained his PhD at the University of California, Berkeley. He has been teaching economics at Cambridge University since 1965. He is currently Fellow and Director of Studies in Economics at Queen's College, University of Cambridge. Since 1987, he has also held the Dr William M. Scholl Visiting Chair in the Department of Economics at the University of Notre Dame in the US. He has been a senior economic advisor to the governments of Mexico and Tanzania and a consultant to various UN developmental organizations. He is the author of *Takeovers: Their Relevance to the Stockmarket and the Theory of the Firm* and co-author of *Growth, Profitability and Valuations*. He has also published extensively in academic economic journals. His most recent books are *Corporate Financial Structures in Developing Countries* (with J. Hamid, 1992), *Economic Crisis and Third-World Agriculture* (co-edited with M. Tabatabai, 1993) and *The State, Markets and Development* (co-edited with A. Dutt and K. Kim, 1994). His essay 'How do developing country corporations finance their growth?' was awarded a Bronze medal in the Amex Awards Competition in 1994.

L. Randall Wray is Professor of Economics, Bard College, and Senior Research Fellow, Jerome Levy Economics Institute. He is President of the Association for Institutional Thought and a member of the Board of Directors of the Association for Evolutionary Economics. His publications include his book *Money and Credit in Capitalist Economies: The Endogenous Money Approach* (1990); and contributions in books and journals which include *Cambridge Journal of Economics, Challenge, International Papers in Political Economy, Journal of Post Keynesian Economics, Monnaie et Production, International Review of Applied Economics, Journal of Economic Issues, Review of Political Economics*.

Introduction

Philip Arestis and Malcolm Sawyer

The approach of the beginning of a new century and indeed a new millennium (whether dated as 2000 or 2001) leads inevitably to crystal-ball gazing into the future and to a consideration of the past century, and this will no doubt apply as much to economic matters as to others. But there are other more substantial reasons for considering and reconsidering economic policies in light of experience for there have clearly been major developments in the past two decades or so which will cast their shadows on to the next century. The first quarter century of the post-war era was largely characterized (at least among the OECD countries) by economic growth, high levels of employment alongside government activism and a widely held belief in the beneficial powers of government. The second quarter century in contrast has been characterized by much lower rates of growth in the OECD countries (though with rapid growth in the Newly Industrialized Countries), persistent and in the main rising levels of unemployment, and a general decline of support for the role of government. 'Let the market decide' has become a powerful slogan in this latter period, and in many countries there has been a rolling back of state activity through privatization and deregulation (though little, if any, reduction in the scale of public expenditure and taxation relative to GDP). Whether the scale of government involvement in industrialized economies has actually declined in a moot point, for alongside privatization has gone regulation, and policies of deregulation (for example, US airlines) can be countered by other policies of regulation (for example, UK financial sector) (and there are some very substantial difficulties in measuring the scale of government involvement other than by simple and often misleading indicators such as degree of public ownership).[1] But it would be undeniable that the intellectual and policy climate has shifted from one which saw an active role for government in economic and social matters towards a generally more sceptical view of the role of government.

In addition to a shift in the intellectual climate, there have been

1

some major changes in the industrialized economies which are often seen as changing the possibilities for government action. Two developments in the world economy between the first and the second post-war quarter-centuries stand out in this regard. First, the power and influence of financial markets have increased substantially. The financial flows across the foreign exchanges have increased dramatically in size (for some figures see Chapter 6 below), making government control of the level of the exchange rate very much more difficult than hitherto (especially compared with the era of the Bretton Woods system). Whereas the first quarter-century was the era of fixed exchange rates, the second quarter-century has been the era of floating exchange rates (though there have been attempts, for example the European Monetary System, to restore a measure of fixed exchange rates). The fixed exchange rate regime was supported and reinforced by controls over capital flows, whereas the floating exchange rate regime has seen financial liberalization and the lifting of most exchange controls. The financial markets now set the exchange rate whereas during the post-war boom (that is until the early 1970s) it was set by governments. Second, the process of globalization has continued apace. While there are debates over the extent of the globalization and specifically how much greater it is now than it was in the early part of the century under the gold standard (see, for example, Hirst and Thompson, 1996), there is little doubt that the degree of globalization increased from the first to the second post-war quarter-century. This is reflected not only in the increased financial flows across the foreign exchanges and higher levels of foreign direct investment, but also in the degree of integration between financial markets in different countries and in the organization of production on a transnational basis. These changes (alongside many others) have arguably cast doubts on the ability of national governments to pursue independent and effective economic policies, particularly in the area of macroeconomic fiscal and monetary policies. The argument is quite simple: globalization severely limits the degree to which one national economy can diverge from another in terms of key economic variables such as the level of unit labour costs, the rate of profit and the rate of interest. As such, it generates pressures against any policy measures (ranging from minimum wages through to prohibition of child labour) which appear to raise labour costs in one country relative to those prevailing elsewhere. In any case, financial markets disapprove of policies which they consider unsustainable (and/or which favour objectives such as low inflation over others such as low unemployment), and would punish governments which sought to adopt reflationary policies.[2] The essays in this volume were first published as separate issues of the *International Papers in Political Economy*, which we have edited since their launch in 1993. We have chosen these essays for the contribution which they make to the construction of economic policies relevant to the twenty-first century.[3] They have not been written to any common prescription, and there are no doubt some conflicts between the analyses and policy implications of the different essays presented here. There are, though, clear common threads, some of which are well summarized by the following:

> The task today is to meet the challenges of the coming millennium without forgetting the valuable lessons of the past, lessons that include: (1) capitalism comes in many varieties; (2) institutions established through public policy play a vital role in determining the performance of capitalism; and (3) laissez-faire is a prescription for economic disaster. (Minsky and Whalen, 1997, p. 161)

These three threads are closely related to the political economy tradition within which these essays have been written, and it may be useful to elaborate briefly on them.[4] It is perhaps self-evident that the capitalism of say Japan or Sweden is substantially different from the capitalism of say the United States or of the United Kingdom. The institutional arrangements are clearly different and that is the case whether institutions are seen in terms of norms and standards of behaviour or in terms of organizations. The roles of trade unions, of large corporations, of the financial sector and the relations between the public sector and the private sector are some of the more notable examples of the different institutional arrangements (see the essay below by Pollin for an indication of some differences in the financial sectors). While the existence of institutional differences may seem self-evident, that perspective stands in some contrast to the implicit view developed within the neoclassical analysis. In that analysis, there is a single underlying representation of a market economy, namely that embedded in the general equilibrium analysis which could be said to be institution-free (though in a broader context the market would be viewed as an institution, and the general equilibrium analysis draws in its formal representation on the institution of an auctioneer: Sawyer, 1992).

There has been the development of the so-called new institutional economics (for example, Williamson, 1985) seen by its proponents as lying within the neo-classical family, and this has largely retained the notion of an optimal set of institutional arrangements (on the basis of efficiency considerations). While the political economy approach stresses that institutional arrangements are relevant for economic performance, it does not have any belief that optimal institutional arrangements will necessarily emerge (and indeed would doubt that there is any single set of optimal arrangements). Though there are these differences, it may be possible to say that there are better capitalisms or worse capitalisms, whether we wish to set criteria in terms of economic performance or in terms of other features of those capitalisms. Or, we may wish to point to features of a capitalism which we feel to be good or bad, which can be summarised in the notion that there are 'high roads' and 'low roads' which capitalist economies can take (for example, Singh, 1997; Gordon, 1996), where the 'high road' would involve the development of high skill levels among the workers, rewarded by appropriately high wages, with an involved and participatory work force, whereas the 'low road' would be involve a low-skill work force with work discipline enforced by a combination of the threat of unemployment and close supervision. The discussion of good and bad features of different capitalism is, of course, frequently undertaken, and the features of the Japanese economy which are seem as responsible for the rapid growth of that economy have, for example, been much discussed. This is not to say that features of one economy can be readily transplanted into another, and specifically institutional arrangements are particularly difficult to transfer especially where norms of behaviour are involved.

The institutions of the public sector are important, according to the political economy approach, in numerous ways (though how beneficial the operations of those institutions are, of course, varies enormously). This is not just a matter that the public sector is usually a major provider of key services such as education and health, or that the central bank underpins the financial system. It is also that the public sector can play a key role in the moulding the institutions of the private sector. It is self-evident that the legal framework will influence institutions and norms of behaviour, but there can be a fuller range of government activities which be of influence (for example, the nature of regulation of the financial sector will have a significant influence on the structure of that sector).

There are many differences between the neo-classical approach and the political economy one (see, for example, Sawyer, 1989, ch. 1). Many of these differences are reflected in the different visions of the workings of markets and the nature of a market economy, and those differences are in turn reflected in quite different approaches to economic policy and the appropriate roles of the market and of the state. The neoclassical approach envisages that a market economy reaches (or could provided that imperfections which restrain free competition were removed) a position of general equilibrium (based on perfect competition) in which there was productive and allocative efficiency and in which there was full employment of labour and of capital equipment. Specifically, full employment would be the norm, and departures from full employment are to be explained either in terms of 'imperfections' (such as trade unions, oligopolies) or in terms of frictions and speeds of adjustment. Although there have been attempts to explain cyclical behaviour in terms of shifting equilibrium (for example, in the real business cycle literature; see, for example, Prescott, 1986), it remains the case that there is little hint of major fluctuations in economic activity and of economic crises. In contrast, the political economy approach sees unemployment as the norm and it is the infrequent achievement of full employment that has to be explained. Unemployment arises for many reasons, but some major ones include the failure of a market economy to generate sufficient aggregate demand to underpin full employment, the inflationary pressures which may arise at full employment, and the 'need' for unemployment as a disciplinary device for generating work commitment' (for further discussion see Sawyer, 1995a, b, c). Economic cycles, arising from variations in aggregate demand, are a major element of economic experience in the political economy approach. The neo-classical approach suggests a perfectibility of markets, with government policy directed towards a combination of removing so-called market imperfections and correcting market failures. In contrast, the political economy approach would regard the search for the perfect market to be futile.

A glance at the list of contents will quickly reveal that the essays are, to a greater or lesser extent, concerned with the influence of the financial sector on the level of real activity and the dangers which an unregulated and powerful financial sector poses. Randall Wray, for example, explores the effects of the deregulation of the savings and loans institutions in the United States. In orthodox writing on the financial sector, two themes can be readily identified (which are not necessarily in conflict). First, the monetary (financial) side of the economy is largely passive with respect to real variables (such as output, employment) and while it may serve to set nominal variables (notably the price level and the rate of inflation) it does not determine real variables. This is particularly evident in the classical dichotomy under which (in a general equilibrium framework) relative prices are determined by real factors (reflected in demand and supply functions) and the price level is set by the money supply (given the overall level of economic activity which is presumed to be at the full employment level). This 'classical' dichotomy has, in effect, lain at the heart of the orthodoxy which has developed under which control of the money supply is seen as the route to controlling inflation, and supply-side measures (which is, in this context, a euphemism for liberalization and deregulation) are to be used to bring the economy closer to the perfectly competitive ideal. Specifically controlling inflation through monetary constraint is viewed as having little, if any, adverse effects on the real side of the economy (since there is a separation between the real and the monetary sectors), and this view has been a powerful ingredient in the arguments advanced for an independent central bank).[5] Second, the regulation of the financial sector by government is likely to be harmful, and hence deregulation and liberalization of the financial sector brings benefits. The paper by Ilene Grabel in this volume is particularly critical of this line of argument as applied to Third World economies (which have been particularly subject to financial liberalization in the past 15 years or so), and one of us has written extensively elsewhere on these matters – see, for example, Arestis and Demetriades (1997).

The underlying view, to which the essays in this volume would generally subscribe, stands in some contrast to that orthodox perspective. The functioning of the financial sector has substantial effects on the real side of the economy. The financial sector influences, *inter alia*, the direction in which funds are allocated between sectors (for example, perhaps favouring sectors with pay-offs in the short term over those with pay-offs in the longer term, that is exacerbating short termism). The financial sector has significant political influence, and as such is likely to favour high interest rates, low inflation and to have little regard for the level of unemployment. Further, the financial sector may exhibit instability which has significant effects on the real sector. Two dimensions of instability may be identified. The first is that prices in the financial sector (such as the price of equity, exchange rates) display a degree of volatility which is much greater than could be explained by the variation in the relevant underlying real factors (for example, in the case of an equity price the variation in the earnings potential of the company concerned and the discount rate). This volatility is further discussed in the essay by Arestis and Sawyer in this volume as perceptions that the foreign exchange rates display excessive volatility with damaging effects on the real economy (especially foreign trade and investment) have lain behind proposals for a 'Tobin tax' on foreign exchange transactions. The second dimension, which has been particularly associated with the work of Hyman Minsky (for example, Minsky, 1986), is that there can be periods of financial fragility and instability (though other periods exhibit financial tranquillity). The financial fragility arises from the increase in debt (relative to some relevant measures of economic activity and wealth), which comes about through the exuberance of the financial sector in the provision of credit and the ways in which credit creation has a pyramiding effect. The debt position is sustainable provided that the expectations of growth of incomes, from which repayment of interest and principal would be made, held when the debt was incurred are realized: when the growth of incomes falter below expectations, difficulties arise in making the repayments of principal and interest, and default on loans follows. This financial fragility is significant in two respects: first, it may lead to a crisis in the financial sector (such as collapse of some financial institutions), which spills over into effects on the level of economic activity. Second, the regulation of the financial system can be used to limit the degree of financial fragility, and the government (usually in the form of the central bank) is required to rescue the financial system from the consequences of the financial fragility. In his essay below, Wray views the US financial system as having evolved from a robust to a fragile system, where he identifies market forces as destabilizing and government interventions as a mixture of stabilizing and destabilizing.

In the essays below, proposals to reform and change the financial system (particularly at the international level) abound. Arestis and Sawyer discuss in detail what in some regards is a modest proposal for the taxation of foreign exchange transactions (often labelled the 'Tobin tax').[6] It is modest in the sense that it does not propose to make major changes in the institutional arrangements of the financial sector but rather to levy a tax, though its introduction would represent a major shift in the balance of power between the financial sector and the productive sectors. But although this is a modest proposal, it does reflect widespread unease over the volatility of the financial sector and the consequences of that volatility for the other sectors of the economy. More broadly, this tax proposal would also comfort the political influence which is yielded by the financial markets over macroeconomic policies.

Wray focuses on what he sees as a crisis in and of the US financial system, which he argues has arisen from the cumulative effects of the interrelated causes of deregulation, the pursuit of monetarist policies, corruption and the evolution to a fragile financial structure. A significant feature of this analysis is that the crisis is seen to arise from the pursuit of private objectives by the firms in the financial sector (what others may term 'market forces') and from the retreat of government from the regulation of that sector. Wray's proposals for remedying the crisis include a range of re-regulation of the financial sector, which would include policies to 'encourage development of alternative community-based, financial institutions that would increase payment, investment, and credit services in targeted (generally, low income) communities.'

Pollin's particular concern is to inject democratic control into the financial markets and over the allocation of credit, where he views 'policies focused on financial institutions and activities ... [as] a central feature of any renewed egalitarian policy project'. He contrasts the capital market based system of the United States and United Kingdom with the bank-based system of Germany and Japan in order to draw out the possibilities for 'voice' effects (using the terminology of Hirschman, 1970) of the latter as compared with the 'exit' effects of the former. In a system drawing on voice effects, the question is whose voice is heard and heeded: and Pollin advances proposals to move from an elite voice system to a democratic voice one.

Grabel is concerned to develop an accurate analysis of the financial system so as to inform a relevant policy discussion. She argues that 'the present orthodox direction of financial policy in developing and former socialist countries is misguided when judged against the developmental imperatives facing these countries.' Specifically she is critical of both the neoclassical and the neostructuralist theory in terms of their theoretical and empirical contributions to the discussions of the financial liberalization programmes which have been promoted in many Third World (and other) economies. Her preferred analysis, which she labels post-Keynesian, leads to proposals for encouraging state-mediated financial intermediation and restraining the degree of financial openness of an economy.

The political economy tradition does not treat the state as a neutral agent acting in some social interest (as so often is the case in the neoclassical market failure tradition). Hence whatever the merits of the broad sets of policies which are proposed below, none of us would expect that solely the power of argument would persuade the state to adopt such policy frameworks. The activities of the state are strongly influenced by and constrained by the requirements of the economically powerful.

But the political economy tradition does not follow the 'New Right' in believing that there is no constructive role for the state, and that state activity is indeed detrimental to economic development and prosperity (and that the free flow of the market is crucial for economic prosperity). The experience of many of the Newly Industrialized Countries (from an earlier era Japan, and more recently South Korea, Taiwan and so on) suggests the importance of the state as an agent of development.[7] At a minimum, the process of development requires the guiding hand of the state, and does not come about through the agency of the market alone. The paper below by Singh provides an important critique of the view that 'competitive markets are the best way yet found for efficiently organising the production and distribution of goods and services. Domestic and external competition provides the incentives that unleash entrepreneurship and technological progress.' (World Bank Study as quoted by Singh).[8] As he argues there, the state in the cases of Japan, South Korea and Taiwan played 'a vigorous role and followed a highly active industrial policy. The government did not supplant the market ... [n]or did it simply follow the market.'

The advocacy of economic policies which require a degree of government intervention raises many issues relating to the integrity of the civil servants, the degree to which they are answerable to the democratic system, and so on. Here we would follow Harcourt (1997) when he wrote that

> I do not wish to deny that there are aspects of the growth of bureaucracies and of the power and influence of policy makers that are disquieting, to say the least. Keynes optimism that ... disinterested and highly intelligent persons desire the common good more than their own good (except indirectly by obtaining

satisfaction from making the world more rational and just than
they found it), has not always been borne out. The structures of
many government departments – the hierarchies, the motions that
have to be gone through for promotion, the drive and ruthless-
ness needed in order to reach the top – are not necessarily the
ideal incentives or channels for ensuring that altruistic, charitable,
and tolerant people (as well as intelligent ones) make it to the
top. Bureaucratic empires built for their own sakes, rather than
to serve useful social purposes, are also not unknown. Those who
favor intervention, as I do, and a flourishing public sector must
seriously come to grips with these problems. (pp. 172–3)

We could note, though, that building bureaucratic empires for their
own sakes is not limited to the public sector.

DeMartino takes the argument to the realm of industrial policies versus competitiveness strategies. He opposes the view that
the ability of a nation to achieve competitiveness in world markets
determines the country's economic activity and prosperity. By contrast, global competition rewards winners and punishes losers quite
harshly. Three broad categories of competitiveness are discussed:
the neoliberal (the position taken by neoclassicals), the competitiveness-enhancing (whereby countries ought to pay attention to
their relative competitiveness) and the competitiveness-reducing
(prosperity should be sought through relationships which govern
economic behaviour rather than through sheer competitiveness).
DeMartino argues for *international egalitarianism* as the best approach in the context of today's global economy. In this sense, the
competition-reducing perspective is the only defensible position.
The viability of this agenda is briefly discussed.

The essays below provide a rich menu for economic policies in
the twenty-first century. While there are differences between the
proposals and different areas of concern are addressed, there are
some important common themes to the essays. These would identify as, first, the shortcomings of the current financial systems and
proposed for rectifying those shortcoming. Second, the policy proposals are intended to shift policy concerns from a focus on promoting the interests of the rich and powerful to a greater concern
for the interests of the poor and the excluded. This would be reflected in a greater concern for the reduction in unemployment
rather than of inflation through to ensuring that the financial system allocated resources for economic and industrial development.

Third, the essays are informed by political economy analysis of the operations of markets which stands in contrast to the starry-eyed view of economic orthodoxy. There is a clear realization that markets can perform valuable economic functions, but that they perform even better when appropriately regulated and controlled. Special thanks must go to the contributors for their willingness to respond to our comments and suggestions with forbearance and good humour. Thanks are also extended to Kevin McCauley for research assistance and June Daniels and Christine Nisbet of the Department of Economics, University of East London, and Eleanor Lynn of the Economics Division of the Leeds University Business School for their secretarial assistance. Finally, Tim Farmiloe of Macmillan and his staff, as always, have provided excellent support throughout the period it took to prepare this volume.

Notes

1. We are talking here of the industrialized capitalist economies: there has obviously been a sea-change in the role of government in most of the former COMECON countries.
2. The experience of the Mitterrand government in France in the early 1980s is an oft-quoted example of what happens to a government which seeks to reflate alone. However, Lombard (1995) concluded that

    the Mitterrand experiment failed not because France embarked alone on a programme of expansionary policies at a time of world recession, nor because Keynesian expansionary policies were outdated in the world economic environment of the 1980s, but because of the way these policies were implemented and more importantly because of the reluctance of the French government to operate outside the EMS guidelines' (p. 371).

    There is also the example of the Reagan administration in the United States in the 1980s, which was able to reflate (albeit through tax cuts and increases in defence expenditure) without incurring the wrath of the financial markets. Further, many governments have been able to run substantial budget deficits for most of the past two decades (and there is the paradox that budget deficits have been much larger in the supposedly monetarist era of the second post-war quarter-century than in the supposedly Keynesian first quarter century.
3. The papers published in Arestis and Sawyer (1997) address more directly the question of the relevance of Keynesian economic policies in the late twentieth century and into the twenty-first century.
4. In the first paper in the *International Papers in Political Economy* (Arestis

and Sawyer, 1993) we sought to provide an account of political economy: see also Arestis and Sawyer (1994).

5. The argument is put that if the 'classical dichotomy' holds, then the pursuit of low monetary growth to achieve low inflation can be undertaken without any detriment to the levels of output and employment.
6. James Tobin has also proposed a tax on transactions in securities to reduce volatility and to encourage long-term holdings of securities: that tax raises some different issues and is not addressed in the essay in this volume.
7. Relevant references here include Amsden (1989), Wade (1990), World Bank (1993).
8. These two sentences may be in some conflict with one another for, as Schumpeter and others have argued, perfectly competitive markets may (under some stringent assumptions) generate an allocatively efficient outcome, but such markets would not be technologically progressive. For a recent popular restatement of this see Kutner (1997).

References

Amsden, A. (1989) *Asia's Next Giant* (New York: Oxford University Press).

Arestis, P. and P. Demetriades (1997) 'Financial development and economic growth: Assessing the evidence', *Economic Journal*, **107**(May), forthcoming.

Arestis, P. and M. Sawyer (1993) 'Political Economy: an editorial manifesto', *International Papers in Political Economy*, **1**(1).

Arestis, P. and M. Sawyer (1994) 'Introduction', in P. Arestis and M. Sawyer (eds) *The Elgar Companion to Radical Political Economy* (Aldershot: Edward Elgar).

Arestis, P. and M. Sawyer (eds) (1997) *The Relevance of Keynesian Policies Today* (London: Macmillan).

Gordon, D.M. (1996) *Fat and Mean* (New York: The Free Press).

Harcourt, G.C. (1997) 'Critiques and alternatives: reflections on some recent (and not so recent) controversies', *Journal of Post Keynesian Economics*, **19**(2): 171–80.

Hirschman, A.O. (1970) *Exit, Voice and Loyalty: Responses to Decline in Firms, Organisations and States* (Cambridge, Mass.: Harvard University Press).

Hirst, P. and G. Thompson (1996) *Globalization in Question: The International Economy and the Possibilities* (Cambridge: Polity Press).

Kutner, R. (1997) *Everything for Sale* (New York: Knopf).

Lombard, M. (1995) 'A re-examination of the reasons for the failure of Keynesian expansionary policies', *Cambridge Journal of Economics*, **19**: 359–72.

Minsky, H.P. (1986) *Stabilizing an Unstable Economy* (New Haven and London: Yale University Press).

Minsky, H.P. and C.J. Whalen (1997) 'Economic insecurity and the institutional prerequisites for successful capitalism', *Journal of Post Keynesian Economics*, **19**(2): 155–70.

Prescott, E.C. (1986) 'Theory ahead of business-cycle measurement', *Carnegie-Rochester Conference Series and Public Policy*, 25(Autumn): 11–44.

Sawyer, M. (1989) *The Challenge of Radical Political Economy* (Hemel Hempstead: Harvester-Wheatsheaf).

Sawyer, M. (1992), 'The nature and role of the market', *Social Concept* (A slightly revised version appeared in C. Pitelis (ed.) *Transaction Costs, Markets and Hierarchies* [Oxford: Blackwell, 1993]).

Sawyer, M. (1995a) 'Overcoming the barriers to full employment in capitalist economies', *Economie Appliquée*, 43(1): 185–218.

Sawyer, M. (1995b) *Unemployment, Imperfect Competition and Macroeconomics* (Aldershot: Edward Elgar).

Sawyer, M. (1995c) 'Obstacles to the achievement of full employment in capitalist economies', in P. Arestis and M. Marshall (eds) *The Political Economy of Full Employment: Conservatism, Corporatism and Institutional Change* (Aldershot: Edward Elgar).

Singh, A. (1997) 'Expanding employment in the global economy', in P. Arestis, G. Palma and M. Sawyer (eds) *Markets, Unemployment and Economic Policy: Essays in Honour of Geoff Harcourt*, Vol. 2 (London: Routledge).

Wade, R. (1990) *Governing the Market: Economic Theory and the Role of Government in East Asian Industrialisation* (Princeton University Press).

Williamson, O.E. (1985) *The Economic Institutions of Capitalism: Firms, Markets, Relational Contracting* (London: Macmillan).

World Bank (1993) *East Asian Miracle: Economic Growth and Public Policy* (New York: Oxford University Press).

1 Industrial Policies versus Competitiveness Strategies: In Pursuit of Prosperity in the Global Economy

George DeMartino

1.1 INTRODUCTION[1]

Competitiveness, like free trade, is one of those concepts that separates orthodox economists not only from their heterodox colleagues, but from most politicians and the general public. For the latter, the ability of a nation's firms to achieve competitiveness in global markets determines the nation's level of economic prosperity. Global competition rewards winners and punishes losers, often quite harshly.

Orthodox economists take pride in their dissent from the prevailing view. Not only is national competitiveness not the primary determinant of national prosperity, it is hardly of any consequence at all. For Krugman (1994a), the 'obsession' with competitiveness distracts attention away from the more important and yet elusive determinants of prosperity. The concern over national competitiveness is exploited by ideologues with ulterior motives wielding dangerous rhetoric in pursuit of ruinous policies. Economists must drive the stake of scientific reasoning through its heart before it leads us down the road of reckless neo-mercantilist economic and geopolitical strategies.

But the demon of competitiveness will not be exorcised. The competitiveness formula for prosperity is prescribed today by political antagonists who agree on little else, from trade unionists, to left/liberal economists, to social democrats, to conservatives, to right-wing neo-populists. While proponents present alternative and in many ways irreconcilable programmes to restore competitiveness, they all identify a powerful causal link that runs from national competitiveness to prosperity. This paper has two chief objectives. First, it seeks to untangle the threads of the competitiveness debate by classifying the contending perspectives into three broad categories. These will be referred to as the *neoliberal*, the *competitiveness-enhancing* and the *competition-reducing* approaches:

• The first is the position of neoclassical economics. Neoclassicals cite domestic productivity growth as the chief lever by which to secure economic prosperity. These economists advocate what will be called 'global neoliberalism', including but not limited to free trade and the removal of political constraints on capital flows. The perfection of a one-world market will enhance global efficiency, the benefits of which will redound to all countries.

• In contrast, advocates of the competitiveness-enhancing position hold that much of what winners gain in the global economy comes at the expense of the losers. Nations are therefore wise to pay close attention to their relative standing *vis-à-vis* their neighbours, and to implement policies that secure an improving position in the global competitive hierarchy.

• Advocates of the competition-reducing approach seek prosperity not through restored competitiveness, but through the establishment of an appropriate set of rules and institutions that govern economic behaviour. On this account, malevolent economic outcomes can be mitigated only by removing critical aspects of social, political and economic life from the market so as to insulate them from the ravaging effects of competition. Proponents often advocate the international harmonization of labour and environmental standards so as to prevent the 'social dumping' that would otherwise occur.

The second objective of the paper is to adjudicate the competitiveness debate from a left progressive perspective. This is hardly a straightforward matter, not least because left progressives can be found within the competitiveness-enhancing and the competition-reducing camps. Both of these positions arose in the 1980s in opposition to the then resurgent neoclassical orthodoxy. But matters are more complicated still: much of the scorn that has been heaped on the competitiveness-enhancers by proponents of neoliberalism resonates with the competition-reducers, as we shall see.

To facilitate this adjudication, the paper presents a normative framework that relies on the binaries egalitarianism/anti-egalitarianism and internationalism/nationalism. The paper will demonstrate that the tensions between the claims of egalitarianism and internationalism lie at the heart of the discord among heterodox contributors. The paper will advocate the joint normative criterion of *international egalitarianism* as best suited to the political projects of left (and other) progressives in the context of today's global economy. Against this criterion, the paper will identify the competition-reducing perspective as the only defensible contribution to the debate.

The paper proceeds as follows. Section 1.2 treats the matter of normative criteria. Section 1.3 surveys briefly the economic and political landscape in the USA and Europe which gave rise to the competitiveness debate. This section will also situate modern competitiveness policy as an adaptation of circa 1970s 'industrial policy' to the rapidly changing global economic environment. Tracing its origins in (and differences from) industrial policy will help to clarify the terms of the dispute that has emerged among the left over competitiveness. Section 1.4 then presents a substantive discussion and critical evaluation of the major positions in the competitiveness debate. This section will ignore the corporate management literature as the explicit concern of the paper is not competitiveness *per se*, but the purported connection between competitiveness policy and prosperity. The paper concludes with a brief discussion of the viability of the competition-reducing agenda.

1.2 NORMATIVE CRITERIA

Notably absent from the competitiveness debate is any explicit discussion of normative criteria. This oversight contributes substantially to the confusion among progressives about competitiveness. We must begin, then, by repairing this omission.

Historically, left progressives have adopted normative criteria that privilege the common interests of all of humanity through the cessation of exploitation, discrimination, and privation. The universalist impulse in left thought has manifested in an enduring commitment to genuine equality. This in turn has served to engender solidaristic political demands, policies and strategies that are seen to be potentially acceptable to all who are concerned about justice. At least rhetorically (if not always substantively), the pursuit of justice as genuine equality has biased left programmes against the pursuit of particularist interests, be they predicated on race, gender, class or nationality.

In recent decades our understanding of justice has been advanced by critical readings of historical experience and by important theoretical debates. Today, there is far less innocence about demands for equality: it is understood that all manner of injustices and violations of important freedoms can and have been paraded under the banner of equality, as the Soviet experience (among others) attests. Such betrayals were often the result of reductionist theoretical narratives, in which (for example) class exploitation was essentialized as the primary injustice from which other injustices flowed. But it is important to recognize that the most insightful of the recent contributions to the theoretical debate over justice to date – such as those by Rawls (1971), Sen (1992), Walzer (1983) and others – do not displace equality as a normative imperative, but rather yield a more nuanced account of what it is that ought to be equalized, and how the demand for equality should be balanced against other valued normative criteria.

This is not the place to reproduce these arguments. Instead, we must only affirm that equality still does and should occupy pride of place among left-progressive normative commitments. Following Sen (1992), we might endorse the notion of the *equality of substantive freedoms to lead valued lives* as a criterion that provides a compelling vision of a better world. In Sen's account, this demand entails that people receive the means they require, including allocations of resources, so that they can secure equal ability to achieve. That is, substantive freedom as an end – not the means – is to be equalized. For example, a wheelchair-bound person might require more resources to achieve the same level of freedom as an able-bodied person. Moreover, in this account arbitrary relative inequalities may be expected to induce absolute deprivations, such as the political impotence suffered by the poor in a wealthy society. The affinities with the Marxian dictum 'to each according to need' are rather direct.

What does this commitment to equality imply in the context of today's global economy? Within a nation's borders, this criterion calls for a much more equal distribution of, for example, income, wealth, educational opportunity, and access to valued work than we presently see. Distributions today are predicated not on need, but on the articulation of historical privilege, class, gender, race, luck and talents. Globally, this criterion impels a strong commitment to internationalism: the life circumstances of inhabitants of the most impoverished countries must be substantially improved to close the gap with wealthy countries.[2] This criterion would not only deem illegitimte beggar-thy-neighbour strategies, but would seem to require the pursuit of policies that ensure rising prosperity for those with the least substantive freedoms. Moreover, to be practically viable, economic strategies and policies must be designed so as to secure the assent of those concerned about justice in the North and the South.

In short, a normative criterion of *internationalist egalitarianism* can and should guide our assessment of the competitiveness debate. Of each contribution to the debate we might enquire: to what degree is it likely to secure equality of substantive freedoms, nationally and internationally?

1.3   ORIGINS OF THE COMPETITIVENESS DEBATE

The contemporary competitiveness debate emerged gradually during the 1980s in the USA and Europe and hit its stride by the latter years of that decade. Notably, the debate arrived on the heels of global economic dislocation that developed during the 1970s, and that marked the end of the post-war 'golden era' which had extended up to the early 1970s.

The post-war period is now seen to have been exceptional in many respects. First, productivity rates rose rapidly in the USA and particularly dramatically in much of Europe and Japan. Second, this productivity growth was coupled to rising living standards for workers throughout the developed world, and was paralleled by impressive economic growth throughout much of the developing world. Third, the link between rising productivity and incomes succeeded in producing global economic growth without severe recessions.

For orthodox theorists, this period validated the mechanical and vitally important neoclassical relation between contribution and reward: workers' incomes rose *because* of and in direct proportion to their rising productivity. The lines of causation in this account therefore run from rising productivity to rising incomes. For many Marxists, in contrast, the outcome was far more complex and, ultimately, precarious. In Marxian interpretations, the period came to be theorized through the lens of the 'regulation', 'social structures of accumulation' and other long-wave theories.[3] In these accounts, the post-war period was marked by a peculiar contingent constellation of institutions (such as the 'capital–labour accord' and Keynesian macro-regulation) that articulated production with demand and mediated power relations between capital, labour and the state. These institutional arrangements provided a fortuitous configuration of power that generated rising incomes which in turn validated robust capital accumulation. The latter process had, as one important effect, rising labour productivity.

In both accounts, the golden era is seen to have begun to unravel by the early 1970s. The following two decades were marked by declining productivity growth and profit rates in most OECD countries, and by severe economic crisis in much of Africa and Latin America.[4] The USA faced the most severe and sustained decline in productivity, extending through the 1970s and 1980s. During this period there have been substantial sectoral shifts that have permanently displaced millions of workers from their previous industries in the USA, Britain and parts of Europe. Particularly in the USA, the majority of these have encountered substantial decreases in income in their new employment. Those who have shifted into the burgeoning non-union 'service sector' have fared especially poorly. Notably, in those countries that permit it, permanent, full-time positions have been steadily replaced by temporary and/or part-time contracts that do not provide employment security, living wages, training, pensions and other benefits that have historically been associated with full-time employment.

The 1970s also heralded the onset of the demise of the capital–labour accord in the USA and eroding union density and influence in Europe (Freeman and Katz, 1994). Employer resistance precipitated a steady erosion in union bargaining power in those industries where labour had always been strongest. In the USA and Britain, unemployment grew fastest in the most heavily unionized regions of the country, as manufacturing operations were downsized, relocated to lower-waged areas at home and abroad, and closed entirely (Bluestone and Harrison, 1982). With the elections of Thatcher and Reagan the assault on labour gathered momentum. The 1980s was the worst decade for organized labour in the USA since the 1920s; by 1990 union density among private sector workers was lower than it had been prior to passage of the Wagner Act. In Britain the 1980s witnessed particularly dramatic defeats for labour, while in Europe the corporatist model came under strain even in those countries where it had seemed most secure, such as Sweden.

In Europe, the past two decades have also witnessed the highest unemployment rates since the Depression. In the USA, in contrast, the same period was marked by a dramatic reversal in the trend toward greater income equality that extended through much of the post-Depression era. The income and wealth shares of the richest quintile – and especially the richest one per cent of US households – have soared to heights approaching those of the 1920s (Phillips, 1990). Indeed, since the mid-1980s the popular press has reported with awe and some consternation the rise of the 'overclass', a phenomenon which has placed into sharp relief the stagnation in real incomes for up to 80 per cent of the work force (*Newsweek*, 1995). And although the rising poverty of the period is not unprecedented, the growth of poverty in the context of a growing economy and low official unemployment rates is indeed new. The long Reagan expansion of the 1980s was characterized by a new phenomenon – the rise of the 'working poor'. Growth, the historic palliative for poverty, was seen to be failing to lift the poor into the ranks of the middle class (see *Business Week*, 1991; and *New York Times*, 1991).

Economic Integration

These trends have developed alongside deepening economic integration, registered in dramatic increases in international flows of goods, services and capital. Integration has begun to erase the geographical fragmentation of markets and production. While this period of deepening integration is by no means the first in history, there are particular aspects that distinguish it from previous episodes (MacEwan, 1991).[5] Financial markets are more effectively integrated today than in the past, due in part to new technologies that facilitate rapid transactions without regard to national borders, but also to explicit 'financial liberalization' policies in developing countries and the former socialist countries (Grabel, 1995). In addition, trade patterns today depart from those predicted by traditional, static models of comparative advantage and reflect instead the global competitive strategies of multinational corporations. Corporations today increasingly locate design, marketing, production and subordinate functions where they can be achieved most inexpensively.

Other forces have also contributed to the intensification of competition in global markets. Developing countries have become a substantial factor in these markets, for two very different reasons.

On the one hand, the Newly Industrializing Countries (NICs) have entered global markets from a position of strength. Influenced by the success of Japan, the NICs adopted export-orientated strategies over the past 20 years and have been able to compete aggressively in a wide range of manufactures. More recently, other developing countries have been forced to undertake aggressive export strategies by virtue of their relative weakness. Under the tutelage of the IMF and World Bank, debt-ridden countries have adopted aggressive strategies to establish balance of trade surpluses so as to be able to meet their debt obligations. The proliferation of 'export processing zones' (EPZs) in debtor nations partly reflects this imperative. Although the EPZs still represent a small proportion of total employment in most developing countries, there has been a substantial growth in production and exports emanating from these areas over the past 15 years.

The globalization of markets and production has occurred against the backdrop of global economic stagnation. Global competition has therefore emerged as a site of contest over the distribution of unemployment and income, as countries have sought to export their way out of economic distress. It is therefore not surprising that the 1980s witnessed significant increases in tariff protection by developed countries against the exports of developing countries. Since the 1980s, the USA has also engaged in rather aggressive sabre-rattling against Japan and other countries that were seen to impair its balance of trade.

Looking on this period, many observers have been particularly troubled by what they perceive to be an erosion of the civic fabric throughout Europe and the USA. Feelings of mutual interdependence that had spawned broad attachments to enlightened self-interest have given way to a pervasive sense of disharmony and to a fragmentation of spheres of obligation and mutuality. These have been replaced by a naked self-interest – by ethnic, regional, racial and class balkanization. The era has been marred by growing hostility to immigration and, especially in the USA, a distrust of supranational entities that would usurp national sovereignty and subordinate 'our' interests to those who might do us harm. The distinction of 'self' from 'other' that attends the eternally-contested process of identity formation and reassertion has acquired a raw and ugly character in recent times.

Economic Integration Dislocation, and 'Competitiveness'

Binding the pervasive economic hardship and uncertainty to a revitalized parochialism in developed countries is the deepening economic integration referenced above. The rapidly-changing international economic landscape has undermined a sense of economic order, security and control. This malaise extends from national policy-making, where national sovereignty itself is seen to be eclipsed, to the private sphere of industrial relations. By dismantling borders that had provided a degree of insulation for a nation's markets, economic integration has deprived the isolated nation state of expansionary macroeconomic policy targeted toward full employment and growth (Crotty, 1989). Similarly, a worker's, a community's, or indeed, an entire nation's economic fate seems more than ever to be driven by forces and agents far removed from local accountability. In the place of a local mill-owner whose decisions could be pointed to as the cause of economic prosperity or hardship, there stands the faceless global market dictating what shall be produced where, who shall prosper, and who shall suffer. Vulnerability to global economic forces has been a commonplace in developing countries for centuries, of course; today it is seen to afflict even the most powerful developed nations.

It is not the intent here to assess whether these apprehensions are warranted. Rather, it is to suggest that these broad economic trends and the interpretations given thereto provided the context for the rise of the competitiveness debate during the 1980s. Looking on these developments with dismay, many analysts surmised that declining prosperity for working people and their communities in Europe and the USA was tied directly to the intensification of competition in global markets. During the 1980s, the association between prosperity and national competitiveness became deeply ingrained in policy circles.[6] The evidence was apparent in aggregate trade, productivity and income statistics: success in global markets – notably by Japan and the NICs – was correlated with rising incomes; failure – by the USA and much of Europe – induced falling real incomes, rising inequality and/or unemployment and social dislocation. From the 1980s onward, a massive literature that seeks to identify the means by which competitiveness and prosperity can be recovered developed in Europe and the USA. Much of this literature invokes the need for government strategies to create conditions for private sector competitiveness. It is sometimes referred to as 'industrial policy' by both proponents and opponents. But this usage is at least misleading, if not entirely incorrect, and it is important for us to see why.

Political Economy of Industrial Policy

Although the post-war period is widely eulogized today as an era of social harmony and growth, the 1940s through the 1970s were marked by rather sharp ideological conflict throughout Europe and even in the USA. Radical parties emerged from the war with strong political bases among workers, students and intellectuals. What is often described in neutral terms today as the 'rebuilding' of Europe and Japan under the auspices of the Marshall Plan was a much more contentious process that comprised intense struggle between partisans of antagonistic social visions. United States assistance and intervention in rebuilding postwar Europe and Japan were driven in part by a concern to save these countries from communist influence. Without overstating the point, it is safe to say that the threat of a radical assault on capitalist privilege was taken to be real and immediate throughout France, Italy, and other European countries. Even within the USA, where political controversy was largely channelled into skirmishes between the Democratic and Republican parties, the influence of radical activists and ideas (especially within the labour movement) was considered to pose a significant threat to national security.

An important aspect of the political struggles of this era concerned the terms by which the inherent conflict between capital and labour was to be mediated so as to contain radicalism. In those countries where US influence was strongest, such as Germany and Japan, efforts were made to construct institutions of labour representation that were 'non-ideological'. Radical labour organizations that had emerged prior to the war were largely suppressed (although France and Italy represent important exceptions). In place of a fragmented, ideologically contested labour movement were built centrist organizations that posed no substantive challenge to the capitalist system. In the USA, where radicalism had been weaker prior to and after the war, the government succeeded in rooting out radicals from the labour movement, often with the help of centrist labour leaders.

No one institutional model for mediating class conflict emerged across post-war Europe, Japan and the USA during this period (cf

Boyer, 1995). Scandinavia moved furthest toward a co-operative corporatist model, a system in which inclusive labour and employer confederations bargain with and under the auspices of the state to determine incomes policies and to define more broadly the terms of the capital–labour and capital–citizen accords. Social democratic systems of mediation (such as in Germany) established substantial constraints on the prerogatives of capital – so much so that these became the preferred model of economic organization among socialists in other countries. In Japan, the appearance of corporatist governance masked a significant subservience of unionism to capital, so that industrial relations served the interests of capital much more directly than in Scandinavia and Germany. In the UK, the terms of the 'bargain' between capital and labour were less acceptable to both parties. Although displaying real strength on the shop floor, British unions failed to wield the kind of unified political power of their Scandinavian and German counterparts. Moreover, in so far as the British model of industrial relations and bargaining remained far more fragmented than on the continent, unions lacked the cohesiveness to institute economywide bargaining in pursuit of collective goals. The USA, finally, exhibited the greatest opposition to legislated constraints on capital, and the least politically efficacious labour movement among these countries (with the possible exception of Japan).

Attributes of Industrial Policy

Abstracting from important cross-national differences, Table 1.1 isolates the salient features of what came to be known as industrial policy.[7] Industrial policy was understood to provide one resolution to the daunting question of the proper role of government in organizing and directing economic affairs. For continental Europe, post-war industrial policy was connected to the need to replace infrastructure and industrial enterprises, of course. But of equal importance, it was tied to the imperative to mediate class conflict. It was therefore often corporatist in structure. In Sweden, where corporatist structures and industrial policy emerged prior to the war, the connection between these institutions and class conflict was especially direct (Korpi and Shalev, 1979).

Notably, industrial policy was promoted as a means to correct inherent failings of the market economy.[8] The latter was seen to be a site of conflict that pitted relatively powerless labour against

Table 1.1 Attributes of industrial policy

Mediation of domestic conflict: capital versus labour
Tripartite corporatism
Protection from the market
Full employment (of labour)
Equity/distribution
Maintenance of stability
Mandated co-operation
'Fixing' capital
National interest promoted through protection of Labour's interests
Equality as end

more powerful capital. This imbalance led to unjust economic outcomes, such as income inequality across classes and regions. Industrial policy sought to address these failings so as to universalize the benefits that market organization could induce.

As a concomitant to this concern for equity, industrial policy was intended to sustain full employment. This was pursued through several means, not least by substantially limiting the ability of firms to shed workers during economic downturns by requiring prior notification of plans to cease or reduce industrial production, state authorization to lay off workers, and restraining of redundant workers. In addition, investment dictates and incentives were also tied in part to the goal of securing full employment.

The free market was seen to induce other forms of suboptimal macroeconomic performance. In the absence of public control over investment decisions, firms might underinvest (or misinvest) with the effect of generating economic stagnation and instability. By constraining the authority of corporate managers, society could smooth out the otherwise inevitable cycles of investment, employment and income. Hence, while Keynesian macro-regulation did not necessarily entail industrial policy (or vice versa), the two could be seen as complementary means to achieve growth and stability.

Although particular industrial policies could take the form of market incentives to bring about beneficial corporate behaviour, the corporatist structures and social democratic influences generally entailed more direct intervention. As such, industrial policy could be thought of as means to 'fix' capital so as to ensure full employment.[9] By fixing capital (for example geographically or industrially), the state stripped the firm of the option of 'exit' in pursuit of profits. Rather than see these constraints as market imperfections, they were posited as necessary parameters within which the market might operate to fulfil paramount social objectives. Mechanisms for fixing capital could range from outright nationalization to corporatist bargaining, to credit control through quasi-public investment banks. While different in important respects, these mechanisms shared a commitment to overriding market signals in the important sphere of corporate investment and location patterns.

In short, industrial policy as it emerged prior to and following the war sought to accomplish two distinct classes of objectives: to promote economic development (which, in postwar Europe took the form of rebuilding and modernizing) and to mediate what were seen to be fundamental social antagonisms. Rather than focus on competitiveness *per se*, industrial policy sought the creation of genuine equality, opportunity, full employment, and stability. For all its virtues, the free market was taken by proponents of industrial policy to fail in these latter regards. For liberal advocates, industrial policy was seen as a chief means to repair once and for all the schisms of capitalism; for radical proponents, it was taken as a step toward the socialization of production and distribution.

From Industrial Policy to Competitiveness

The economic turbulence of the 1970s and 1980s had contradictory effects on industrial policy and the broader Keynesian macroregulatory and social democratic regimes in which it was embedded. Economic crisis in Britain led the Labour Party to advocate a comprehensive industrial policy (first in 1964 and then again more ambitiously in 1974) (Sawyer, 1991). The left wing of the Labour Party proposed extensive nationalization of large firms in major industries as a means to ensure sufficient investment to generate employment and rising incomes. The Labour Party adopted resolutions that proposed the formation of what came to be called the National Economic Board (NEB) which would acquire substantial ownership stakes in major industries. By increasing investment in the nationalized firms, the NEB would establish a moving target to be emulated by competing firms, leading to an economywide rationalization of industry, growth and rising employment. But this initiative was largely stillborn: the minority Labour Government failed to acquire substantial ownership stakes during the mid-1970s. Thatcher's victory in 1979 signalled the growing influence of a resurgent neoclassical orthodoxy in Europe. With Thatcher's elections, industrial policy was abruptly dismantled in favour of an embrace of neoliberal policies. On the continent, the 1980s marked a gradual two-pronged ideological transition. On the right, neoclassicals came to articulate the neoliberal critique of the interventionist state. For neoclassicals, European industrial policy was identified as inefficient and counterproductive. Growing unemployment was attributed in part to the rigidities embedded in social-democratic market interventions which prevented rapid adjustment to the changing demands of an increasingly dynamic global economy. The result was seen by neoclassicals to be 'Eurosclerosis': having fought a rearguard action to insulate society from the vagaries of the market, social democratic industrial policy had undermined the ability of European capital to innovate. The pursuit of stability had stifled the entrepreneurial spirit and had brought about precisely the stagnation, insecurity and punishment by the market that it had been intended to prevent.

The social democratic left developed a more complicated relationship to industrial policy during the 1980s. Still suspicious of the effects of the free market, but now tarred by neoliberals with responsibility for growing unemployment and stagnation, some social democrats began to rethink the goals, instruments and efficacy of industrial policy. In the context of deepening economic integration, policy discussions turned increasingly toward the troubling matter of European competitiveness in global markets. This intellectual transition was reflected in a series of reports by the European Community and European analysts on competitiveness. Competitiveness became a means by which to salvage state intervention in pursuit of socially benevolent outcomes.[10] But the shift from industrial to competitiveness policy represented something more than a strategic manoeuvre; it marked a fundamental transition in progressive thought concerning political aspirations and, more importantly, the proper role of the market in society. It therefore reflected a change in left ontology which has brought in its train a changing set of normative commitments.[11] To appreciate these transitions, we need take a close look at the emergent competitiveness debate.

1.4 THE COMPETITIVENESS DEBATE

The diverse contributions to the competitiveness debate can be classified into three categories: the neoliberal; the competitiveness-enhancing; and the competition-reducing approaches. Like any broad classification scheme, this one necessarily abstracts from distinctions that might be salient in other contexts. This classification is chosen because it best serves the purpose of the paper, which is to adjudicate this debate from a left progressive perspective.

Neoliberalism

The first perspective originates in orthodox neoclassical theory. It claims simply that the competitiveness of a nation's firms simply does not matter for national prosperity. National prosperity is tied directly to a nation's productivity. A nation's stagnating income can therefore be traced to stagnation in its own productivity growth – not to decreasing competitiveness *vis-à-vis* other nations.

What separates this perspective from most others is its focus on absolute rather than relative productivity gains. A nation is better off when its own productivity rate is high, but lower than that of its trading partners, than when its own productivity rate is low, but higher than that of its competitors (Krugman, 1994a; McCloskey, 1993). The error of those who embrace the concept of national competitiveness is to draw on interfirm competition to analogize relations between nations. In a market, one corporation's gain necessarily comes at the expense of the welfare of another corporation. But in the international realm, British citizens are not generally hurt – and indeed are likely to be helped – by the increasing productivity gains of the Japanese economy. With Japanese productivity rising, British consumers can acquire Japanese goods more cheaply through trade.

The neoclassical antipathy to competitiveness policy follows directly. A focus on declining national competitiveness as the source of economic malaise is apt to generate harmful national policy, including but not limited to neo-mercantilist trade initiatives (Krugman, 1994b). The competitiveness obsession also contaminates discussion of other policy initiatives that ought to be thought through on their own merits, not by reference to their supposed effect on national competitiveness. On a global level the concern with competitiveness distracts our attention away from the truly pressing problems in today's global economy: we debate the insignificant question of why Britain has slipped from number one to number ten when we ought to concern ourselves with why so many countries remain so poor at a time when it would seem that there exist the means to alleviate their plight (McCloskey, 1993).

Table 1.2 Adjudication of contributions to the competitiveness debate

	Market ideal	Egalitarian	Internationalist
Neoliberalism	Yes	No	Yes
Competitiveness enhancing perspective	Yes	Yes	No
Competition reducing perspective	No	Yes	Yes

Adjudicating Neoliberalism

Despite the objections of left critics, the orthodox neoliberal project is inherently internationalist (see Table 1.2). Market liberalization is promoted on the basis that it benefits all countries. The defence invokes a notion of enlightened self-interest that is deep-seated in orthodox thought – each country stands to gain from the increasing efficiency and incomes enjoyed by others. Efforts to promote one's own interests by means that penalize others (such as tariffs) are ultimately self-defeating.

In the neoclassical view, global neoliberalism may also be expected to equalize factor prices, with the effect of ensuring that the same contribution to production earns the same reward globally. Although the achievement of factor price equalization will entail declining reward for scarce factors (such as unskilled labour in developed countries), the growing efficiency of the global economy yielded by neoliberalism will ultimately lead to rising incomes for all factors in the long run.[12]

The internationalist impulse of orthodox theory is perhaps best indicated in its rather radical view of the nation state. In the ideal liberalized world economy, national borders would indeed become *economically* meaningless. Neoliberal global policy regimes would efface the segmentation of markets for goods, factors and finance, while removing virtually all political barriers to the globalization of production and even to the free flow of labour. For the orthodoxy, national borders are impediments that can be partially overcome through free trade; ideally, they should be cancelled as determinants of market transactions. In short, orthodox neoliberals are 'one-world' advocates in pursuit of a global economy free of neo-mercantilism or other particularist national strategies.

Nevertheless, the orthodox neoliberal perspective is hardly egalitarian. The commitment of neoclassical theory to welfarist normative criteria weighs against demands for equality of incomes or other egalitarian criteria.[13] Welfarism is founded in a steadfast relativism regarding preference orderings. In modern orthodox thought, this is codified in a hostility to interpersonal utility comparisons and an associated refusal to distinguish between legitimate needs and superfluous desires. These biases preclude examination of whether social welfare would be enhanced by policies that redistribute income from the wealthy to the poor and that (correspondingly) reorientate production away from luxury goods and toward the satisfaction of more important needs (DeMartino 1996).

Neoclassical theory also pays insufficient attention to the manner in which institutional configurations condition peoples' substantive freedoms. By largely abstracting from the analytical categories of class and power, orthodox thought can produce a theory of distribution in which each factor is rewarded in proportion to its contribution. But productivity is hardly the only (or even the most important) determinant of distribution. Distribution is fundamentally conditioned by the social context within which production and market transactions occur. The neoliberal error is to presume equality of opportunity; inequality of incomes can therefore be read as deserved, reflecting, for example, inter-personal differences in aptitudes, predilections and preferences that influence decisions about the acquisition of human capital.

The abstraction from schisms such as class and race that produce inequality of substantive freedoms weakens the kind of internationalism that neoliberalism embraces. At worst, neoliberal accounts tend to treat nations as representative economic actors so that trade between countries is analogized as exchange between individuals. At best, the nation is seen to be the site of pluralist political interests, in which different constituencies contest on a relatively equal footing in pursuit of their interests. In the absence of an appreciation of the very different political capabilities that positions of wealth, class and so forth induce, there is no recognition of how global neoliberalism might deepen systemic inequality. For example, the ability of a firm to relocate in pursuit of lower costs may substantially erode the ability of its workers to secure decent incomes or economic security, leading in Marxian terms to an increasing rate of exploitation. Here, the neoclassical view of the mutual interests of two countries in free trade – the internationalism of the neoliberal account – is sustained only by its ignorance of class and power.

In short, while the neoliberal view seeks a world of international co-operation, in which a commitment to enlightened self-interest engenders mutually beneficial policies, it does not demand (or indeed, countenance) measures that would interfere with market signals in pursuit of egalitarian distributions of rewards. Its mechanical view of distribution prevents it from grasping the degree to which its internationalism may induce greater inequality.

The Progressive Competitiveness-Enhancing Perspective

The competitiveness-enhancing perspective is expansive – housing management theorists, social democrats, institutionalist economists and others. The focus here will be on what will be called the 'progressive' competitiveness-enhancing perspective. This admittedly cumbersome term refers to the heterodox theorists who share two views:

- protecting and/or promoting the prosperity of a nation's workers ought to be a (if not the) central goal of economic policy; and
- the achievement of this goal under the conditions obtaining in today's global economy requires the enhancement of national competitiveness.

The most important contributions to the progressive competitiveness-enhancing perspective are the flexible specialization, corporate governance, and human capital approaches. Most recent writings on competitiveness fit within one of these categories, or embrace some mix of the three. The following discussion will first identify the salient features of each, drawing attention to their distinctiveness; this will be followed by a more general discussion of their shared premises which distinguishes competitiveness policy from industrial policy, and a normative assessment.

Flexible Specialization

The most important contribution to the competitiveness debate remains Piore and Sabel's *The Second Industrial Divide*, which appeared in 1984. The persuasiveness of this book has been such that a recent critic of the approach has rightly drawn attention to what he calls the 'flexibility fetish' (Curry, 1992).
Piore and Sabel's central themes can be summarized as follows.

First, industrial organization is necessarily *institutionally embedded*: a nation's industrial organization is always situated in a dense web of social, political and economic institutions. Second, economic development is necessarily *path-dependent*. Once a commitment to an industrial paradigm is made, alternatives often recede to the margins of the economy not because of their inherent weaknesses, but because of their failure to secure the kinds of institutional supports that they require to flourish. Having committed itself to the paradigm, then, a society may lack the institutional means or vision to establish a new model that is better adapted to changed economic circumstances. Together, institutional embeddedness and path-dependence therefore breed *industrial inertia*.

For Piore and Sabel, the early nineteenth century marked a contest between two distinct paradigms. This 'first industrial divide' pitted mass production against craft production. In the event, mass production came to dominate the industrial landscape in the USA, Britain and parts of Europe. Craft production was seen to be eclipsed by a *superior* form of industrial organization. Where craft production survived, governmental policy often sought consciously to replace it with 'national champions' patterned on the US mass-production model.

For Piore and Sabel, we are living now through the 'second industrial divide'. Mass-production has been threatened by growing instability in global markets, increasing sophistication of consumers, and new technologies that allow manufacturing firms to innovate more quickly and to secure economies of scale at much lower levels of output. These changes have given a competitive advantage to 'flexible' firms that can quickly respond to changing demand. While mass producers require stable demand conditions in order to validate high capacity, the flexible firm thrives in the context of uncertainty, rapid change and enhanced consumer sophistication that rewards attention to quality and innovation.

The two industrial paradigms differ in their use of technology and labour. Mass production requires use-specific technology which is suited to long production runs of standardized products. Flexible specialization uses generalized technologies that can be easily reorientated to different production tasks. Complementing this difference, the mass-producing firm employs large numbers of relatively unskilled workers who retain little control over the production process; in Marxian terms, they are appendages of the machine, in which is located the knowledge and skill, rather than vice versa. In contrast, the flexible firm employs broadly skilled workers who possess sufficient knowledge to be able to innovate on the shop floor to develop new products and production methods.

Piore and Sabel draw attention to successful examples of flexible specialization, focusing in particular on the widely studied and celebrated 'Third Italy'. The industrial districts of northern Italy comprise thousands of small firms that have evolved complex webs of co-operation and competition in the textile and other artisan industries. The regional clustering of these firms is a key determinant of their success. In the view of its proponents, clustering of this sort induces external economies by attracting and retaining a highly skilled work force that can move from firm to firm as circumstances warrant, and various forms of interfirm co-operation in production, marketing, research, and risk-sharing. Clustering also gives these firms sufficient political weight to ensure that local government will adopt policies that are supportive of flexible specialization, such as co-ordinating marketing and enforcing labour policies to prevent ruinous forms of competition.[14]

Piore and Sabel emphasize that either paradigm could take benevolent or malevolent forms as concerns the effects on workers' prosperity. Nevertheless, they have been interpreted fairly as advocates of flexible specialization as a viable means of restoring prosperity through the restoration of competitiveness. Provided a suitable institutional structure is established to protect workers' interests, flexible specialization might be expected to enrich workers' lives on the job while providing a basis for increased wages reflecting enhanced skills.

It should be clear that for Piore and Sabel, the achievement of competitiveness through flexible specialization requires institutional changes that reach beyond the firm. A successful transition to flexible specialization would entail a reorientation in the institutions that have historically supported the mass-production paradigm, not least education and labour policies and social welfare arrangements. In this perspective, then, the concept of national competitiveness makes sense – success in global markets will depend on the policies that national governments pursue in support of one industrial paradigm or another.

The Corporate Governance Approach

A second approach will be called here the 'corporate governance' perspective. Like flexible specialization, this perspective highlights the ways in which firms respond to increasing competition as a key determinant of national prosperity. The distinctive feature of this approach is its emphasis on the social, economic and political environment of the firm – its 'corporate culture' – as a pivotal factor affecting intra-firm co-operation and conflict. Of the various progressive competitiveness-enhancing contributions, this speaks most directly to corporate managers and least to government policy-makers, although it implies certain policy reforms.

Lazonick (1991) exemplifies this perspective. Lazonick follows Piore and Sabel in paying careful attention to the manner in which past decisions shape present day corporate strategies and economic outcomes. Forms of industrial organization that yielded success in the past may become fetters to success in the present, as those with vested interests resist fundamental change. Lazonick demonstrates how the forms of corporate governance that propelled British and US firms to success, in the nineteenth and twentieth centuries respectively, ultimately blocked the kinds of innovations that were required to remain competitive.

A key analytical distinction in Lazonick's work is that between the 'innovative' and the 'adaptive' firm. The former is willing to invest in long-term strategies that promise to enhance 'value-creation' (the production of useful commodities at low cost) over the long run, even though they entail higher costs in the short run. In contrast, the latter attempts to remain competitive by intensifying production on the basis of existing technologies and social relations of production. The former entails continual reskilling of workers and the search for new products and better production processes. The latter entails the sweating of labour and other means to reduce costs within the confines of existing products and processes. The former looks ahead, and takes initiatives now to position itself for future competition; the latter looks backward, and seeks to remain competitive by living off past innovations.

For Lazonick, the choice that a nation's firms make regarding these alternatives shapes the level of prosperity that its inhabitants can expect to achieve. To be prosperous a nation needs a critical mass of innovative firms that outperform foreign rivals. The innovative strategy promises better prospects for workers, including higher standards of living and greater workplace satisfaction. But the innovative strategy entails substantial risks. Innovation entails incurring high fixed costs in the short run, as the firm must create the factors of production (for example, new skills and tools) that will ultimately provide it with competitive advantage. Only by producing factors of production not generally available on the market can the firm hope to secure an enduring competitive advantage. The innovative firm is therefore continuously engaged in discovery, in the identification of new problems and the successful design of novel solutions. The learning-by-doing inherent in new techniques requires the full co-operation of a firm's front line workers, upon whom the firm must depend to see the innovation through. And in so far as the innovative strategy requires a lengthy gestation period during which time costs will be high and profits low, the firm must also secure the co-operation of its suppliers and financiers. Like the firm's workers, these parties must provide the firm with 'privileged access' to their services; that is, they must be willing to provide these services at less than the market rate.

How is the firm to secure this co-operation? Lazonick argues for the incorporation of the firm's work force, suppliers and financiers as stakeholders in the firm's corporate community so that they identify their interests with the long-term viability of the firm.[15] For workers, this requires that the firm make long-term commitments in the form of lifetime employment contracts and profit sharing. For all three groups, the firm must replace its market-based (or 'arms-length') relationships with organizational co-ordination. The promise of long-term rewards that are higher than those provided through market-based relationships must induce input suppliers to grant privileged access in the short run if the firm is to realize internal economies in the future.

For Lazonick, the ultimate competitive crisis in the UK and later in the USA reflected a failure of firms to pursue the innovative path. An exclusion of key input providers from the corporate community denied firms the cooperation necessary to risk the innovative strategy. When confronted with external competitive threats, first British and then US firms responded with adaptive strategies that ultimately undermined national prosperity.[16] In contrast, Japan's success stems from the organizational co-ordination that binds workers, financiers and suppliers to the goals of the corporation. The strategy implications follow directly. Firms must make long-term commitments to their stakeholders so as to secure willing co-operation to allow them to pursue the innovative strategy. For its part, the state must take steps to encourage the innovative approach. This would entail the institution of high capital-gains tax rates on short-term holdings, changes in anti-trust laws and, most

importantly, the use of short-term protective tariffs to insulate innovative firms from foreign competition.[17]

The Industrial Relations Approach. An important offshoot of the
corporate governance approach focuses on industrial relations as a
key determinant of competitiveness. The resurgence of neoclassical theory, coupled with the electoral successes of conservatives in
the USA, Britain and on the continent of Europe in the 1970s and
1980s, posed a theoretical and political challenge to trade unions.
Especially in the USA and Britain, unions were identified as key
obstacles to innovation, flexibility and competitiveness. In this supply-
side view, the path to restored national competitiveness and prosperity ran right though the heart of organized labour.

In reaction, institutionalist economists have come to emphasize
not just the salutary effect of unionism on the distribution of economic power within society, but also on corporate performance. For
example, Freeman and Medoff (1984) rely on Hirschman's 'exit/
voice' dichotomy to theorize the effects of unionism. By empower-
ing workers within a firm and by providing them with a vehicle to
mobilize in defence of their interests, unions provide workers with
a vehicle to achieve the 'voice' option within the firm. Unionized
workers are encouraged to seek redress of grievances rather than
avail themselves of the option of 'exit' by quitting. The unionized
firm is therefore the beneficiary of lower labour turnover.[18] Longevity
gives the firm an incentive to invest in worker training, thereby
enhancing their productivity. Higher wages also give the firm the
incentive to seek competitiveness through improved technology and
productivity improvements rather than through efforts to sweat labour.
In short, Freeman and Medoff find that unionized firms achieve
higher productivity than non-union firms in the same industries.

Freeman and Medoff do not focus explicitly on the connection
between unionism and competitiveness, but their work inspired many
contributions to the competitiveness debate. Paralleling the arguments of Lazonick, institutionalists have emphasized the connection between workers' security and willingness to promote the
objectives of management. Mishel and Voos (1992) argue that the
presence of unionism enhances the effects of shopfloor participation schemes that arose especially during the 1980s in the USA in
response to intensifying competition. The protections afforded by
unionism are also necessary to ensure the success of the flexible

specialization model described by Piore and Sabel. In Mishel and Voos' view, the workforce of the successful flexible firm

> must be highly skilled, involved, and motivated – willing to be deployed and redeployed flexibly . . . Unions are a positive force in that they can facilitate a key ingredient of this high-performance business system: a secure, motivated, and participative workforce. (p. 8)

For Mishel and Voos, 'the fundamental point is that high productivity, worker rights, flexibility, unionisation, and economic competitiveness are not incompatible' (p. 10).[19]

In keeping with the tenets of institutionalist theory, this perspective focuses on national competitiveness rather than on the isolated strategies of individual firms. These accounts emphasize the effect of the environment within which competition unfolds on corporate behaviour. Under present institutional and economic conditions, the individual firm that attempts the progressive, high-waged path may face daunting obstacles, not least the unfair competition from firms pursuing the scorched-earth, low-waged path. The switch to the high-performance path may therefore require an orchestrated transformation in the behaviours of firms, unions and the state.

The Human Capital Approach

The flexible specialization and corporate governance approaches call for rather pronounced changes in social and economic organization, to be sure. But in an important sense these analyses remain rather conventional. Both equate the prosperity of a nation's citizens with the competitive success of *its firms*.

The human capital approach, best articulated by Robert B. Reich, Secretary of Labor in the Clinton Administration, rejects this association as symptomatic of 'vestigial thought.' Reich (1991) contends that the competitiveness of a nation's firms is an increasingly meaningless determinant of national prosperity in the global economy. Corporations today are global webs that place each function where it can be performed most cheaply. Post-war technological advances in telecommunications and transportation allow for the efficient co-ordination of far-flung industrial operations, reducing the need for close geographic proximity among research and design, marketing, production and assembly. Hence, a 'British' corporation might create more high-paying jobs in the USA than in Britain, rendering the nationality of the corporation relatively meaningless.

But if competition between nations' firms has come to mean little, competition between nations' *workers* has achieved paramount importance. With firms scouring the globe in search of the best site for each corporate activity, workers now compete for the best jobs. The nation that produces the best trained, most skilled work force is likely to attract the best jobs and, thereby, the highest incomes for its inhabitants (see Cuomo Commission, 1992; Prowse, 1992; and Lynch, 1994).

National prosperity in the new global economy depends on a nation's ability to entice corporations to locate what Reich calls their 'symbolic analytic' functions within its borders. Symbolic analysts are the researchers, managers, creative problem-solvers and other high-skilled professionals. These jobs require high levels of education, add high levels of value to production, and consequently command high remuneration. To achieve prosperity a nation must therefore invest heavily in education, producing the most qualified potential symbolic analysts in the world. As corporations select a nation for such functions, a virtuous cycle develops: 'well-trained workers attract global corporations, which invest and give workers good jobs; the good jobs, in turn, generate additional training and experience' (1990a, p. 59). For the USA, Reich prescribes substantial increases in investment in human capital, ensuring that every reasonably talented child be given the chance to become a symbolic analyst. Notably, Reich argues that virtually all Americans can become symbolic analysts in the new global economy.

Industrial versus Competitiveness Policy

We can now draw out the ways in which contemporary competitiveness policy differs from industrial policy (see Table 1.3). Most fundamentally, competitiveness policy is intended to mediate international, *intra-class* conflict. For most contributors, policy must enhance the ability of domestic firms to outcompete foreign rivals; for Reich, policy must address competition between domestic and foreign workers. For the former, workers and their firms are seen to have largely harmonious interests, provided firms can be cajoled into pursuing mutually beneficial competitiveness strategies. For Reich, although the link between a nation's own firms and national

Table 1.3 Industrial versus competitiveness policy

Industrial policy	Competitiveness policy
Mediation of domestic class conflict: capital versus labour	Mediation of international intra-class conflict: — domestic *vs.* foreign capital — domestic *vs.* foreign labour
Tripartite corporatism	Bilateral, capital–state partnership
Protection from the market	Protection through the market
Full employment (of labour)	Efficient employment (of capital)
Equity/distribution	Efficiency
Maintenance of stability	Adaptation to instability via innovation/flexibility
Mandated co-operation	Enlightened, voluntary paternalism
'Fixing' capital	'Romancing' capital
National interest promoted through protection of labour's interests	National interest promoted through protection of corporate interests
Equality as end	Equality as means

prosperity is severed, workers' interests are nevertheless best served by preparing themselves to meet corporate needs. By serving the corporation best, a nation's workers can outcompete their primary combatant, namely, foreign workers. In short, both efface the social antagonism between capital and labour that figured so prominently in policy formation in the postwar period, replacing it with an inevitable international, intra-class conflict.

As a consequence, tripartite systems of governance have given way in the competitiveness literature to bilateral capital–state partnerships. The role of the state is to provide a context within which corporations can pursue benevolent paths to competitive success, while providing the resources they need to meet global competition. This is tied to a further, fundamental shift away from industrial policy: the (global) market is now taken to be the optimal form of economic integration. The liberalized global market sets the context within which firms must prosper or perish. Rather than shape market outcomes by overcoming the market – as through national planning, for example – desirable outcomes are to be secured by altering the strategies that firms pursue. This is true even for the corporate governance approach of Lazonick, despite his emphasis on the advantages of organizational co-ordination over arms-length market mediation. Organizational co-ordination is deemed superior precisely by virtue of its ability to outcompete market-based micro-co-ordination in the marketplace. In the competitiveness-enhancing approach, to conclude, the protection of workers' livelihoods must occur *through* the market, in place of industrial policy's emphasis on protecting workers *from* the market. Writ large, 'the market' is taken to be the inevitable and/or most desirable form of economic organization, so that industrial strategies must conform to its dictates. If prosperity is to be protected, this must be achieved through market-respecting initiatives.

Respect for the market yields a further distinction between competitiveness policy and its progenitor. Whereas industrial policy was intended to yield *full employment of labour*, competitiveness policy seeks the *efficient employment of capital*. In so far as labour's interests are now tied to that of capital and its ability to outcompete foreign rivals, policy most promote efficiency as the chief means to protect workers' prosperity.

Advocates of industrial policy took the chaotic nature of capitalist competition to be an inherent weakness of the market economy, one that could be overcome through a combination of supply-side and demand-side policies. Industrial policy combined with Keynesian macro-regulation could ensure sufficient investment so as to secure macroeconomic stability. Competitiveness-enhancing policy, on the other hand, takes instability to be ineradicable. Successful strategies are therefore those that *accommodate* instability rather than resist it. The flexible specialization approach is explicit in this regard: the industrial district is a site of continuous reconstitution of interfirm relationships, while workers move quickly from firm to firm in response to changing circumstance and market dictate. The corporate governance approach emphasizes enduring commitments between firms and stakeholders, as we have seen. But this is also justified on the basis of its purported dynamism in meeting competition. Reich's human capital approach, for its part, features a vision of the corporation as a whirling dervish of spin-offs, spin-ins, subcontracting arrangements and kaleidoscopic configurations. Indeed, what is most pronounced about the new corporate form is its impermanence. Competitiveness policy seeks to harness this instability in service of prosperity.

The respect for the market is associated as well in a shift away from state-mandated behaviour to an enlightened, voluntary paternalism. The main thrust of much of the progressive competitiveness-enhancing literature is that business can do better for itself by doing better for its workers. In a complementary way, rather than developing policies that attempt to 'fix' capital, nations are encouraged to pursue policies that 'romance' capital. The human capital approach is most explicit in this regard: the strategy is to build a first-class work force so as to influence firms' location decisions.

Finally, while industrial policy seeks equality as an end in itself, competitiveness-enhancing policy seeks equality as a means toward a more important end, that is, competitive success. Having accepted the dictates of the market as inexorable, the progressive competitiveness-enhancers have undertaken to show how market success can be tied to socially benevolent outcomes. This is not an insignificant achievement, to be sure. But it does substantially break with traditional left defences of equality and economic opportunity and security: now, these must be defended in terms of their effects on capital.

Adjudication of the Competitiveness-Enhancing Perspective

The progressive competitiveness-enhancing perspective differs from the neoliberal view on both nodes of the normative criterion adopted here, which may help to explain why the debate between the two camps has been so sharp (see Krugman, 1994b).

Despite whatever other virtues it may have, the competitiveness-enhancing perspective is explicitly nationalist. By tying a nation's prosperity to *relative* performance – either of its own firms or its own work-force – advocates construct an inherently nationalist and conflictual worldview. In place of the mutual self-interest of orthodox theory, this perspective presents a vision in which national interests are tied to besting foreign rivals. Contra orthodox thought, a nation is better off when its low productivity growth exceeds others' rates rather than when its high productivity growth falls short of that of its competitors.

This nationalism presents practical difficulties for the various competitiveness-enhancing proposals surveyed above. All suffer from a fallacy of composition: what might yield rising prosperity for any one country that pursues these paths is not likely to succeed when all countries do so. Within the interpretive frame of the competitiveness-enhancing perspective, if all enjoy rising productivity at equal rates as a result of enlightened corporate governance, for example, *no one gains*. Paradoxically, this is not the case within the worldview of orthodox theory, where what matters is absolute productivity gains. In this approach, if enlightened corporate governance yields higher productivity growth, then all countries can become better off by pursuing it.

The nationalist impulse is evident in the policies dictated by these approaches as well; again, an aggregation problem emerges. Lazonick's call for protective tariffs to insulate firms as they undertake the innovative path can succeed only if others do not mimic the policy or retaliate. But why should other countries not do so? The answer might be that Lazonick's explicit focus is in promoting the competitiveness of the USA – one of the few countries with the political and economic muscle to influence the trading strategies of at least some of its partners. The policy prescription therefore requires *exploitation of national power in the international arena* – hardly a prescription for internationalism. Moreover, in so far as the innovative approach requires high-volume production and sales to be efficacious, competitor countries can sabotage this strategy by protecting their markets. Rather than each country risking the expensive innovative path – which would require a degree of international co-operation that this approach makes unlikely – the scene is set for a non-cooperative low-level equilibrium wherein each protects its markets to insulate its adaptive firms.

When we recall that the proponents of the competitiveness-enhancing perspective surveyed here are motivated by progressive impulses, there is also an ethical problem associated with the nationalism of their work. Indeed, they seem to be aware of this, although none of those surveyed here grapples explicitly with the global consequences of their perspectives (and in this they are representative of the progressive contributions more generally). For Piore and Sabel, this concern leads to a vision in which developing countries become the site of low-waged mass production, while developed countries specialize in flexible specialization. For Reich, the ambivalence is particularly acute. In his major work, the emphasis is entirely on the USA struggling to lure the good jobs away from other countries so as to promote rising US prosperity. In this account, low-paid routine production jobs migrate to the poor countries. While this might cement existing inequalities between the North and the South, Reich defends this distribution of jobs on grounds that any increase in employment will help poor countries. But elsewhere he expresses uneasiness about this implicit nationalism. In work published a year before *The Work of Nations*, he proposes 'multilateral, rule-oriented negotiations designed to allocate [symbolic analyst] jobs among nations according to some set of agreed-upon criteria' (1990b, p. 42). It must be emphasized that this call for the sharing of good jobs represents a repudiation of the central thesis of *The Work of Nations*. It repudiates not only the right of corporations to allocate these jobs according to competitive interests, but it also obviates the need for the USA to expend any additional resources on education to compete for these jobs.

Domestically, however, each of these proposals is egalitarian, as we have seen. In each case, greater equality of income and substantive opportunities is taken to be a critical determinant of renewed competitiveness and, thereby, prosperity. This feature has given the progressive competitiveness-enhancers wide credibility among the left. But as emphasized above, the commitment to equality is *instrumental* rather than *intrinsic*. This subjects equality to a daunting test: not whether it is defensible in its own right, but whether it can outcompete other models of industrial organization founded on inequality. Hence, market competition is to be the arbiter of whether society can and should sustain equality.

Is it reasonable to expect that equality can meet the test of global economic integration? It must be emphasized that, like neoliberalism, the competitiveness-enhancing perspective takes global market liberalization as a desirable and/or inevitable form of economic integration. Both accept the rules of the game of global neoliberalism as given; disagreement is reserved for the determinants of prosperity and, consequently, the strategies that will ensure it.

On what grounds, then, should we assume that the progressive approaches will outcompete less benevolent competition strategies? If other countries are able to mimic the training or forms of industrial organization promoted by the competitiveness-enhancers, but are able to secure the willingness of workers through repression, might not they be able to succeed in global markets? Critics of 'Toyotism' have argued persuasively that Japanese firms have secured competitiveness precisely by denying workers independent representation on the shopfloor (Dohse *et al.*, 1985; Tomaney, 1990; Curry, 1992). In this context, lifetime employment coupled with the associated practice of firms' hiring only at the entry level strips workers of the ability to switch firms mid-career. Hence, they are deprived of Hirschman's 'voice' *and* 'exit'. In the absence of strong workers' rights, the 'organizational co-ordination' and 'privileged access' that Lazonick celebrates are transmogrified into indentured subservience, workplace coercion and super-exploitation. Similarly, as Piore and Sabel note, flexible specialization may acquire exploitative forms in the absence of strong worker protections. In the latter case, egalitarianism may be sacrificed in pursuit of corporate interests.

The Competition-Reducing Perspective

A third perspective in the competitiveness debate has been advanced by certain radical institutionalists, neo-Marxists, Keynesians and other heterodox theorists. The defining feature of this perspective is its attention to the nature of the regimes that facilitate global economic integration. These theorists reject the claims that are made on behalf of neoliberalism, on the one hand, and the progressive competitiveness-enhancing proposals on the other. In their place, this school calls for the implementation of new rules of economic engagement that promote socially benevolent outcomes by tempering competition. Rather than seek renewed prosperity via enhanced competitiveness, this school seeks to advance the interests of working people by *reducing international competition*.[20]

This approach calls for the *upward global harmonization of standards* (including minimum wages, environmental protections and worker rights) by conscious design to prevent capital from exploiting regional differences that would otherwise exist. The presumption is that under the neoliberal regime capitalist competition will generate pressure toward a downward levelling in conditions of life by rewarding capital that operates in those regions where social regulations are lowest.

Although advocates of this approach range across theoretical perspectives, the demand for harmonization reflects an implicit commitment to central tenets of institutionalist theory as advanced by Commons (1924) and others. For institutionalists, the market is seen to be a socially and politically instituted process rather than a natural outcome of social evolution. Unlike neoclassical theorists, who see most forms of state intervention into the market as interferences, institutionalists recognize that the market is not *constrained* but actually *defined by* the rules, norms, and institutions that give rise to it (cf. Dugger, 1989). In this account, the market is always overdetermined by a broader social, natural and cultural matrix. In this account, then, the neoclassical abstraction of 'the market' is thoroughly misleading, as it implies an entity with a unified, essential nature that stands apart from society. In place of this distortion, institutionalists emphasize the diversity of market processes and market outcomes: 'the market' is presented as a heterogeneous entity taking a variety of forms as it develops across time and place. This perspective is critical of the idealized neoclassical free market economy. Institutionalists view market outcomes as valid only to the degree that they are 'fair', that is, to the degree that they result from voluntary agreement between parties that exhibit genuinely equal power. But in an unregulated labour market, fairness of this sort does not obtain: with its greater ability to withhold agreement, capital holds substantial power over labour. Hence, the worker does not receive 'reasonable value' when she sells her labour power. This imbalance can only be overcome through regulation that protects labour, such as legislation that promotes union bargaining (Ramstad, 1987).

The globalization of the neoliberal market ideal is likewise seen to threaten prosperity by undermining fairness in the labour market. While global neoliberalism may or may not enhance global economic efficiency – by no means a certainty for institutionalists – it simultaneously undermines the institutional foundations of prosperity for working people, income equality, and fairness. For example, by allowing firms to take advantage of cross-national differences in labour and environmental standards and wage levels, neoliberalism threatens the hard-won historical protections of workers and communities from the most ravaging effects of market processes. To the degree that neoliberalism makes the threat of capital flight more credible, communities may be forced to lower standards or make wage and tax concessions even in the absence of plant relocation.

In keeping with its view of market processes more generally, this institutionalist perspective understands that market competition generates diverse effects depending on the broader social context within which it occurs. Proponents of the competition-reducing perspective therefore investigate rules, norms and institutions in order to determine which constellation of these are most apt to promote desirable outcomes via market competition. Advocates investigate which aspects of social life can be taken out of competition,[21] short of the elimination of market integration altogether, without eroding whatever progressive effects competition is able to induce (DeMartino and Cullenberg, 1995). In addressing this question, the institutionalist premise concerning the social construction of the market leads to the conclusion that what must be 'in' competition in order for it to generate benevolent effects is variable and subject to change through public policy and political mobilizations. There is therefore *no natural or essential limit to what can be taken out of competition*. The institutionalist perspective therefore embraces a twofold theoretical and political project: to determine which important aspects of social life can be taken out of competition at a particular moment without impairing the beneficial effects of competition; and to investigate how society might be reformed through public policy so as to allow for the removal of other aspects of social life from competition in the future.

The institutionalist view also provides a basis for interrogating the *qualitative nature of innovation* that market competition might induce. Institutionalists emphasize that the rules and institutions governing competition affect not just how the spoils of innovation will be distributed, but also the *kinds* of innovations that are permitted and encouraged. Rather than treat innovation as a necessarily benevolent outcome of market competition, we are encouraged to investigate the forms that innovation takes, and to understand that society can exert decisive influence over the qualitative nature of economic development. When wages, hours and work intensity are removed from competition, the sweating of labour ceases to be a viable innovation; when strict environmental standards are enforced, new technologies which increase external social costs while reducing private costs are eclipsed by other technologies that reduce social costs. Hence, taking aspects of social life out of competition becomes a means to alter the fundamental character not only of competition, but of innovation as well – to exert social control over this powerful determinant of the quality of social life (cf. Piore, 1990, and Herzenberg *et al.*, 1990).

Policy Proposals

Advocates of this perspective have offered various policy proposals that are intended to remove fundamental aspects of social life from international competition. Typically, these entail proposals to harmonize labour, environmental and other standards, and/or to offset international differences in such standards to prevent 'ruinous competition'.

Conditioning Trade on Standards

The simplest means for a country to institute protections from competition based on low standards is to restrict access to its market to those countries that meet some minimum level of social protections. For example, the United States has banned the import of goods produced with prison labour since 1890 (Perez-Lopez, 1988). During the 1980s the US government also tied trade preferences to the protection of labour rights. Access to the US market has also been tied to environmental standards. This approach is unilateral, and hence allows each country to tie market access to its own standards. This is both a strength and a weakness: while unilateralism facilitates action, it nevertheless creates opportunities for each nation to use standards as a pretext in order to protect the domestic market.

The Social Charter Approach

A far more ambitious approach entails the adoption of a social charter. To date, the most notable instance of countries adopting a social charter is the EU. The stated purpose of the Charter is to harmonize certain social and labour standards throughout Europe. Included in the Charter are fundamental rights ranging from employment protections to the protection of children, elderly and disabled persons (Kraw, 1990).[22]

In recent years many have argued that a social charter should be established as part of the process of North American integration (for example, Castañeda and Heredia, 1992; Brown, Goold and Cavanagh, 1992). These proposals include provisions for harmonization of minimum environmental and labour standards, greater community and worker participation in their enforcement, and a strengthened social safety net.

The Sullivan Principles Approach

Under an alternative approach suggested by Bhagwati (1993) for North America, a high-standard country would require domestic corporations that undertake direct investment in low-standard countries to enforce its own national worker, social and environmental protections in its foreign subsidiaries. This approach is inspired by the Sullivan Principles of the 1980s which governed the behaviour of US multinational corporations with subsidiaries in South Africa during the apartheid era. Bhagwati argues that this approach would prevent social dumping while respecting national autonomy of developing countries. In his view, a nation may legitimately enforce behaviours on firms of its own nationality without undermining the sovereignty of other nations.

The Social Tariff Approach

A fourth proposal is the social tariff approach (Ramstad, 1987; Lebowitz, 1988; Chapman, 1991; Dorman, 1992). Under this regime, countries with relatively high standards would levy tariffs on imports from countries with lower standards. The goal is to protect gains in labour and environmental protections achieved in high-standard countries by cancelling the competitive advantage enjoyed by firms operating in low-standard countries. Ultimately, it is hoped, such trade restrictions would induce low-standard countries to improve their social protections.

The Social Index Tariff Structure (SITS)

DeMartino and Cullenberg (1995) propose a new approach intended to remove important aspects of social life from competition. A Social Index Tariff Structure (SITS) trading regime would reward those countries that perform well in promoting the human development of their inhabitants relative to their means through tariff protection against those countries that perform poorly in this regard. Rather than being punished in global markets for promoting rising wages or taxing corporations to fund universal health care or education, a country would attain open access to the markets of other good performers while being insulated from foreign competition based on low wages and standards. Unlike the social tariff approach summarized above, this approach would be rule-based and would result from multilateral negotiations that would determine the criterion for establishing the social tariffs.

As a first approximation, the Human Development Index (HDI) computed by the United Nations Development Programme (UNDP) can serve as a measure of each country's performance in promoting human development. The HDI is a composite measure that combines information on each country's literacy and mortality rates and welfare (computed from income). It is intended to capture the fact that human development reflects peoples' full set of economic, political and cultural capabilities and is therefore not reducible to any one indicator (such as GDP per caput). Ideally, the index would include information on other important aspects of social life, such as income equality and political freedoms; to date, lack of sufficient data and methodological controversies have prevented the extension of the HDI to include such indicators. Wealthy countries generally perform better than poor countries in HDI rankings because income appears as one term in the index, and because national income affects the other components. As such, HDI performance alone cannot provide a basis for the institution of social tariffs, as this would merely penalize poor countries for being poor. Instead, we must correct for per caput income so as to measure each country's performance relative to its means. DeMartino and Cullenberg (1995) divide countries into income deciles, and compute for each country the ratio of its HDI to the average HDI for its income decile. Hence, good performers achieve a ratio value greater than one; poor performers exhibit values less than one.

The 'means-corrected' HDI does not include information on how well workers are compensated. If wages are to be taken out of international competition, the SITS regime must incorporate some measure of employment practices. International differences in productivity levels complicate this goal.[23] One crude way to handle this complication is to weight the means-corrected HDI by the earnings share of value added in manufacturing. This weighting yields a 'class-means adjusted HDI', a measure of performance which can provide the basis for establishing a multilateral, rule-based social tariff structure. Countries that export to other nations with significantly higher performance would face a social tariff, while those countries that export to equal or lower performers would gain free access to their markets.

The goal of a SITS regime is to promote human development by providing countries with the incentive to improve, and by penalizing countries that seek growth or competitiveness via strategies that impede human development. But in so far as some poor performers will be poor countries, the regime might penalize the worst off. The SITS approach provides a remedy to this problem: a SITS regime would generate new sources of development funds that could be targeted to poor countries that demonstrate good faith efforts to promote human development.

Finally, a SITS regime should ideally be instituted alongside a strong social charter which spells out the minimum labour, environmental and social standards that all countries must adopt in order to be able to join a trading system. As lagging member countries improve their standards in order to enhance their positions in the SITS, the minima specified in the charter could be raised. Hence, a SITS-augmented charter would include a dynamic toward improving social protections over time.

Adjudication of the Competition-Reducing Perspective

The competition-reducing perspective is explicitly internationalist. Notably, it shares the neoclassical antipathy to the nationalism that informs the progressive competitiveness-enhancing perspective. In this vision, gains made at the expense of others are ill-gotten. Rather than pursue success in a game that blesses winners with the sacrifices of the losers, the competition-reducing approach seeks rules that promote mutual benefits. But unlike the orthodoxy, the competition reducers refuse the notion that global neoliberalism represents a regime of mutually beneficial rules.

The competition reducers presume a worldview that breaks sharply with the orthodoxy. For the former, society is marked by deep divisions and enduring fissures that yield very different levels of economic and political capabilities across groups. Hence, notions like 'national' interest make little sense, as they obscure the differential impact of events on society's members. This view rejects the pluralism underpinning the orthodox view of politics, replacing it with a conception of unequal access to power. Hence, the kind of internationalism endorsed by the competition-reducers refuses the orthodox notion of nation as unified economic actor. This internationalism probes into the fabric of a nation, to interrogate how any particular global economic regime affects the diverse groups that constitute a given society.

This approach is also egalitarian. While the orthodoxy refuses to make value judgements about preference orderings and interpersonal utility comparisons, the critics see this refusal as a value judgement that has the effect of cementing the *status quo*, no matter how unequal (cf. Daly, 1991). Rather than read formal freedom in markets an indicator of equality of substantive freedoms, the competition-reducers presume the existence of fundamental inequalities that bias economic outcomes toward the interests of some and against others. In diverse ways, the various proposals of the competition-reducing perspective seek to inaugurate increasing equality – not as a means to something else deemed more important, as in the case of the competitiveness-enhancers – but as a vital end in itself.

Hence, the competition-reducing perspective breaks with both of the other approaches in fundamental ways. Rather than treat the liberalized global market as an ideal or an inevitable form of economic organization, the competition-reducing perspective understands all forms of economy to be historically contingent, socially constructed and hence, malleable. Rather than seek ways to accommodate what it sees to be an inherently flawed mode of organization, it develops alternatives that accommodate those normative criteria that are most highly valued. In short, rather than prove that equality can survive neoliberalism, it seeks forms of economic organization that ensure equality, both domestically and internationally.

1.5 CONCLUSION

This paper has suggested that the competitiveness debate arose out of the economic difficulties and sense of economic malaise of the 1970s and 1980s in the USA and across Europe. In the face of a resurgence of neoclassical orthodoxy and apparent weaknesses in social democratic institutions and policies, many on the left came to advocate competitiveness strategies that were progressive in the sense that they seemed to retain traditional left commitments to equality and economic security and opportunity for working people. The progressive competitiveness-enhancers have sought to reverse the fortunes of working people by envisioning strategies that at once yield competitive viability and economic prosperity.

But this approach will not do. As orthodox economists rightly argue, the approach is nationalistic and is undeserving of support by left progressives. In its place, the paper has presented and advocated the competition reducing perspective on the grounds that it is uniquely internationalist and egalitarian.

This is not to say that the competition-reducing approach yields simple solutions to the pressing problems of economic privation and inequality. This approach cannot succeed in the absence of other, far-reaching structural changes in the global economy, to be sure. It must also resonate for progressive activists and theorists in the North and the South, and so must span chasms of economic and political capabilities, but also enduring disagreements over cultural norms. Rather than be imposed on the South by a North that is fearful of losing economic hegemony, it must take forms that speak directly to the needs and aspirations of the most impoverished.

This requirement is not trivial. To date, efforts to reduce competition in the global economy have tended to be pursued by activists of the North, often over the objections of activists of the South. Southern activists have opposed revisions of US trade law that tie trade privileges to efforts by trading partners to protect labour rights; more recently, developing nations objected to the linking of trade to labour rights in the Uruguay Round of GATT negotiations and in recent negotiations within ASEAN. Southern activists interpreted these initiatives as guises to mask protectionism by the North. Efforts of activists in the North to ban child labour have met with similar resistance.

These challenges seem to require a transformation in the manner in which activists in the North develop national strategies (cf. Robinson, 1995; Cavanagh, 1993; Hunter, 1995). While the temptation for Northern activists to use the state power of the USA and other OECD countries in pursuit of benevolent outcomes is substantial, unilateral steps of this sort may be counter-productive to the degree that they rely on and may reinforce existing disparities in power and privilege in international relations. Northern activists may be loathe to forfeit the autonomy provided to them by this state of affairs, but unless they take this risk, they may find Southern activists increasingly allied with neoliberals or the competitiveness-enhancers against competition-reducing initiatives. And this would amount to a defeat for activists of the North and South.

Notes

1. The author would like to thank Philip Arestis and Malcolm Sawyer for their extremely helpful comments on an earlier draft of this paper, and Kerry Riccono for her research assistance.
2. DeMartino (1996) explores these matters more extensively. See also the discussion of upward harmonization in Hunter (1995).
3. These literatures are voluminous. On regulation theory see Aglietta (1979) and Lipietz (1987); on the social structures of accumulation, see Bowles, Gordon and Weisskopf (1990) and several of the essays in Marglin and Schor (1990); and on long-wave theory see Mandel (1980). For a variety of such perspectives see the essays in Schor and You (1995).
4. For a detailed discussion of productivity and profitability in OECD countries see Glyn, Hughes, Lipietz and Singh (1990) and Armstrong, Glyn and Harrison (1991).
5. For a critical view of the contemporary focus on globalization, see

Hirst (1996), Panitch (1994), Zevin (1992) and Gordon (1988). In various ways, each problematizes the notion that global forces are overwhelming national government authority, and/or are responsible for the current economic malaise. In this paper I take no position on this debate, as it is beyond my present purposes. The salient point is that the widely-held presumption of globalization accounted (in part) for the rise of the competitiveness debate, as discussed below.

6. For examples see Magaziner and Reich (1982), Adams and Klein (1983), the President's Commission on Industrial Competitiveness (1985), Lenz (1991) and the Cuomo Commission on Competitiveness (1992). Stokes (1992) surveys the various competitiveness councils formed in the USA in the late 1980s and early 1990s.
7. For discussions of industrial policies in OECD countries see Zysman (1983), Curzon Price (1981), Hall (1986) and Amable and Petit (1996). For a discussion of industrial policy in East Asia see Chang (1994), Johnson (1985), Vestal (1993) and Wade (1993).
8. Chang (1994) and Sawyer (1992) present alternative theoretical justifications for industrial policies.
9. This term was used by Joel Rogers in a presentation at the University of Denver, December 1995.
10. For example, see Beje et al. (1987), Frohlich (1989), Hirst and Zeitlin (1989), Cowling (1990), Hughes (1993), Sandholz (1995) and the numerous OECD and EC reports cited in Montagnon (1990). Curzon Price's (1981) study of European industrial policy exemplifies this ideological transition.
11. For example, Cousins (a Labour member of Parliament and spokesperson for Labour on industry) sums up the British Labour Party's view on the revival of the British economy: 'Building the basis for competitiveness and social cohesion is a task for the left' (1993, p. 170).
12. The World Bank's 1995 *World Development Report* exemplifies this internationalist perspective.
13. A welfarist normative framework evaluates economic states by sole reference to the subjective judgements of individuals about their own condition under these states.
14. See also Best (1990). Note that some critics charge that the advocates of flexible specialization err in their interpretation of the Third Italy – of its origins, desirability and the degree to which it can (and should) be generalized. Curry (1992) provides a particularly astute examination of these matters. He argues that the Third Italy is far from the worker Utopia portrayed by its advocates; that the global trend toward flexibility (such as it exists) generally occurs within large firms and concerns innovation of style rather than content, and continued use of de-skilled, casualized labour; and that flexible specialization is necessarily associated with labour market fragmentation which benefits the minority of workers and consumers at the expense of the ever-more vulnerable majority.
15. This entails giving pride of place to all manner of extra-market relationships and institutional arrangements that neoclassicals would identify

as rigidities or sources of inefficiency. The essays collected in Matzner and Streeck (1991) make this point especially forcefully. See also Traxler and Unger (1994); on the need for cooperation see Hart (1992), Magaziner and Reich (1982), Lodge and Vogel (1987) and Reich (1995).

16. Cf the arguments advanced by Marshall (1987), Best (1990), Bowles, Gordon and Weisskopf (1990), Thurow (1992) and Bluestone and Bluestone (1992).

17. While the parallels between the corporate governance approach and the developmental state approach as pursued by Japan and the East Asian NICs are explicit in Lazonick's work, he does not envision a central role for state agencies. Instead, the state is to assume an accommodating role, while the chief impetus for reform is to come from corporate leaders once they come to appreciate the benefits of enlightened self-interest and interfirm linkages.

18. See also Cutcher-Gershenfeld (1991), Magaziner and Reich (1982), Ehrenberg (1990), Freeman (1994) and OECD (1995).

19. For theorists in this camp, a progressive industrial relations system is the key building block for the construction of what is today called a 'high performance economy'. Appelbaum and Batt (1994) and Bluestone and Bluestone (1992) argue that strong unions committed to co-operation with management provides the most progressive means to achieve restored competitiveness (cf. van Liemt, 1992).

20. This perspective finds historical precedent in the classical doctrine of labour organization. Unions seek to remove wages and working conditions from competition to ensure that competition finds alternative bases, such that no firm can win competitive advantage by exploiting its work force beyond some codified level.

21. Such as the harmonization of wages (via union bargaining) or labour standards (via government regulation).

22. Substantial debate exists over the significance of the EU social charter. See Addison and Siebert (1994), Lange (1993) and Streeck (1994) for contrasting perspectives.

23. The institutionalist perspective rejects the view that international wage differences simply reflect productivity differences. See Mead (1990).

References

Adams, F.G. and L.R. Klein (1983) 'Economic evaluation of industrial policies for growth and competitiveness: overview', in F.G. Adams and L.R. Klein (eds) *Industrial Policies for Growth and Competitiveness* (Lexington, Mass.: Lexington) pp. 3–11.

Addison, J. and W.S. Siebert (1994) 'Recent developments in social policy and in the new European Union', *Industrial and Labor Relations Review*, **48**(1): 5–27.

Aglietta, M. (1979) *A Theory of Capitalist Regulation* (London: NLB).

Amable, B. and P. Petit (1996) 'New scale and scope for industrial policies in the 1990s', *International Review of Applied Economics*, **10**(1): 23–41.

George DeMartino 55

Appelbaum, E. and R. Batt (1994) *The New American Workplace: Transforming Work Systems in the United States* (Ithaca: ILR).
Armstrong, P., A. Glyn and J. Harrison (1991) *Capitalism Since 1945* (Oxford: Blackwell).
Beje, P.R., J. Groenewegen, I. Kostoulas, C.W.A.M. van Paridon and J.H.P. Paelinck (1987) *A Competitive Future for Europe?* (London: Croom Helm).
Best, M. (1990) *The New Competition* (Cambridge, Mass.: Harvard University Press).
Bhagwati, J. (1993) 'American rules, Mexican jobs', *New York Times*, 24 March, p. 13.
Bluestone, B. and I. Bluestone (1992) *Negotiating the Future* (New York: Basic).
Bluestone, B. and B. Harrison (1982) *The Deindustrialization of America* (New York: Basic).
Bowles, S., D. Gordon and T. Weisskopf (1990) *After the Wasteland: A Democratic Economics for the Year 2000* (Armonk, NY: M.E. Sharpe).
Boyer, R. (1995) 'Capital–labour relations in OECD countries: from the Fordist Golden Age to contrasted national trajectories', in J. Schor and J.-I. You (eds) *Capital, the State and Labour* (Aldershot: Edward Elgar) pp. 18–69.
Brown, G. Jr, J.W. Goold and M. Cavanagh (1992) 'Making trade fair', *World Policy Journal* (Spring) pp. 309–27.
Business Week (1991, August) 'What happened to the American Dream?' pp. 80–5.
Castañeda, J. and C. Heredia (1992) 'Another NAFTA: what a good agreement should offer', *World Policy Journal* (Fall/Winter) pp. 673–85.
Cavanagh, J. (1993) 'Strategies to Advance Labor and Environmental Standards: A North–South Dialogue', *Capitalism, Nature, Socialism*, **4**(3): 1–6.
Chang, H. (1994) *The Political Economy of Industrial Policy* (New York: St Martin's).
Chapman, D. (1991) 'Environmental standards and international trade in automobiles and copper: the case for a social tariff', *Natural Resources Journal*, **31**(3): 449–61.
Commons, J.R. (1924) *Legal Foundations of Capitalism* (New York: Macmillan).
Cousins, J. (1993) 'Labour's policies for the revival of British competitiveness', in K. Hughes (ed.) *The Future of UK Competitiveness and the Role of Industrial Policy* (London: Policy Studies) pp. 166–70.
Cowling, K. (1990) 'A new industrial strategy: preparing Europe for the turn of the century', *International Journal of Industrial Organization*, **8**(2): 165–83.
Crotty, J. (1989) 'The limits of Keynesian macroeconomic policy in the age of the global marketplace', in A. MacEwan and W.K. Tabb (eds) *Instability and Change in the World Economy* (New York: Monthly Review) pp. 82–100.
Cuomo Commission on Competitiveness (1992) *America's Agenda: Rebuilding Economic Strength* (Armonk, NY: M.E. Sharpe).
Curry, J. (1992) 'The flexibility fetish: a review essay on flexible specialisation', *Capital and Class*, **50**: 99–126.

Curzon Price, V. (1981) *Industrial Policies in the European Community* (London: St Martin's).

Cutcher-Gershenfeld, J. (1991) 'The impact on economic performance of a transformation in workplace relations', *Industrial and Labor Relations Review*, 44(2): 241–60.

Daly, H.E. (1991) *Steady-State Economics* (2nd edn, Washington, DC: Island).

DeMartino, G. (1996) 'Against global neoliberalism: normative principles and policy alternatives', *New Political Science*, 35 (Spring): 21–42.

DeMartino, G. and S. Cullenberg (1995) 'Economic integration in an uneven world: an internationalist perspective', *International Review of Applied Economics*, 9(1): 1–23.

Dohse, K., U. Jürgens and T. Malsch (1985) 'From "Fordism" to "Toyotism"? The social organization of the labor process in the Japanese automobile industry', *Politics and Society* (June) pp. 115–46.

Dorman, P. (1992) 'The social tariff approach to international disparities in environmental and worker right standards: history, theory and some initial evidence', in C. Lehman and R. Moore (eds) *Multinational Culture: Social Impacts of a Global Economy* (Westport, CT: Greenwood) pp. 203–23.

Dugger, W. (1989) 'Radical institutionalism: basic concepts', in W. Dugger (ed.) *Radical Institutionalism: Contemporary Voices* (New York: Greenwood Press) pp. 1–20.

Ehrenberg, R. (1990) 'Introduction: do compensation policies matter?', *Industrial and Labor Relations Review*, 43 (February): 3–12.

Freeman, R.B. (1994) 'How labor fares in advanced economies', in R.B. Freeman (ed.) *Working Under Different Rules* (New York: Sage) pp. 1–28.

Freeman, R.B. and L.F. Katz (1994) 'Rising wage inequality: the United States vs. other advanced countries', in R.B. Freeman (ed.) *Working Under Different Rules* (New York: Sage) pp. 29–62.

Freeman, R.B. and J.L. Medoff (1984) *What Do Unions Do?* (New York: Basic).

Frohlich, H. (1989) 'International competitiveness: alternative macroeconomic strategies and changing perceptions in recent years', in A. Francis and P.K.M. Tharakan (eds) *The Competitiveness of European Industry* (London: Routledge) pp. 21–40.

Glyn, A., A. Hughes, A. Lipietz and A. Singh (1990) 'The rise and fall of the Golden Age', in S. Marglin and J. Schor (eds) *The Golden Age of Capitalism* (Oxford: Clarendon) pp. 39–125.

Gordon, D. (1988) 'The global economy: new edifice or crumbling foundations?', *New Left Review*, 168: 24–65.

Grabel, I. (1995) 'Speculation-led economic development: toward a post-Keynesian interpretation of financial liberalization programs in the third world', *International Review of Applied Economics*, 9(2): 127–49.

Hall, G. (1986) *European Industrial Policy* (New York: St Martin's).

Hart, J. (1992) *Rival Capitalists* (Ithaca: Cornell University Press).

Herzenberg, S., J.F. Perez-Lopez and S.K. Tucker (1990) 'Introduction: labor standards and development in the global economy', in S. Herzenberg and J.F. Perez-Lopez (eds) *Labor Standards and Development in the Global*

Economy (Washington, DC: US Department of Labor) pp. 1–16.

Hill, S. (1993) *Fostering Competitiveness in the High Technology Industries* (NY: Garland).

Hirst, P. (1996) 'Globaloney', *Prospect* (February) pp. 29–33.

Hirst, P. and J. Zeitlin (1989) 'Introduction', in P. Hirst and J. Zeitlin (eds) *Reversing Industrial Decline?* (Oxford: Berg) pp. 1–16.

Hughes, K.S. (1993) 'Introduction: internationalisation, integration and European competitiveness', in K.S. Hughes (ed.) *European Competitiveness* (Cambridge University Press) pp. 1–7.

Hunter, A. (1995) 'Globalization from below? Promises and perils of the new internationalism', *Social Policy* (Summer): 6–13.

Johnson, C. (1986) 'The institutional foundations of Japanese industrial policy', *California Management Review*, **27**(4): 59–69.

Korpi, W. and M. Shalev (1979) 'Strikes, industrial relations and class conflict in capitalist societies', *British Journal of Sociology*, **30**(2): 164–87.

Kraw, G. (1990) 'The Community Charter of the Fundamental Social Rights of Workers', *Hastings International and Comparative Law Review*, **13**: 471–7.

Krugman, P. (1994a) 'Competitiveness: a dangerous obsession', *Foreign Affairs*, **73**(2): 28–44.

Krugman, P. (1994b) *Peddling Prosperity: Economic Sense and Nonsense in the Age of Diminished Expectations* (New York: Norton).

Lange, P. (1993) 'Maastricht and the social protocol: why did they do it?', *Politics and Society*, **21**(1): 5–36.

Lazonick, W. (1991) *Business Organization and the Myth of the Market Economy* (New York: Cambridge University Press).

Lebowitz, M. (1988) 'Trade and class: labor strategies in a world of strong capital', *Studies in Political Economy*, **27** (Autumn): 137–48.

Lenz, A.J. (1991) *Beyond Blue Horizons* (New York: Praeger).

Lipietz, A. (1987) *Mirages and Miracles* (London: Verso).

Lodge, G.C. and E.F. Vogel (1987) *Ideology and National Competitiveness* (Boston: Harvard Business School).

Lynch, L.M. (1994) 'Payoffs to alternative training strategies at work', in R.B. Freeman (ed.) *Working Under Different Rules* (New York: Sage) pp. 63–96.

MacEwan, A. (1991) 'What's "new" about the "new international economy"?', *Socialist Review*, **3–4**: 111–31.

Magaziner, I. and R. Reich (1982) *Minding America's Business* (New York: Harcourt Brace, Jovanovich).

Mandel, E. (1980) *Long Waves of Capitalist Development* (Cambridge University Press).

Marglin, S. and J. Schor (1990) *The Golden Age of Capitalism* (Oxford: Clarendon).

Marshall, R. (1987) *Unheard Voices: Labor and Economic Policy in a Competitive World* (New York: Basic).

Matzner, E. and W. Streeck (eds) (1991) *Beyond Keynesianism* (Aldershot: Edward Elgar).

McCloskey, D.N. (1993) 'Competitiveness and the antieconomics of decline', in D.N. McCloskey (ed.) *Second Thoughts: Myths and Morals of U.S.*

Economic History (Oxford University Press) pp. 167–73.

Mead, W.R. (1990) *The Low-Wage Challenge to Global Growth: The Labor Cost–Productivity Imbalance in Newly Industrialized Countries* (Washington, DC: Economic Policy Institute).

Mishel, L. and P. Voos (1992) 'Introduction', in L. Mishel and P. Voos (eds) *Unions and Economic Competitiveness* (Armonk, NY: M.E. Sharpe) pp. 1–12.

Montagnon, P. (ed.) (1990) *European Competition Policy* (New York: Council on Foreign Affairs).

New York Times (1991), Business section, 17 November, p. 1.

Newsweek (1995) 'Special Report: The rise of the overclass', 31 July, pp. 32–46.

OECD (1995) *Employment Outlook*, July (Paris: OECD).

Panitch, L. (1994) 'Globalisation and the State', in R. Miliband and L. Panitch (eds) *Socialist Register* (London: Martin Press) pp. 60–3.

Perez-Lopez, J. (1988) 'Conditioning trade on foreign labor law: the U.S. approach', *Comparative Labor Law Journal*, **9**(2): 253–92.

Phillips, K. (1990) *The Politics of Rich and Poor* (New York: Random House).

Piore, M. (1990) 'Labor standards and business strategies', in S. Herzenberg and J.F. Perez-Lopez (eds) *Labor Standards and Development in the Global Economy* (Washington, DC: US Department of Labor).

Piore, M. and C. Sabel (1984) *The Second Industrial Divide* (New York: Basic).

President's Commission on Industrial Competitiveness (1985) *Global Competition: The New Reality, vol. II* (Washington, DC: US Government).

Prowse, M. (1992) 'Is America in decline?', *Harvard Business Review*, **70** (4): 34–45.

Ramstad, Y. (1987) 'Free trade versus fair trade: import barriers as a problem of reasonable value', *Journal of Economic Issues*, **21**(1): 5–32.

Rawls, J. (1971) *A Theory of Justice* (Cambridge, Mass.: Harvard University Press).

Reich, R.B. (1990a) 'Who is us?', *Harvard Business Review*, **68** (January–February): 53–64.

Reich, R.B. (1990b) 'We need a strategic trade policy', *Challenge* (July–August) 38–42.

Reich, R.B. (1991) *The Work of Nations* (New York: Knopf).

Reich, S. (1995) 'Ideology and competitiveness: the basis for US and Japanese economic policies', in D. Rapkin and W. Avery (eds) *National Competitiveness in a Global Economy* (Boulder, Colo.: Lynne Rienner).

Robinson, I. (1995) 'Globalization and democracy', *Dissent* (Summer) 373–80.

Sandholtz, W. (1995) 'Cooperating to compete: the European experiment', in D. Rapkin and W. Avery (eds) *National Competitiveness in a Global Economy* (Boulder, Colo.: Lynne Rienner).

Sawyer, M. (1991) 'Industrial Policy', in M. Artis and D. Cobham (eds) *Labour's Economic Policies, 1974–1979* (Manchester University Press) pp. 158–175.

Sawyer, M. (1992) 'Reflections on the nature and role of industrial policy', *Metroeconomica*, **43**(1–2): 51–73.

Schor, J. and J.-I. You (eds) (1995) *Capital, the State and Labour* (Aldershot: Edward Elgar).

Sen, A. (1992) *Inequality Reexamined* (Cambridge, Mass.: Harvard University Press).

Stokes, B. (1992) 'Is Industrial policy now mentionable?', *National Journal*, **24**(10): 576–7.

Streeck, W. (1994) 'European social policy after Maastricht: The "social dialogue" and "subsidiarity"', *Economic and Industrial Democracy*, **15**: 151–77.

Thurow, L. (1992) *Head to Head* (New York: William Morrow).

Tomaney, J. (1990) 'The reality of workplace flexibility', *Capital and Class*, **40**: 29–60.

Traxler, F. and B. Unger (1994) 'Governance, economic restructuring and international competitiveness', *Journal of Economic Issues*, **28**(1): 1–23.

United Nations Development Programme (1990–5) *Human Development Report* (Oxford University Press).

van Liemt, G. (1992) 'Economic globalization: labour options and business strategies in high labour cost countries', *International Labour Review*, **131**(4–5): 453–70.

Vestal, J. (1993) *Planning for Change* (Oxford: Clarendon).

Wade, R. (1993) 'The visible hand: The state and East Asia's economic growth', *Current History*, **92**(578): 431–40.

Walzer, M. (1983) *Spheres of Justice* (New York: Basic).

World Bank (1990–5) *World Development Report* (Oxford University Press).

Zevin, R. (1992) 'Are world financial markets more open? If so, why and with what effects?', in T. Banuri and J. Schor (eds) *Financial Openness and National Autonomy* (Oxford University Press) pp. 43–84.

Zysman, J. (1983) *Governments, Markets and Growth* (Ithaca: Cornell University Press).

2 Competitive Markets and Economic Development: A Commentary on World Bank Analyses*

Ajit Singh

2.1 INTRODUCTION

One of the more important studies published by the World Bank in recent years has been *The World Development Report 1991: The Challenge of Development* (hereafter referred to as *The Development Challenge*). The significance of this publication lies in the fact that it 'synthesises and interprets forty years of development experience'[1] as seen by World Bank economists. This study also introduced the concept of the 'market friendly' approach to development which continues to be the Bank's main policy gospel for developing countries. Although there have been subsequent Bank Reports and other publications on this subject, none of them provide as comprehensive an account of Bank economists' analytical and policy approach to development issues as *The Development Challenge*. More recent Bank documents simply endorse the main theses of this study or attempt to defend them against criticism.[2]

The main object of the present chapter is to provide a full analysis of the intellectual approach of *The Development Challenge* and the evidence underlying its conclusions. It sets out *inter alia* a systematic critique of the central analytical thesis of the World Bank Study: 'Competitive markets are the best way yet found for efficiently

*This is a revised version of the paper originally presented at the joint World Bank/UN University Symposium on *Economic Reform in the Developing Countries: Issues for the 1990s* held in Washington DC on 6 February 1993. An earlier version, Singh (1993c), see p. 91, was brought out as a working paper by Universitat–Gesamthochschule – Duisburg, Institut fur Entwicklung und Frieden, for circulation to German scholars and to research institutions in that country. Singh (1994) contains in an abridged form some of the material reported here.

organizing the production and distribution of goods and services. Domestic and external competition provides the incentives that unleash entrepreneurship and technological progress' (p. 1).

The starting point for *The Development Challenge* is the question: why during the last four decades some developing countries have been successful in the narrow but important sense of substantially raising their per caput incomes whilst others have not? The basic analytic argument is that economic growth is determined essentially by the growth of the total factor productivity of capital and labour. The analysis comes to the conclusion that the more open an economy, the greater the degree of competition and the higher its investment in education, the greater will be its growth of total factor productivity and hence its overall economic growth. Although the significance of the international economic factors is recognized, a major argument is that domestic policy matters far more for raising per caput incomes than world economic conditions.

The centrepiece of *The Development Challenge*'s policy conclusions is its recommendation of a so-called 'market-friendly' approach to development. The Report states: 'Economic theory and practical experience suggest that (government) interventions are likely to help provided they are market-friendly' (p. 5). Now 'market-friendly' is a seductive phrase and it can mean different things to different people. To save the concept from being a mere tautology, *The Development Challenge*, to its credit, defines 'market-friendly' fairly precisely in the following terms:

(a) *Intervene reluctantly.* Let markets work unless it is demonstrably better to step in ... [I]t is usually a mistake for the state to carry out physical production, or to protect the domestic production of a good that can be imported more cheaply and whose local production offers few spillover benefits.

(b) *Apply checks and balances.* Put interventions continually to the discipline of international and domestic markets.

(c) *Intervene openly.* Make interventions simple, transparent and subject to rules rather than official discretion.

The state's role in economic development in this 'market-friendly' approach is regarded as being important but best limited to providing the social, legal and economic infrastructure and to creating a suitable climate for private enterprise. *The Development Challenge* implicates other development economists in its policy recommendations by suggesting that there is now a growing consensus around the 'market friendly' approach to development (p. 1).

2.2 POINTS OF AGREEMENT AND DISAGREEMENT WITH THE DEVELOPMENT CHALLENGE: A SUMMARY

I have a number of reservations about *The Development Challenge*'s analysis and its conclusions. However, it would be best to begin with significant points of agreement. I concur with the general methodological approach of examining the question why over the last four decades some countries were able to achieve high rates of economic growth and others not. Secondly, I agree with the study's generally optimistic outlook on the possibilities for development for the poor countries. I also read the last 40 years of development experience as indicating that these countries have an enormous potential for economic growth. In principle, in the right international economic circumstances, and with appropriate economic policies, these countries can in general achieve what may be called their 'socially necessary' rates of economic growth. The latter represent the rates of economic expansion which developing countries require to provide employment for their fast growing labour forces and to meet the minimum basic needs of their people, including food, clothing and shelter, over a reasonable time span. Such growth rates, which are estimated to be of the order of 5–6 per cent per annum need not be out of reach of the developing countries.[3] I also welcome the recognition that there is no automatic trickle down of the fruits of economic progress in a market economy, and that it is therefore necessary for governments to provide a 'safety net' for the most disadvantaged in society during the course of economic development. Moreover, the emphasis on the importance of the objective of establishing stable macroeconomic conditions in developing countries is also common ground.

My principal reservations concerning *The Development Challenge* are summarized below and will be elaborated in the following sections.

1. I have difficulty in accepting the analysis of the relative importance of the international conditions and domestic policy in determining economic outcomes in developing countries. *The Development Challenge*, in my view, does not give adequate recognition

to the fact that during the 1980s world economic forces had a far greater adverse impact on countries in Latin America and Sub-Saharan Africa relative to these in Asia which was a main reason for the poor performance particularly of the Latin American countries during the last decade. There are a number of important implications of this point which are ignored, thus leading to incorrect conclusions being drawn with respect to some of its central themes.

2. A fundamental argument of *The Development Challenge* is that the greater the degree of international economic integration (for example, the larger the share of trade), the better it is for any particular economy or for the world economy as a whole. A corollary of this view is that the less the distortions from international competitive prices in an economy, the greater would be its economic growth. I am afraid I cannot accept these propositions either at a theoretical level or empirically.

3. The intellectual foundation of the study is the total factor productivity approach to economic growth. The implicit underlying paradigm here is that the more competitive the product, labour and capital markets in an economy, the more efficient will be the utilization of resources, the faster will be its technical progress and hence economic growth. In my view this paradigm is analytically flawed. It is also not as good at explaining empirical evidence as an alternative theoretical approach which does not regard greater market competition as an unalloyed good, and which gives a far bigger role to demand factors and to overall national and world economic growth as an explanation of changes in productivity growth.

4. I find it particularly difficult to accept *The Development Challenge's* account of the economic history of the successful East Asian economies – Japan, South Korea and Taiwan. Nor am I at all comfortable with the analysis of, and the lessons to be learnt from the experience of the 'unsuccessful' countries.

5. In addition to these analytical differences, I also find that there are important omissions from the Bank economists' examination of 40 years of development experience (for instance, what lessons do they draw from the Bretton Wood institutions' own role in the international debt crisis of the 1980s?). There are also a number of relatively minor points of disagreement – interpretations of the econometric evidence which is presented, places where even in its own terms the conclusions do not follow from

the data put forward. These points will be referred to as appropriate in the course of the analysis below.

In view of the above reservations, it is no surprise to say that I arrive at very different policy conclusions from those contained in this study.

2.3 THE MARKET-FRIENDLY APPROACH TO DEVELOPMENT AND THE EAST ASIAN EXPERIENCE

I begin with *The Development Challenge*'s analysis of the experience of the successful East Asian economies. The study observes:

> Extraordinary progress is possible even when countries seem doomed to fail. Forty-three years ago an influential government report in an important developing country observed that labour today shunned hard, productive jobs and sought easy, merchant-like work. The report showed that workers' productivity had fallen, wages were too high, and enterprises were inefficient and heavily subsidized. The country had virtually priced itself out of international markets and faced a severe competitive threat from newly industrializing China and India. It was overpopulated and becoming more so. This would be the last opportunity, concluded the prime minister in July 1947, to discover whether his country would be able to stand on its own two feet or become a permanent burden for the rest of the world. That country was Japan. *The central question of this Report is why countries like Japan have succeeded so spectacularly while other have failed.* (pp. 13–14; my italics)

The study is quite right to stress the case of Japan since the experience of that country in the period following the Second World War is highly relevant to the developing countries, particularly the large semi-industrial economies. In the early 1950s, Japan produced less steel (about 5 million tons) and fewer cars (about 50 000) than countries like Brazil, India and Mexico do today and it was largely an exporter of labour-intensive products. The US annual steel output at that time was about 100 million tons and the American automobile industry produced around 6 million cars every year. Yet less than two decades later Japan was producing more steel, and by 1980 more cars than the USA. The Japanese workers, starting from Asian wage levels in the 1950s, were well on their way to reaching European standards of living 25 years later (Singh, 1989). In analysing this, arguably the most spectacular case of successful industrial development in the history of mankind, the relevant question in the present context is to what extent, if any, the Japanese followed *The Development Challenge*'s prescriptions and a 'market-friendly' approach to development. Did the Japanese government intervene in the markets 'reluctantly'? Did it, for example, leave the prices and production priorities to be determined mostly by market forces and simply provide the necessary infrastructure for private enterprise to flourish? How 'transparent' was the government intervention in Japanese industry? To achieve this colossal economic success, how closely did the Japanese economy integrate with the world economy? The study does acknowledge the inescapable fact that there was considerable government intervention in the course of post-war Japanese development. The important issue, however, is whether the study's characterization of this intervention and the lessons to be drawn from it are valid.

There is overwhelming evidence which is generally accepted among the scholars in the field that the government in Japan did not intervene in the markets 'reluctantly'. On the contrary, it pursued a forceful and aggressive industrial policy to change the unsatisfactory economic situation faced by that country – so eloquently described in *The Development Challenge*'s paragraph quoted above. The cornerstone of this industrial policy was the so-called 'structural policy' aimed at adaptation and technological development of certain specific industries (steel, chemicals, machinery and other heavy industries) thought to be vital for the rapid growth of productivity and per caput incomes (Singh, 1979). The role of the government in promoting these industries and hence bringing about Japanese economic success has been so crucial that, as the Japanese industrial economist Professor Nino (1973), remarked, 'whereas [the] USA is said to be a country of [the] military industrial complex . . . in this sense, Japan may be called a country of the Government industrial complex' (p. x).

At the end of the Second World War, the bulk of Japanese exports consisted of textiles and light manufactured goods. In the view of the Ministry of International Trade and Industry (MITI), although such an economic structure may have conformed to the theory of comparative advantage (Japan being a labour-surplus economy at the time), it was not viable in the long run. It is worth quoting in full Vice-Minister Ojimi's rationale for the ministry's industrial policy:

> The MITI decided to establish in Japan industries which require intensive employment of capital and technology, industries that in consideration of comparative cost of production should be the most inappropriate for Japan, industries such as steel, oil-refining, petro-chemicals, automobiles, aircraft, industrial machinery of all sorts, and electronics, including electronic computers. From a short-run, static viewpoint, encouragement of such industries would seem to conflict with economic rationalism. But, from a long-range viewpoint, these are precisely the industries where income elasticity of demand is high, technological progress is rapid, and labour productivity rises fast. It was clear that without these industries it would be difficult to employ a population of 100 million and raise their standard of living to that of Europe and America with light industries alone; whether right or wrong, Japan had to have these heavy and chemical industries. According to Napoleon and Clausewitz, the secret of a successful strategy is the concentration of fighting power on the main battle grounds; fortunately, owing to good luck and wisdom spawned by necessity, Japan has been able to concentrate its scant capital in strategic industries.[4]

The government used a wide variety of instruments to bring about this extraordinary structural transformation of the Japanese economy between 1950 and 1973 the period of its most rapid growth. The most important of these were bank finance and directed credit, import controls and protection, restrictions on entry and exit of firms in the domestic market, control over foreign exchange and importation of foreign technology (OECD, 1972; Boltho, 1975; Nino, 1973; Caves and Uekusa, 1976; Dore, 1986; Yamamura, 1988).

The significance of these policies, and particularly the economic rationale underlying them, will be considered further in the next two sections. In the meantime we note that the Japanese government did not only use these methods of intervention to concentrate resources for the promotion of specific industries, its role in the country's industrial development was deeper and even more intrusive. It extended to the level of the individual firm – MITI accorded favourable treatment in a variety of ways to the specific firms which were thought to fulfil its aims best and were therefore in its good books. As for the 'transparency' of this intervention, it was the exact opposite of the 'market-friendly' specification. Thus Professors Caves and Uekusa (1976) on the operations of the Japanese industrial policy:

Each sector of the Japanese economy has a cliental relation to a ministry or agency of the government. The ministry, in addition to its various statutory means of dealing with the economic sector, holds a general implied administrative responsibility and authority that goes well beyond what is customary in the United States and other Western Countries. While the Ministry of International Trade and Industry (MITI) plays the most prominent role, its operations are not distinctive. 'The industrial bureaus of MITI proliferate sectoral targets and plans; they confer, they tinker, they exhort. This is the economics by admonition to a degree inconceivable in Washington or London. Business makes few major decisions without consulting the appropriate governmental authority; the same is true in reverse'. (p. 149, including quotation from Lockwood, 1965)

Moreover, as we shall see in section 2.4, the Japanese government did not seek 'close' but rather what may be called a 'strategic' integration with the world economy. For example, it made extensive use of formal or informal import controls and protection. It also restricted foreign direct investment by multinationals. These points will be taken up further when the concept of 'strategic integration' is developed below.

South Korea and Taiwan

As several scholars have noted, the other East Asian tigers, notably South Korea and Taiwan, have also each followed a purposive and comprehensive industrial policy (see among others Johnson, 1987; Amsden, 1989a; Wade, 1990). These countries have been greatly influenced by the Japanese example and practice. In view of their relative backwardness compared with Japan, state intervention in these economies has been even more far-reaching than in Japan. Very briefly, in the case of South Korea, attention may be drawn to the following aspects of the country's industrial policy:

- the use of long-term credit at negative real interest rates to foster particular industries;
- the 'heavy' subsidization and the 'coercion' of exports;
- the strict control over multinational investment and foreign equity ownership of Korean industry;
- a highly active state technology policy;
- state promotion of large-scale conglomerate firms, government encouragement of mergers of specific corporations, and general state restrictions on the free entry and exit of firms.

Table 2.1 summarizes the industrial policy instruments used in the development of core Korean industries (as well as textiles) in the late 1960s and 1970s.

Similarly, for Taiwan, Wade (1990) documents the widespread and intensive use of state industrial policy to guide the market economy purposefully. It is certainly not a picture of some nightwatchman state intervening 'reluctantly'. Until the early 1980s, both South Korea and Taiwan had nationalized banks (and most of their banks are still state-owned), and in both countries, state-directed credit to favoured sectors and firms was an important device for planned industrial development. Moreover, the authors of *The Development Challenge* overlook the fact that the public enterprise sector in Taiwan is one of the largest among the developing mixed economies. It is bigger than India's or that of Argentina, Brazil or Mexico. The public enterprises have contributed 13–14 per cent of GNP and a third of gross fixed capital formation in Taiwan throughout the years 1950 to 1975, a period which witnessed the most rapid economic and industrial growth in that country (Chang and Singh 1993; Short 1984). Wade observes that:

> In many sectors public enterprises have been used as the chosen instrument for a big push. This is true for the early years of fuels, chemicals, mining, metals, fertilizer, and food processing; but even in sectors where public enterprises did not dominate, such as textiles and plastics, the state aggressively led private producers in the early years. Later, during the late 1950s and 1960s, public enterprises accounted for a large part of total investment in synthetic fibres, metals, shipbuilding, and other industries ... To say that public enterprises have often played a central role in creating new capacities is not to say that private firms have been left alone. Incentives and pressure are brought to bear

Table 2.1 The Chief provisions of industrial promotional laws in Korea

Major Content (year of enactment)	Machinery (1967)	Ship building (1967)	Electronics (1969)	Petro- chemical (1970)	Iron & Steel (1970)	Non- ferrous metal (1971)	Textile (1979)
Regulations							
Entry restriction	x	x	x	x	x	x	x
Capacity regulations							
Setting up facility standard	x	x					
Capacity expansion approval				x	x		x
Incentives to use domestically produced facilities	x		x				
Production Regulation							
Regulation of material imports					x	x	
Production standard and its inspection	x	x	x		x	x	
Restrictions on technology imports	x		x				
Price Control				x	x		
Reporting and inspection	x	x	x	x	x	x	x
Rationalisation							
Rationalisation programmes	x	x	x	x			x
R&D support							
Subsidies to R&D	x		x	x	x		
Joint R&D projects			x				
Financial support							
Special Purpose Fund	x	x	x		x	x	x
Financial assistance subsidies	x	x	x		x	x	x
Direct subsidy	x					x	
Reduced public utility rates	x				x		
Tax Preferences							
Special depreciation	x					x	
Tax-reduction/exemption	x	x	x	x	x	x	
Special industrial complex	x		x	x			x
Administrative assistance							
Facilitating overseas activities			x		x		
Purchase of raw materials					x	x	
Producers' association	x	x	x				x

Source: Reproduced from Chang (1994) pp. 115–16.

on them through such devices as import controls and tariffs, entry requirements, domestic content requirements, fiscal investment incentives, and concessional credit. Even in the case of machine tools, a small-scale industry relatively neglected until recently, the state nevertheless has provided subsidized design help, subsidized credit, and quantitative import restrictions. And large-scale private firms are often exposed to more discretionary government influence, taking the form of what in Japan is called 'administrative guidance'. (pp. 110–11)

In view of the useful and important role played by public enterprises in Taiwan as well as in Korea, the World Bank Study's blanket admonition to the states in developing countries not to engage in 'direct production' – not to produce steel and cement (p. 31) – would appear to be misconceived. The reference to steel is particularly inappropriate since Posco, the Korean state-owned steel company, is the most efficient steel producer in the world. In the mid-1980s, Posco produced 467 tons of crude steel per person compared with an average of 327 tons for Japan's five biggest steel producers. The company's efficiency advantage was passed on to its Korean customers. It charged domestic steel consumers \$320 per ton – far less than US or Japanese car makers who (according to Posco) paid \$540 and \$430 respectively (*The Economist*, 21 May 1988: for a more detailed discussion of Posco's efficiency advantage over other steel producers, see Amsden, 1989a, pp. 298–9).

Assessment

To sum up, between them, Japan, South Korea and Taiwan did all the things which the 'market-friendly' approach to development is not supposed to do. Above all, all three countries followed an 'industrial strategy' – a set of policies to deliberately change the vector of prices and incentives facing the producers – which is explicitly ruled out by this approach. *The Development Challenge* acknowledges that there was heavy state intervention in all these three countries but argues that 'these economies refute the case for thorough going dirigisms as convincingly as they refute the case for laissez-faire' (p. 5). The experience of these countries is certainly an argument against laissez-faire; it also does not provide any support for 'command' planning of production of the Soviet-type, which in effect supplants the market altogether. However, *for*

mixed-economy developing countries with effective states, it is unequivo-
cally an argument for adopting an industrial strategy, for guiding
the market, and *not* following the hands-off 'market-friendly' approach as enunciated by the World Bank. Moreover, as mentioned
in the case of Japan, it will be suggested below that the experience
of all three East Asian countries is an argument against seeking
'close integration' with the world economy; rather it is an argument for choosing 'strategic integration' with the latter. These concepts of 'guiding' the market and of 'strategic integration with the
international economy' will become clearer when we discuss the
role of domestic and international competition in these economies
in the following sections.

Other neoclassical accounts, not just *The Development Challenge,*
also have a difficult task in accommodating the facts of pervasive
interventions of the East Asian states in their internal and external
economies, with the theoretical and policy framework used in such
analyses. Some have even argued that these countries would have
grown faster still if the state had not intervened in these economies (Lal, 1983). Others have suggested that in countries like Korea,
the state has followed a 'prescriptive' rather than a 'proscriptive'
policy and that accounts for the success of state intervention in
that economy. Still others have suggested that the essential reason
for the state's success in these countries is that it has followed the
market rather than leading or guiding it. The World Bank's follow-
up study, *The East Asian Miracle,* has proposed what I have elsewhere called the 'industrial policy ineffectiveness' doctrine. This
argues that industrial policy in the East Asian countries can be
regarded as being unsuccessful, in part, because the industrial structure which emerged in these countries is no different from what it
would have been had there been no industrial policy: that is, the
market would have produced the same outcome. Such arguments
have been carefully analysed by Wade, Amsden, Chang (1994), Singh
(1994c) and others and found to have very little merit.

What does distinguish the industrial policies of Japan, South Korea,
and Taiwan from those of many other countries, both developed
and developing, is the ability of the state in the former countries to
use not only 'carrots' (for example, incentives and subsidies) but also
'sticks' (punishments) to influence firm behaviour. In that sense,
the state in these countries has been much more powerful and has
what the political scientists call greater 'autonomy' than in many other
economies (see further Amsden, 1989a; Wade, 1990; Fishlow, 1991).

2.4 THE DEVELOPMENT CHALLENGE: THE ANALYTIC FOUNDATION

The theoretical foundation of the World Bank analyses is the TFP (Total Factor Productivity) approach to economic growth. It is suggested that inter-country and inter-temporal variations in growth rates are caused by variations in total factor productivity of capital and labour. Changes in the latter variable are thought to be determined mainly by economic policy – the degree of openness of an economy, the extent of competition in the product and factor markets, and investment in physical and human capital (education), particularly the last. The underlying chain of causation is that competition and education promote technical progress, and therefore TFP growth and hence economic expansion. 'Free mobility of people, capital, and technology' and 'free entry and exit of firms' are regarded as being particularly conducive to the spread of knowledge and technical change.

The role of 'openness' and international competition, as well as domestic competition, as critical determinants of productivity growth is repeatedly stressed throughout *The Development Challenge* (see chs 1, 2, 4, 5, and 8). In relation to domestic competition it notes: 'systems of industrial licensing, restrictions on entry and exit, inappropriate legal codes concerning bankruptcy and employment, inadequate property rights, and price controls – all of which weaken the forces of competition – have held back technological change and the growth of productivity' (p. 7). In the analysis below, I shall concentrate mainly on the study's arguments with respect to the role of competition. Questions of external competition, 'openness' and the 'integration of countries with the global economy' will be examined in section 2.5 and those relating to domestic competition in the product, labour, and financial markets in section 2.6. The rest of this section will take up two issues. First it will examine more closely the TFP approach to economic growth. Second it will comment briefly on *The Development Challenge*'s analysis of the relationship between education and economic growth.

The TFP Model

At a theoretical level there are several well-known objections to the causal model underlying the TFP approach to economic growth. The model assumes, for example, full employment of resources and perfect competition, neither of which obtain in the real world. It is, moreover, a wholly supply-side model which ignores altogether the role of demand factors.[5] This, as we shall see below, is a critical weakness which creates serious difficulties for the Bank's analyses of the East Asian as well as other economies.

With respect to empirical evidence, even a cursory consideration of the data presented by Bank economists themselves in *The Development Challenge* (see Table 2.2) reveals the serious limitations of the TFP approach. The table provides figures for the growth of GDP, capital and labour inputs and TFP separately for each of the sub-periods, 1960–73 and 1973–87, for each of the five developing regions as well as for a group of 68 developing economies. In addition, it also provides similar information for each of the four leading industrial economies. These data show that in every region, and for each country or group of countries shown in the table except South Asia (that is, for nine out of ten observations), the rate of growth of TFP fell substantially during 1973–87, compared with 1960–73. For example, TFP growth fell in East Asian developing economies from 2.6 per cent per annum in the first period to 1.3 per cent per annum in the second period. In Latin America, the corresponding figures were 1.3 per cent per annum and −0.4 per cent per annum. For the group of 68 developing economies, the TFP growth fell from 1.3 per cent to −0.2 per cent over the two periods. However, in South Asia – notably the only region which registered a trend increase in its GDP growth between the two periods – TFP growth rose from zero in 1960–73 to 1.2 per cent per annum during 1973–87.

In terms of the causal model underlying the World Bank analysis, this almost universal fall in TFP growth in the recent period would be due to policy mismanagement – low rates of technical progress caused by distortions, for example lack of competition, or lack of integration with the world economy. The evidence, however, is not compatible with such an analysis, since (as Bank economists themselves note) there has actually been more competition, greater integration of the world economy, less distortions in most developing countries in the latter period (particularly in the 1980s) than in the former.[6]

These facts are much more in accord with an alternative theoretical model (Verdoorn's Law) which would suggest that the fall in the world and the national economic growth rates in the post-1973 period was responsible for the decline in the rate of growth

Table 2.2 The growth of GDP, inputs, and Total Factor Productivity 1960–73 and 1973–87, different regions, groups and individual economies (%)

Region, group and economy	GDP			Capital			Labour			TFP		
	1960–73	1973–87[a]	1960–87[a]	1960–73	1973–87[a]	1960–87[a]	1960–73	1973–87[a]	1960–87[a]	1960–73	1973–87[a]	1960–87[a]
Developing economies												
Africa	4.0	2.6	3.3	6.3	6.3	6.3	2.1	2.3	2.2	0.7	-0.7	0.0
East Asia	7.5	6.5	6.8	9.8	10.7	10.2	2.8	2.6	2.6	2.6	1.3	1.9
Europe, Middle East, and North Africa	5.8	4.2	5.0	7.7	7.5	7.6	1.4	1.9	1.7	2.2	0.6	1.4
Latin America	5.1	2.3	3.6	7.4	5.6	6.3	2.5	2.8	2.6	1.3	-1.1	0.0
South Asia	3.8	5.0	4.4	8.0	7.2	7.7	1.8	2.3	2.1	0.0	1.2	0.6
Sixty-eight economies	5.1	3.5	4.2	7.4	7.1	7.2	2.2	2.4	2.3	1.3	-0.2	0.6
Industrial economies												
France	5.5	2.1	3.9	5.7	3.8	4.8	0.4	-1.0	-0.2	2.3	0.9	1.7
Germany[b]	4.3	1.8	3.1	5.3	3.0	4.2	-0.3	-0.9	-0.6	1.9	0.9	1.4
United Kingdom	3.3	1.3	2.4	3.6	2.6	3.1	0.1	-0.5	-0.2	1.7	0.6	1.2
United States	3.7	2.2	3.0	3.8	2.8	3.4	1.8	1.9	1.8	1.0	-0.1	0.5

Notes:
[a] Until 1985 for industrial economies
[b] The Federal Republic of Germany before reunification with the former German Democratic Republic

Source: Reproduced from *The Development Challenge*, p. 43.

of productivity in most regions. Verdoorn's Law[7] predicts that the faster (slower) the growth of production, the faster (slower) the growth of productivity. Regression analysis shows the following relationship between the two variables in Table 2.2.

$$p = -0.17 + 0.59q$$
$$(-0.54) \quad (3.8)$$
$$R^2 = 0.60$$

Where p is the change in the growth rate of productivity and q is the change in the growth rate of output between the two periods. Parentheses give t values of the coefficients.

The decline in world economic growth after 1973, in terms of this model, was due to a *lower rate of growth* of world and national demand caused by a whole range of factors (for example the collapse of the Bretton Woods system, the growth of real wages in a number of industrial countries outstripping productivity growth in the wake of the first oil shock) connected with the fall of the Golden Age of development of the OECD economies.[8]

It is a serious shortcoming of *The Development Challenge* that it does not even consider this alternative causal model, let alone systematically test it against empirical evidence. Without such an examination of the data in terms of competing causal hypotheses emanating from these two paradigms – both of which have well-established pedigrees in the subject – the study's policy conclusions are unconvincing. Regrettably, the failure to consider different causal explanations of the data is commonplace in *The Development Challenge*, leading often to misleading and erroneous policy conclusions. Some further examples of this will be provided in the following sections.

Education and Economic Growth

I now turn to *The Development Challenge*'s analysis of the relationship between education and economic growth.[9] On the basis of an inter-country cross-section examination of 60 countries over the period 1965–87, the study arrives at the following empirical conclusion with respect to the relationship between education and economic growth:

> Research for this Report suggests that increasing the average amount of education of the labour force by one year raises GDP

by 9 per cent. This holds for the first three years of education; that is, three years of education as compared with none raises GDP by 27 per cent. The return to an additional year of schooling then diminishes to about 4 per cent a year – or a total of 12 per cent for the next three years. These results are consistent with earlier studies (p. 43).

Although the study correctly observes that such correlations do not imply causation, it nevertheless goes on to draw the conclusion that: 'both better policies and more education contribute to growth. Furthermore, they seem to interact. Thus, the effect on growth of better policy and more education together is greater than that of each separately . . .' (p. 46).

From these and other similar analyses, the World Bank's economists arrive at the policy recommendation that, in order to enhance economic growth, the developing countries should promote primary and secondary education. Such recommendations, however, can unfortunately be misleading. To illustrate, it will be difficult to argue that the Latin American economic performance over the medium term (say the next five to seven years) would be improved by further investment in early education. The economic failure of the Latin American countries during the 'lost decade' of the 1980s can scarcely be ascribed to a deficit in education. There is a large literature (reviewed in section 2.7 below) on the question of why the Latin American countries failed so comprehensively in the 1980s while the Asian countries continued to enjoy economic success. None of this literature, however, suggests that this phenomenon could be explained in terms of a skills or educational deficit in the Latin American economies. Broadly speaking, these writings instead emphasize the role of the debt crisis or internal mismanagement in the Latin American countries to explain the differences in performance of the economies on the two continents. It will be hard to demonstrate that education, let alone primary or secondary education, is currently a constraint on economic growth in these countries.

Even for African countries, where *The Development Challenge*'s policy conclusions in this area may be regarded as being more applicable, a detailed investigation is required to show that it is the lack of primary or secondary education, rather than other factors (for example world economic conditions or deficiencies in university education) that have been responsible for slow economic growth in these countries during the last decade. The study does not provide such an analysis. Any policy conclusion that expansion of primary education will increase economic growth in the medium term or for that matter during the rest of this decade, even for the African countries, is therefore hazardous.

There are two basic flaws in the World Bank's analysis and policy conclusions with respect to the role of education. First, the economic paradigm underlying the Bank's analysis implicitly assumes that there will be full employment of resources – that those who are educated will find productive and remunerative employment. The paradigm also assumes that there is perfect competition and that factors are paid their marginal products. Neither of these assumptions are suitable for the vast majority of developing economies.

Secondly, *The Development Challenge*'s empirical conclusions are based on cross-section regression analyses of countries from different continents and over time periods which, from an economic point of view, it may be inappropriate to aggregate.[10] Equally importantly, at the methodological level, it is not valid to draw policy conclusions of the kind emphasized by the Bank's economists from cross-sectional analysis. This is because such analyses at best indicate the nature of long-term equilibrium relationships between the variables. They do not provide any information on the time path of movement from one long-term equilibrium position to another. That kind of information, which is essential for policy purposes can only come from dynamic time-series analysis (Pesaran and Smith, 1992). However, the latter are hard to implement for the developing economies because of deficiencies of the available data.

There are important aspects of the relationship between education, skills and economic growth which are usually not captured by econometric or statistical analyses. These may be illustrated by the following example from the Punjab (India). Punjab has an outstanding record of the growth of agricultural production as well as productivity per acre over the last two decades. Food grain production in the state has increased at a long-term rate of nearly 5 per cent per annum over the period 1967–89, an exceptional performance by comparative international standards (Rao, 1992). The net result is that Punjab, with less than 2 per cent of the country's arable area as well as its population, produces three-quarters of the country's entire food grain surplus.[11]

This transformation of Punjab's agrarian economy over the last two decades has been made possible by the introduction and widespread adoption by the Punjabi peasantry of the new green revolution technology. Yet Punjab's literacy and primary school education levels were by no means as good as those in other parts of the country which have been unable to adopt such technology. The government played a major role in propagating the new technology, for example by providing demonstrations of the success of new seeds at farms throughout the state. Certainly, the lack of formal education does not seem to have prevented the peasantry from acquiring the skills necessary for understanding and implementing this technical revolution in agriculture.

Nevertheless, it is important to note that, at a different level, formal education and skills did play a central and critical role in this process. Punjab's agricultural revolution was spawned by the state's agricultural university at Ludhiana. Although the green revolution technology came from abroad, it was adapted and developed to meet the local soil and climatic conditions by scientists and agronomists at the agricultural university. The university played a crucial role also in providing new seeds, training agricultural extension workers as well as in demonstrations of the success of the new technology at experimental farms. Thus in this significant case, it was not the primary or secondary education but rather the availability of higher level training, education and skills which contributed to the observed trend increase in the state's agricultural and overall growth rates.[12]

The Development Challenge is of course right to note that 'progress in education is to be sought mainly as an end in itself' (p. 56). However, for the reasons outlined in the previous paragraphs, its general policy conclusion that investment in primary and secondary education will promote economic growth may not be valid for many developing countries over the next five to ten years.

2.5   OPENNESS, EXTERNAL COMPETITION AND INTEGRATION WITH THE WORLD ECONOMY

The Development Challenge's assertions with respect to the role of openness, external competition and closer integration with the world economy do not stand up to serious examination either at a theoretical level or empirically, particularly in terms of the experience of the East Asian countries it holds up as models of successful development. In the discussion below, I shall first comment on the empirical evidence presented by the study itself to support its contention of an important positive relationship between these variables. Next I shall provide information bearing on these issues for the East Asian economies. It was suggested in Section 2.3 that these countries had sought a 'strategic' but not a 'close' integration with the global economy – that is, they integrated up to the point where it was useful for them to do so for promoting national economic growth. I shall put forward an alternative theoretical framework for examining the relationship between openness, international economic integration, and economic growth. This will help to provide an analytical rationale for the 'strategic integration' path pursued by Japan, South Korea and Taiwan.

The Development Challenge's own empirical analysis of the relationship between trade openness, 'distortions' from international prices, and productivity growth is presented in Chapter 5. This evidence (see Figure 5.3 on p. 100 and Table note 5.3 in the technical Appendix p. 163), even in its own terms is extremely weak. Notwithstanding countless permutations of the indicators used to denote distortions and openness, only 12 of the 37 regression coefficients reported in Table note 5.3 are statistically significant at the 5 per cent level. The R^2s range between 0.03 and 0.3. The interpretation of the econometric results on page 164 is less than exemplary: it is implied, for instance, that it makes no difference to the verification of the economic hypotheses under discussion whether one considers 'levels' of or 'changes' in the values of some of the independent variables. The tentative character of this empirical evidence are acknowledged in the text of Chapter 5 but, despite that, far-reaching and firm policy conclusions are drawn from it in the study's overview chapter.[13]

With respect to the nature and extent of 'openness' practised by the East Asian economies, I provide here some relevant data on Japan. Table 2.3 gives comparative figures on imports of manufacturers into Japan and other industrial countries between 1961 and 1978. During this period, as a proportion of GDP, Japanese imports rose by 66 per cent. This compares with a threefold increase in the corresponding US imports, more than tripling of the UK imports and a nearly 250 per cent growth in the imports of other European Economic Community countries. In 1978, manufactured imports constituted only 2.4 per cent of the Japanese GDP; the corresponding proportion in Britain and other countries of the EEC was five to six times larger. Even in the United States, which traditionally because of its continental size has a relatively closed economy,

Table 2.3 Import penetration in manufactures in advanced industrial countries, 1961–78 (ratio of manufactured imports to GNP)

	1961	1965	1969	1973	1979
USA	1.5	2.1	3.4	4.0	4.5
UK	4.6	6.7	8.0	11.7	14.2
Rest of EEC 9	6.1	7.6	10.1	13.0	15.8
Japan	1.8	1.5	2.2	3.0	2.4

Source: CEPG (1979).

the volume of imported manufacturing goods in the late 1970s was proportionally almost twice as large as in Japan. Clearly, during the 1960s and 1970s (and even more so in the 1950s) the Japanese economy operated under a regime of draconian import controls, whether practised formally or informally.

With respect to the questions of overvalued exchange rates and distortions, the Japanese Government maintained exchange controls and kept a steady nominal exchange rate with respect to the US dollar over almost the whole of the period of that country's most rapid growth (1950–73). Purchasing power parity calculations by Sachs (1987), using Japanese and US price indices, show a 60 per cent real appreciation of the exchange rate between 1950 and 1970. As for close integration with the international capital markets and foreign direct investment, Sachs notes that domestic capital markets were highly regulated and completely shut off from the world capital markets for most of this period. Only the government and its agencies were able to borrow from and lend abroad. Foreign direct investment was strictly controlled. Foreign firms were prohibited, either by legal or administrative means, from acquiring a majority ownership in Japanese corporations.

To appreciate how the Japanese policy of protection worked at a microeconomic level, consider the specific case of the celebrated Japanese car industry. Magaziner and Hout (1980) note that 'government intervention in this industry was characterized by three major goals: discouragement of foreign capital in the Japanese industry and protection against car imports, attempts to bring about rationalization of production, and assistance with overseas marketing and distribution expenditure' (p. 55). They point out that the government imposed comprehensive import controls and adopted a variety of measures to discourage foreign investment in the car industry. Quotas and tariffs were used to protect the industry. The former were applied throughout the mid-1960s, and prohibitively high tariffs till the mid-1970s. Moreover,

> the government controlled all foreign licensing agreements. To make technology agreements more attractive to the licensor, it guaranteed the remittance of royalties from Japan. The policy stipulated, however, that continued remittances would be guaranteed only if 90 percent of the licensed parts were produced in Japan within five years

– about as powerful a domestic content arrangement as you can get. *The Development Challenge* acknowledges that the Japanese protected their industry (as did Taiwan and Korea) but it is silent on the question of restrictions on foreign direct investment and government controls over foreign capital inflows for industrial development. Even with respect to protection, it does not tell you how large and pervasive its use in effect was in a country like Japan. In general, the Bank economists are embarrassed by the East Asian protection. The study's overall tone is to suggest that it is a miracle that these economies did as well as they did despite the protection.

There is little recognition of the fact that protection has played an extremely important, positive role in promoting technical change, productivity growth and exports in a country like Japan. Protection provided the Japanese companies with a captive home market leading to high profits which enabled the firms to undertake higher rates of investment, to learn by doing and to improve the quality of their products. These profits in the protected internal market, which were further enhanced by restrictions on domestic competition (see section 2.6), not only made possible higher rates of investment but also greatly aided exports. Yamamura (1988) explains the mechanism involved:

> Because increased output meant reduced cost per unit it translated into increased profits on the product sold at high fixed prices in the domestic market, even if the increased output had to be exported at no profit or even at a loss.... Manufacturers enjoyed a margin of error when making ... major investment decisions. Essentially, even in the face of the high probability that the increase in output would have to be sold unprofitably on the international market the expansion was still worth the risk. The stronger the 'home market cushion' – or the more effective the

cartels and protection on the domestic arena – the smaller the risk and more likely the Japanese competitor was to increase capacity boldly in anticipation of demand growth. This can give the firm a strategic as well as a cost advantage over a foreign competitor operating in a different environment who must be more cautious (p. 177).

The Development Challenge echoes the view of some neoclassical analysts who suggest that although the governments in East Asian countries imposed protection, they were careful 'to offset the bias against exports that is usually a feature of trade protection' (p. 39). This suggests that the governments maintained a rough neutrality of incentives between selling in the home and the foreign markets: that is, despite intervention, there were 'level playing fields' between different sectors of the economy and between internal and external markets.[14] However, as Scott (1991) rightly points out, this is simply an incorrect characterization of the commercial and industrial policies pursued in the East Asian economies. Scott notes that the level playing fields between selling in the national and international markets prevailed in the USA and the UK economies which have been relatively unsuccessful in world competition. Countries like Japan and Korea on the other hand, particularly during their periods of rapid growth, had a positive bias in favour of exports through the wide panoply of industrial policy instruments discussed above, including notably the use of performance criteria on exports and market share. The Japanese and Korean corporations could only receive favoured government treatment in terms, for example, of loans or foreign exchange allocations, if they met such criteria. Thus despite often low short-run financial returns on exports, they were obliged to fulfil their export targets.

To sum up, the experience of Japan comprehensively contradicts *The Development Challenge*'s central thesis that the more open the economy, the closer its integration with the global economy, the faster would be its rate of growth. Although, for reasons of space, the cases of Taiwan and South Korea have not been considered above, their stories, subject to certain modifications, also point in the same direction.[15] If, as stated, the study's central purpose was to find out why countries like Japan have been so successful in economic development during the last 40 years, it has clearly been using the wrong paradigm for examining Japanese economic history.

The basic problem is that the underlying assumptions of this paradigm are greatly at variance with the real world of static and dynamic economies of scale, learning by doing, and imperfect competition. In such a world, even neoclassical analysis now accepts that the optimal degree of openness for an economy is not 'close' integration with the global economy through free trade.[16] In that case, what *is* the optimal degree of openness for the economy? This extremely important policy question is not, unfortunately, addresse seriously by orthodox theory.[17]

Chakravarty and Singh (1988) provide an alternative theoretical framework for considering this issue. Very briefly, they argue that 'openness' is a multi-dimensional concept. Apart from trade, a country can be 'open' or 'not so open' with respect to financial and capital markets, in relation to technology, science, culture, education, inward and outward migration. Moreover a country can choose to be open in some directions (say trade) but not so open in others such as foreign direct investment or financial markets. Chakravarty and Singh's analysis suggests that there is no unique optimum form or degree of openness which holds true for all countries at all times. A number of factors affect the desirable nature of openness including the world configuration, the past history of the economy and its state of development, among others. The timing and sequence of opening are also critical. Chakravarty and Singh point out that there may be serious irreversible losses if the wrong kind of openness is attempted or the timing and sequence are incorrect. The East Asian experience of 'strategic' rather than 'close' integration with the world economy is fully compatible with this kind of theoretical framework.

2.6 COMPETITION IN DOMESTIC MARKETS

Contrary to *The Development Challenge*'s homilies about the virtues of 'free mobility of capital and labour', 'free entry and exit of firms' and the importance of competition in the domestic market, the practice of the successful East Asian countries has been rather different. As in relation to the question of integration with the world economy, these countries appear to have taken the view that from the dynamic perspective of promoting investment and technical change, the optimal degree of competition is not perfect or maximum competition. The governments in these countries have therefore managed or guided competition in a purposeful manner: it has been both encouraged but notably also restricted in a number of ways.

In Japan, in the years immediately following the war, the Zaibatsu were disbanded, and antitrust laws of the US type were enacted under the tutelage of the occupation authorities. However, over time these pro-competition measures were greatly diluted. The government permitted or encouraged a variety of cartel arrangements in a wide range of industries including export and import cartels, cartels to combat depression or excessive competition and rationalization cartels. Table 2.4 provides information on cartels which were exempted during the period 1964–73 from Japan's anti-monopoly laws. According to Caves and Uekusa (1976), cartels accounted for 78.1 per cent of the value of shipments in textiles, 64.8 per cent in clothing, 50.0 per cent in non-ferrous metals, 47 per cent in printing and publishing, 41.2 per cent in stone, clay and glass, 34.5 per cent in steel products, and 37.2 per cent in food products. Caves and Uekusa note that although these cartels varied in their effectiveness, 'their mere presence in such broad stretches of the manufacturing sector attests to their importance' (p. 147).

More importantly, the Japanese government has regarded the antitrust laws as a part and parcel of its overall industrial strategy. As Magaziner and Hout (1980) point out, in young industries, during the developmental phase, the government discouraged competition in order to provide firms with a secure environment for profitable investment. When these industries became technologically mature, competition was allowed to flourish. Later, when industries are in competitive decline, the government again discourages competition and attempts to bring about an orderly rationalization of the industry. Magaziner and Hout observed that 'MITI's greatest strength appears to be its understanding of the competitive stages through which an industry moves and its ability to fashion appropriate policy' (p. 38).

Students of the Japanese economy provide many examples of the above pattern from a number of different industries. In steel, for example, Scott (1991) observes that during the expansion phase of the industry, individual companies were not allowed to build new plants except at world-class scale. This meant

spacing out investments to build large-scale plants without at the same time generating an excess capacity. Japanese firms were

Table 2.4 Japanese cartel agreements exempted from anti-monopoly law by Fair Trade Commission or competent ministry, by exempting statute, 1964–73[a]

Statutory basis for exemption	1964	1965	1966	1967	1968	1969	1970	1971	1972	1973
Depression cartels	2	2	16	1	0	0	0	0	9	2
Rationalization cartels	14	14	14	13	13	12	10	13	10	10
Export cartels	201	208	211	206	213	217	214	192	175	180
Import cartels	1	2	3	4	3	4	4	3	2	2
Cartels under Medium and Small Enterprises Organization Act	588	587	652	634	582	522	469	439	604	607
Cartels under Environment Sanitation Act	106	122	123	123	123	123	123	123	123	123
Cartels under Coastal Shipping Association Act	15	14	16	15	22	22	22	21	19	19
Cartels under other statues	43	50	44	44	47	48	56	53	34	42
Total	970	999	1079	1040	1003	948	898	844	976	985

[a] Number in force in March of each year.

Source: Japanese Fair Trade Commission, Staff Office, The Antimonopoly Act of Japan (1973), p. 27. Reproduced from Caves and Uekusa (1976), p. 158.

required to wait their turn to build a new plant while a competitor built new capacity and achieved high volumes. Next time the roles will be reversed. This kind of coordination was carried out under the aegis of the government – by MITI. Later the system required the scrapping of old capacity as a condition for permission to build new. As a result Japan with a smaller home market than the U.S. built ten plants larger than any in the US (p. 54).

Yamamura (1988) provides a useful model of Japanese industrial policy and the role of competition within it. The government essentially organized an 'investment race' among large, oligopolistic firms in which exports and world market share were significant performance goals. In the real world, where markets are always incomplete, such a race without a coordinator will lead to ruinous competition, price wars and excess capacity, inhibiting the inducement to invest. In the Japanese economic miracle, MITI provided this crucial co-ordinating role (with the help of industry associations) and orchestrated the dynamic combination of collusion and competition which characterizes Japanese industrial policy. 'In a nutshell,' Yamamura observes

> what MITI did was to 'guide' the firms to invest in such a way that each large firm in a market expanded its productive capacity roughly in proportion to its current market share – no firm was to make an investment so large that it would destabilize the market. The policy was effective in encouraging competition for the market share (thus preserving the essential competitiveness of the industrial markets) while reducing the risk of losses due to excessive investment. Thus it promoted the aggressive expansion of capacity necessary to increase productive efficiency in output (p. 175).

Domestic Product Markets in South Korea

Again for reasons of space, I briefly note here that Korea also did not follow a policy of maximum domestic competition or unfettered market-determined entry and exit of firms.[18] The Korean government, if anything, went one step further than the Japanese in actively helping create large conglomerates, promoting mergers, and directing entry and exit of firms according to the requirements of technological scale economies and domestic and world demand conditions (see Table 2.1). It also helped organize the 'investment race' among the Korean giant conglomerates along the Japan lines. It is sometimes argued that competitive market forces have played a relatively greater role in Taiwan's domestic economy, but I note that both Taiwan and South Korea possess some of the most highly concentrated industrial structures among market economy countries (see Table 2.5).[19]

Factor Markets

Turning to the factor markets, in Japan both the domestic labour and capital markets have operated rather differently than envisaged in *The Development Challenge*'s recipes for faster economic growth and successful development. Although in South Korea and Taiwan, the labour market may have worked with 'minimum labour laws', as the study approvingly notes (p. 80), the situation in Japan has been quite different. A large proportion of the labour force has effectively a lifetime security of employment. Many leading scholars of the Japanese economy ascribe the international competitive success and technical leadership of the Japanese corporations precisely to these 'rigidities' in the labour market. Security of employment encourages workers to undertake firm specific investments in human capital, to promote technical change rather than to thwart it (for the fear of being made redundant). Not least, it also lets workers identify their interests with those of the corporation (see further Dore, 1986, and Aoki, 1990, among others).

Similarly, in relation to the capital market, a growing number of scholars in the USA and the UK today believe that the Japanese economic success is also in part due to the fact that the Japanese industrial corporations have been spared, unlike their Anglo-Saxon counterparts, the tender mercies of a stock market and a freely functioning market for corporate control (see Dore, 1985; Odagiri and Hase, 1989; Cosh, Hughes, and Singh, 1990). There are important analytical and empirical reasons for the view that the stock-market-based competitive financial systems are not conducive to promoting industrial investment, technical progress and productivity growth.[20] In none of the exemplar East Asian countries did a competitive capital market play a significant role in financing industrial growth. As mentioned earlier, the banks in South Korea were state-owned until the early 1980s. Although some of them are now under majority private ownership, the state has enormous influence and control over their activities. Taiwan's leading banks

Table 2.5 Per cent distribution of manufacturing value-added[a] by firm size, selected countries, 1973

Country	Number of workers			
	1–9	*10–99*	*100–499*	*500 or more*
Korea	5.8	13.8	27.7	52.7
Taiwan[b]	4.4	16.7	22.5	56.4
Hong Kong	7.4	30.2	32.1	30.2
Brazil	3.4	23.7	36.1	36.6
Turkey[c]	11.7	10.1	27.5	48.4
Peru	4.0	23.9	46.4	25.7
Japan[d]	8.7	28.4	24.9	37.9
Canada[d]	2.0	21.1	37.4	39.3
Czechoslovakia	0.2	5.4	18.2	76.11
Austria	0.8	21.5	36.2	41.5
UK	15.7[e]		24.4	60.0
USA	2.4	18.3	30.5	48.7

[a] Generally, value-added in producers' values
[b] Value-added in factor values, 1971
[c] 1970
[d] Net value-added in factor values
[e] 1–99

Source: Reproduced from Amsden (1989a).

continue to be under state ownership even today. The Japanese financial system, during the period of the economic miracle (1950–73), although not under state ownership, was bank-based, oligopolistic and subject to considerable state direction.

In conclusion, I turn to *The Development Challenge*'s argument that '[government] intervention in the market in East Asian economies was, in an overall sense, more moderate than in most other developing economies' (p. 39). How does one quantify the extent of government intervention – for example, how is the crucial co-ordinating role of MITI in Japanese industrial investment outlined above to be measured? Such government support for industry in Japan was much more significant than cash expenditure or subsidies. Moreover, MITI's co-ordinating functions were not simply ones of completing the 'incomplete' markets in the neoclassical sense. Rather, it was a much broader role in the political economy of Japan, to help create a social and business consensus in favour of MITI's specific restructuring and developmental goals. Thus, as Magaziner and Hout (1980) note: 'The process of discussion and debate between MITI and the companies in response to developments in the marketplace creates a dynamic decision making process. MITI aptly refers to Japan as a "plan-oriented market economy"' (p. 39).

2.7 DOMESTIC POLICY, EXTERNAL SHOCKS AND ECONOMIC PERFORMANCE

Another central thesis of *The Development Challenge* is that domestic policy matters far more than international conditions in determining a country's economic performance. This proposition ignores the far-reaching consequences of the historically unprecedented and massive external shocks which many Third World countries suffered at the end of the 1970s and into the 1980s. These shocks had a devastating effect on production, employment, inflation, as well as the political economy of these nations. It will be suggested below that if rich countries like the UK and the USA had been subjected to international economic disturbances of a similar magnitude, they would most likely have fared worse and suffered a decade-long depression. Although *The Development Challenge* recognizes that during the last decade the Latin American and Sub-Saharan African countries were subject to greater external shocks than the Asian countries, it does not adequately consider the differential impact of these shocks for the respective economies on the three continents.

The above points are best illustrated by considering the case of Asian and Latin American economies. Between 1965 and 1980, the Latin American countries grew at much the same rate as the Asian countries – at about 5.5 per cent per annum on average. On the basis of the growth rate in that period, the two groups of countries could not be statistically distinguished.[21] However, during the 1980s the Latin American growth rate collapsed to about 1.5 per cent per annum while the Asian countries continued to grow at much the same rate as before. An important question, therefore, is what part of this reduction in Latin American growth was due to international forces and what due to domestic policy mismanagement and other internal factors. A significant related issue is that if external economic shocks were largely responsible for the Latin American decline during the 1980s, how did the Asian countries continue to prosper in that decade?

The reasons for this differential economic performance of Asian and Latin American countries in the wake of the post-1979 world economic slow-down have been the subject of considerable controversy (see Balassa, 1984; Sachs, 1985; Maddison, 1985; Singh, 1986; Fishlow, 1991; Hughes and Singh, 1991; Ros, 1991). In the present context, the treatment of this question will necessarily be brief.[22]

A priori, there are three main factors which may help to explain the superior economic record of the Asian countries relative to those in Latin America:

- differences in economic structure and other initial conditions;
- differences in the economic policies pursued;
- differences in the size of the economic shocks experienced by the countries on the two continents.

Balassa (1984) and Sachs (1985) – and *The Development Challenge* endorses their analysis – suggest that a very important reason for the better Asian economic performance is that these countries have more open and export-orientated economic structures, compared to those in Latin America. Differences in economic and industrial structures between the Asian and Latin American economies have been examined in detail in Singh (1985) and Hughes and Singh (1991), but this analysis reveals very little evidence in support of the Balassa–Sachs openness hypothesis. The least open Asian economies – like China and India, for example – were able to cope at least as effectively with the world economic crisis in the 1980s as the highly export-orientated Korean economy.[23]

Hughes and Singh (1991) and Singh (1986) argue that certain exogenous shocks emanating from the post-1979 world economic crisis had a much greater impact on the economies of the Latin American countries than on the Asian economies. First, it is suggested that the rise in interest rates had a far bigger effect on Latin American countries than on those in Asia, since a larger proportion of the Latin American debt was of the floating rate variety. Moreover, the Latin American countries were starting from much less favourable initial conditions. In the period preceding the post-1979 world crisis – that is, during 1973 to 1979 – the median debt service to exports ratio of the Latin American countries was more than twice as high as that of the Asian countries: 22.9 per cent compared with 10.7 per cent.

Sachs (1985) suggests that with a few exceptions the impact of the rise in interest rates on the developing economies was not particularly significant. He writes 'at the peak the measured US real interest rate rises by about 10 percentage points and is multiplied by a debt/GDP ratio of the order of 20%, producing a peak annual loss of 2% of GDP and an average annual loss of about 1% of GDP.' This, however, is not a valid argument since, as Hughes and Singh (1991) report, the median current account deficit in the Latin American countries was only about 3 per cent of GDP in the late 1970s. The impact of the increase in interest rates (whether measured in nominal or real terms) on the current balance of these economies was therefore highly significant. The dynamic consequences (particularly in terms of capital flows) of an increase (or decrease) in the current account deficit by nearly a third for a balance of payments constrained economy, cannot be exaggerated.

Second, Hughes and Singh emphasize that the Latin American countries were far more subject to capital supply shocks than the Asian economies (on this point, see also the excellent detailed analysis of Fishlow, 1991). To illustrate the nature of these shocks, consider the case of Mexico. During the oil boom years, 1977 to 1981, the Mexican economy had been growing at a rate of 7–8 per cent per annum with even the non-oil GDP rising at a roughly similar rate. But despite the enormous increase in oil exports, the balance of payments position had been deteriorating. The current account deficit rose from nearly $5 billion in 1979 to almost $7 billion in 1980 and to $11.7 billion in 1981. Notwithstanding this deterioration, the international banking community was happily willing to lend Mexico ever increasing amounts to finance the deficits. Thus from 1978 to 1981, while international bank loans to developing countries as a whole increased by 76 per cent they rose by 146 per cent to Mexico, already a large debtor in 1978. To meet the Mexican government's increased demand for foreign loans to finance the current account deficit, the international banks accelerated their lending to Mexico in 1981, albeit with an increasing shortening of the term structure of the new loans (Ros, 1986). In 1981, the capital account of the balance of payments indicate Mexico's net public short term liabilities rose by $12.7 billion (compared with $6 billion in 1980 and $1.7 billion in 1979). However, in the crisis year of 1982, these capital flows were abruptly halted and the capital account shows that Mexico's net public external short-term liabilities actually *decreased* by $614 million. Brailovsky and Barker (1983) rightly note that this capital supply shock had a devastating effect on the Mexican economy.

Most of the other Latin American economies were subject to similar capital supply shocks. These emanated from what Williamson (1985) has named the 'contagion effect' whereby, following the Mexican debt crisis in 1982, voluntary private capital flows to most Latin American countries were greatly reduced if not stopped altogether. The important point is that because of the 'contagion effect', capital flows were reduced much more to the Latin American than to the Asian economies. This in turn will have worsened the balance of payments constraint in the Latin American countries more so and *more suddenly* than in the Asian countries.

Third, Hughes and Singh (1991) suggest that reduced world economic growth and world trade during 1980–2 had a differential impact on the normal export markets for countries in the two continents. In particular, the Middle Eastern market, which was the most rapidly expanding market during this period, was much more significant for many of the Asian countries than for Latin America. There are two important channels by which the Asian countries benefited from the economic prosperity in the Middle East: workers' remittances; and the growth of merchandise exports.

Relative to the Asian countries it is argued that the above three factors together made the balance of payments constraint on the Latin American economies much more severe.[24] It may be appreciated that a deterioration in the balance of payments position of the developing country has extremely serious consequences for all spheres of the economy, real as well as financial. The effect on industrial production is direct and for many countries immediate. The external payments constraint can become so binding that the country has to curtail not only the import of luxuries, or other consumer goods, but also the essential imports required for maintaining the existing level of domestic production. Agricultural production is affected both directly by the foreign exchange constraint and indirectly by reduced industrial production. Reduced imports as well as lower domestic production of fertilizers and other agricultural inputs, together with lowered oil imports, hamper agriculture production directly. Indirectly there is an unfavourable effect on production because of the reduced availability of the so-called incentive goods to farmers (for example, soap or bicycles). Import compression, however, not only threatens agricultural and industrial production but paradoxically also lowers exports. Khan and Knight (1988) provide empirical evidence in support of this phenomenon. Import strangulation and a balance of payments constraint also generate inflation and disequilibrium in government finances. As in many developing countries, sales and excise taxes on industrial production as well as import duties are a major source of government revenue, the balance of payments constraint was directly and indirectly responsible for the enormous increases in budget deficits or the public sector borrowing requirements which these countries experienced in the 1980s. In the institutional circumstances of the heavily indebted Latin American economies, there was an important additional reason why such a constraint generated a fiscal crisis. This arose from the fact that after the debt crisis foreign debt was consolidated in these countries to become largely the liability of the government and there was therefore a huge burden of interest payments on the budget. Sachs (1987) provided data to show that in Argentina and Mexico, in the mid-1980s, interest payments represented nearly a third of the government's revenues.

As the government in many Latin American countries has a direct and major role in undertaking or financing industrial activity and investment, the fiscal crisis leads particularly to reduced industrial and infrastructural investment. A number of WIDER studies on macroeconomic adjustment in developing countries (see Taylor, 1988) have shown that in general, in the South, public investment 'crowds in' rather than 'crowds out' private sector investment. This compounds the effects of the fiscal crisis on long-term economic development.

In view of all the direct and indirect effects of the foreign exchange constraint and the balance of payments crisis brought about by world economic developments, it is not surprising to observe the poor industrial and overall economic record of the Latin American countries during the last three decades relative to the Asian countries.[25]

There are, however, three other points which also deserve attention in this context. First it should be observed that the external shocks which a wide range of developing countries suffered in the early 1980s were gigantic. It requires an enormous economic and social effort as well as a considerable period of time to recover from the disruptions caused by such shocks. To illustrate, the quantitative impact of the demand shock, the terms of trade shock, and the interest rate shock on the balance of payments was estimated by the World Bank in 1985 for a small number of individual developing countries. The combined average annual negative effect of these shocks during 1981–2 amounted to 19.1 per cent of GDP in Kenya, 14.3 per cent in Tanzania, 18.9 per cent in the Ivory Coast, 8.3 per cent in Brazil, and 29 per cent in Jamaica. Even excluding the capital supply shock, which for many countries was extremely significant, these estimates of losses suffered by the developing countries are huge. To put these figures into perspective, it may be recalled that the impact of the adverse movements in the terms of trade for the UK (not then an oil exporter) as a result of the first oil shock in 1974–5, is estimated to have been equivalent to a reduction in GDP of about 4 per cent. This led to an enormous redistributive conflict and to a near doubling of the rates of inflation and unemployment. The government was obliged to undertake extraordinary measures (including for an advanced economy the rare step in 1976 of a recourse to the IMF) to restore economic stability. Yet the developing economies, which are much poorer, suffered in the early 1980s relatively far greater external shocks than did the UK in the mid-1970s.

Second, apart from the huge task of adjustment to these shocks at the beginning of the decade, it needs to be borne in mind that for many developing countries, particularly in Latin America and Africa, a number of the same adverse external factors continued to operate throughout the 1980s (Singh, 1992c, 1993b).

Third, an essential part of my analysis here is that it is not the case that the Latin American countries were incompetent or unaware of the desirability, for example, of balanced budgets, but that the economic shocks many of them suffered were so gigantic that their social and political institutions simply could not deal with the ensuing redistributive struggles over a diminished national cake. Hence many of them experienced episodes of hyperinflation as well as capital flight.

In view of the above, I find *The Development Challenge*'s treatment of this subject – the impact of external shocks – for the developing countries to be very unsatisfactory. I also find that the study is led into a number of other analytical errors by not properly considering the effects of world economic conditions for national economic performance. In view of these significant external shocks suffered by Latin American economies in the 1980s, it is not valid to aggregate their performance in that period with those of the 1960–80 period, as it would produce misleading results. Rather different rankings of economic performance of developing countries and hence very different conclusions with respect to 'successful' economic policies emerge if the periods 1960–80 and 1980–90 are examined separately rather than together.

2.8 RATES OF RETURN ON WORLD BANK-FINANCED INVESTMENT PROJECTS

The last point above concerning incorrect aggregation bears on *The Development Challenge*'s empirical analysis at several places (the reader may recall our earlier discussion in section 2.4 of the study's evidence on the relationship between education and economic growth). It is also directly relevant to the study's examination of the rates of return on investment projects carried out by the Bank and by the IFC over the previous 20 years (1968–87). *The Development Challenge* sets a great deal of store by the evidence presented on this issue (see chs 1 and 4, Table 4.2 and Figure 5).

This evidence purports to show that where the 'distortions' were low, the 'economic rates of return' (ERR) on these investment projects were considerably higher. It is further argued that the greater the rate of return on investment projects, the greater will be the overall economic growth. Thus *The Development Challenge*:

> By every measure, ERRs are highest in undistorted markets, and lowest in distorted markets. Projects implemented in an undistorted policy climate can have, on average, an ERR that is at least 5 percentage points higher than in a distorted climate (Table 4.2). To put this finding another way, with a few exceptions, undistorted policies makes an investment at least one and a half times as productive. The implication for growth is striking: a difference in the ERR of 5 percentage points, if achieved across the economy, would translate into a difference in the annual rate of GDP growth per capita of more than 1 percentage point every year. (p. 82)

There are two objections to this analysis. First, the robustness of the results to the time periods and countries chosen. For the reasons discussed above, because of the economic crisis in Latin America and Sub-Saharan Africa, during the 1980s, the rates of return on projects in these two developing continents during the last decade will be low and aggregating all countries and time-periods together will therefore lead to incorrect inferences. *The Development Challenge* says that the results are robust with respect to industries and sectors, but it does not say anything about robustness with respect to time-periods and countries.[26] Second, and more important, the causation may well be the other way round. The study's causal chain is: the lower the distortions in an economy, the larger the economic rate of return on its investment projects, the greater its economic growth. The alternative Kaldorian causal model, mentioned earlier, is more plausible: the higher the rate of growth of aggregate demand in an economy, the greater its rate of economic growth and therefore the more productive the investment projects carried out in such an economy. Without an empirical analysis of such competing hypotheses, *The Development Challenge's* conclusion on this point cannot be accepted.

2.9 CONCLUSION

As the main points of this paper were summarized at the start, it is not necessary to repeat them in this concluding section. The chief lesson to be drawn from the experience of Japan, Korea, and Taiwan – countries which the study rightly holds up as models of successful development – is not in favour of some neutral, passive state with a 'market-friendly approach to development'. Nor did these nations seek or practice a deep and unconditional integration with the world economy during their periods of rapid growth.

Rather, the state in these economies played a vigorous role and followed a highly active industrial policy. The government did not supplant the market altogether as the 'command' planning of production of the Soviet type did. Nor did it simply follow the market. Instead, in line with MITI's description of Japan as a 'plan-orientated market economy', the government guided the market towards planned structural change. Moreover the three East Asian countries integrated with the world economy in the directions and extent to which it was useful for them to do so.

This paper has argued that in a world of imperfect competition, economies of scale and learning by doing, there are sound analytical grounds for following such policies to promote technical change and economic growth. In such a world, the optimal degree of openness or the optimal degree of domestic competition for an economy is not maximum openness or perfect competition. *The Development Challenge* seems to have been led into a misinterpretation of the

East Asian experience because it is wedded to a theoretical paradigm whose assumptions do not correspond to the real world of manufacturing. Its analysis and the lessons it purports to draw from the last 40 years of development experience are not therefore helpful to developing countries.

It is important to emphasize that the present paper has mainly been concerned with the question of what are the correct analytical and policy conclusions which should be drawn from the historical experience of the 'successful' and 'unsuccessful' countries in the post-war period. The important issue of whether the successful East Asian model can be replicated in other developing countries is a large subject which has not been examined here. There must be left for another occasion.[27]

In conclusion, I note that in a document which is supposed to reflect the synthesis and interpretation of the lessons of the last four decades of development experience by the World Bank's economists, there is a curious omission. There is very little explicit discussion of what lessons the Bank's economists draw from the Bretton Woods institutions' own important role in the developing countries' debt crisis during the last decade. Normally, the Bretton Woods Institutions (BWIs), and implicitly the present *Development Challenge*, view their intervention in the debt crisis in a very positive light and regard their so-called case-by-case approach to adjustment as being not only correct but also successful. However, from the point of view of the developing countries, the role of these institutions is seen rather differently, essentially as that of a debt collector for the private Western banks. In the bargaining between creditors and debtors during the last decade, the IMF is thought to have been a powerful influence on the side of these banks with the result that the burden of adjustment has been one-sidedly borne by the debtor countries rather than being equitably shared with the banks and other parties. The case-by-case approach has involved the extraordinary spectacle of all the creditor banks banding together, *de facto* under the IMF auspices, and confronting each debtor country separately. It is notable that the BWIs discouraged the formation of debtors' cartels as a response to this situation.

The adjustment process in the debtor countries since 1982 can be regarded as successful only from the standpoint of the banks but not from that of the countries themselves. By the end of the decade the debtor countries were able to achieve massive trade surpluses and large turn-round in their current account balance, but this 'success' was obtained at an enormous cost in terms of capacity under-utilization, unemployment, low economic growth, reduction in real wages, rise in inflation and essentially the 'lost decade' of the 1980s. During the mid-1980s, instead of a normal flow of capital from the rich to the poor countries, the world witnessed a reverse flow from the South to the North, amounting on average in the Latin American countries to as much as 4 per cent of their GDP. BWIs are faced with the further embarrassment that their star pupil for the last decade or more, namely Mexico, has so far been unable to achieve either stabilization or growth.

The significant analytical questions about the role of the BWIs in the debt crisis are the following: has the BWI-inspired adjustment process been economically efficient from the point of view of either the debtor countries or that of the world economy? Would, for example, the losses to output and employment have been lower if the BWIs had acted differently? It is a pity that *The Development Challenge* does not address these issues, not least in order to draw appropriate lessons for the future.

Notes

1. These are the words used by Barber Conable, then President of the World Bank, in his Foreword to *The Development Challenge*.
2. The most important of these studies is World Bank see p. 92 (1993), hereafter referred to as *The East Asia Miracle*. In some areas, this study goes beyond *The Development Challenge* (Singh 1994c), but its final conclusion is nevertheless to endorse the policy analysis of the earlier study. Thus in analysing the East Asian Miracle it proceeds:

   What are the main factors that contributed to the HPAE's (High Performing Asian Economies) superior allocation of physical and human capital to high yielding investments and their ability to catch up technologically? Mainly, the answer lies in fundamentally sound, market oriented policies. Labour markets were allowed to work. Financial markets . . . generally had low distortions and limited subsidies compared with other developing economies. Import substitution was . . . quickly accompanied by the promotion of exports . . . the result was limited differences between international relative prices and domestic relative prices in the HPAEs. Market forces and competitive pressures guided resources into activities that were consistent with comparative advantage (p. 325)

   In other words the final policy conclusion is still essentially the 'market-friendly' approach to development albeit in a new packaging. Devel-

oping countries are recommended to seek their comparative advantage, to get the prices right, to have free markets as far as possible.
3. See further Singh (1984, 1992a), Taylor (1991).
4. OECD (1972), quoted in Singh (1979, pp. 217–18).
5. There is an enormous literature on the subject. For a lucid analysis of the relevant issues under discussion here, see Nelson (1981).
6. See also Singh (1989, 1990) on this point.
7. The classic references here are Verdoorn (1949) and Kaldor (1966). For a review, see Ref. McCombie (1987).
8. The period 1950–73, when the OECD economy grew at an unprecedented rate of almost 57 per cent per annum – twice its historical trend rate of growth – has rightly been termed the Golden Age of capitalism. Glyn, Hughes, Lipietz and Singh (1990) provide a detailed analysis of how the Golden Age rose in the first place and why it fell following the 1973 oil shock. See also Maddison (1982), Bruno and Sachs (1985) and see Ref. Kindleberger (1992). To avoid misunderstanding, it must be emphasized that I am not considering here short term monetary demand management, but rather the forces which affect the long term rate of growth of real demand.
9. In this section I have borrowed passages from Singh (1994a).
10. On this issue, see Fanelli, Frenkel, and Taylor (1993). See also sections 2.6 and 2.7 below.
11. This surplus has been primarily responsible for allaying the international concern, widespread in the mid-1960s in the wake of Indian harvest failures of the time, that the country would continue to be a basket case, would not be able to meet its food needs and hence would be a perpetual burden on the international community. The adoption of the green revolution technology, however, even in a few states like Punjab covering only a small proportion of the arable land, transformed the Indian food outlook. Notwithstanding a rate of population growth of over 2 per cent per annum, the country has been comfortably self sufficient in food over the last two decades.
12. For a fuller discussion of Punjab's agrarian revolution, see Gill (1979), Singh (1983), Bhalla and Chadha (1983), Bhalla and Tyagi (1989).
13. In relation to other empirical studies on this subject, the Report states in the text on p. 98: *Most of the studies* which have analysed GDP growth and openness to trade have found a positive relation (Box 5.3) (my italics). However, when one turns to Box 5.3, the conclusion is much more tentative. We are told: '*The majority of the evidence* now available shows a positive relation between openness – however measured – and growth' (p. 99, my italics). For the record, I note here that other surveys of the empirical evidence on this issue by independent scholars (see Pack, 1988; Rodrik, 1991) are even more sceptical about a positive relationship between openness and economic growth.
14. Some neoclassical economists take this argument even further and suggest that the government intervention in the East Asia economies did no more than what the market would have done anyway, i.e. the government policy was simply simulating the market. There are serious analytical and empirical flaws in this market simulation thesis. See Wade (1990) and Singh (1994c).

15. For a detailed analysis, see Wade (1990), Amsden (1989a).
16. See for example Krugman (1987) and Rodrik (1992).
17. On this point, see the interesting review by Lucas (1990) of Helpman and Krugman (1989).
18. For a fuller discussion of the role of competition and competition policy in South Korea and Japan, see Amsden and Singh (1994).
19. For different perspectives on the relative role of large and small firms in Taiwan's economic development, see Scitovsky (1986) and Amsden (1985b, 1989, 1989b).
20. There is a large literature on the subject. For the UK see Cosh, Hughes and Singh (1990), Singh (1992b). For the USA see, for example, MIT Commission on Industrial Productivity (1990). See also Singh (1993a).
21. Unless otherwise indicated, the source of the figures cited in this section are Hughes and Singh (1991) and Singh (1993b), which are based on a comparative analysis of the records of nine Asian and nine Latin American countries over the period 1960–70, 1970–80, and 1980–90.
22. For a recent review of this literature and for a fuller discussion of these issues, see Singh (1993b). See also Singh (1992a, 1994b).
23. There is a complex relationship between 'openness' and the vulnerability of an economy to external shocks. For a fuller analysis, see Hughes and Singh (1991).
24. In the early 1980s, the terms of trade shock and the reduction in OECD economic activity had in general a larger impact on the Asian countries than on the Latin American countries. However, Fishlow's (1991) analysis shows that even for this period, if the interest rate and the capital supply shocks are also included, as a proportion of exports, the magnitude of external shocks suffered by the Latin American countries was on average much greater than that experienced by the East Asian countries. Fishlow's sample did not include South Asian countries. He also did not consider the effects of workers' remittances and the growth of the Middle Eastern markets.
25. For reasons of space the questions of misallocation of resources and macroeconomic mismanagement by the Latin American economies are not discussed above. For an analysis of these issues, the reader is referred to Singh (1992b, 1993b), Fishlow (1991), and Hughes and Singh (1991), where it is shown that the Latin American record was no worse in the former respect than that of the Asian countries. For example, contrary to the mainstream conventional wisdom, Fishlow's analysis of the consumption functions indicates that the Latin American countries did not use external borrowings to finance current consumption any more than the Asian countries did. He notes: 'At the margin, therefore, there was an expected substitution for domestic saving. But there seems to be no difference in this respect between Indonesia and Korea, on the one hand, and Brazil and Mexico, on the other' (Fishlow, 1991, p. 153). As far as the allocation of investment resources in concerned, with negative real interest rates, it was not just Mexico or Brazil but also South Korea which used foreign borrowings in the 1970s to launch an ambitious programme of import substitution and development of heavy industries. All these programmes ran into teething

troubles of various kinds, but a major reason why the Korean programme nevertheless succeeded in the 1980s while those of Brazilian and the Mexican failed was because of the far more severe foreign exchange constraints to which the latter two countries were subject. It is also important to remember in this context that, prior to the economic crisis of the last decade, Brazil's rate of growth of manufactured export (in value terms) during the 1970s was much the same as that of South Korea, while those of Mexico and Argentina were significantly higher than that of India.

Similarly, questions of macroeconomic policy errors, issues of 'inappropriate' exchange rates and 'capital flight' are also examined in the above contributions to challenge the orthodox views on these matters. The capital flight, it is suggested, for example, was as much a consequence as a cause of the crisis in many of these countries. The basic argument is that these large external shocks led to enormous economic and social disruption and financial instability in these economies in the way outlined in the text here. This in turn led to capital flight which exacerbated financial instability in a negative feedback dynamic. Hughes and Singh argue that the adoption of policies to stem the capital flight was not a simple technical matter, but involved complex questions of the political economy of macroeconomic management in the affected countries.

26. There is evidence that this point about aggregation is not just of theoretical significance but has real empirical relevance. The results reported in ch. 4 of *The Development Challenge* are based on an aggregate data set of about 1200 projects carried out either by the World Bank or the IFC during the two decades 1968 to 1989. However, the IFC economists have been unable to confirm the aggregate results reported in the study with respect to the IFC projects considered on their own. These projects are the private sector ones and constitute about a third of the total number of projects. This embarrassing detail which is not reported in *The Development Challenge* but has been intimated to me by the economists in the Economics Department of the IFC, must cast some doubt on the robustness of the study's conclusions on this point.

27. These issues are taken up in Singh (1995).

References

Amsden, A. (1985) 'The state and Taiwan's economic development' in P. Evans, D. Rueschemeyer and T. Skocpol (eds) *Bringing the State Back In* (Cambridge University Press) pp. 78–106.

Amsden, A. (1989a) *Asia's Next Giant* (New York: Oxford University Press).

Amsden, A. (1989b) 'Big business and urbanisation in Taiwan: the origins of small and medium size enterprise and regionally decentralised industry', *mimeo* (Cambridge, Mass.: Massachusetts Institute of Technology).

Amsden, A and A. Singh (1994) 'The optimal degree of competition and dynamic efficiency in Japan and Korea', *European Economic Review*, 38(3–4): 941–51.

Aoki, M. (1990) 'Toward an economic model of the Japanese firm', *Journal of Economic Literature*, 28(1): 1–27.

Balassa, B. (1984) 'Adjustment policies in developing Countries: a reassessment', *World Development*, 12(9): 955–72.

Bhagwati, J. (1988) *Protectionism* (Cambridge, Mass,: The MIT Press).

Bhalla, G.S. and G.K. Chadha (1983) *Green Revolution and the Small Peasant* (Delhi: Concept Publishing House).

Bhalla, G.S. and D.S. Tyagi (1989) *Patterns in Agricultural Development: A District Level study* (Delhi).

Boltho, A. (1975) *Japan: An Economic Survey* (London: Oxford University Press).

Brailovsky, V. and T. Barker (1983) 'La politica económica entre 1976 y 1982 y el plan national en desarrollo industrial,' paper presented at the Seminar on Mexican Economy at El Cologio de Mexico, 8–10 August 1983.

Bruno, M. and J. Sachs (1985) *Economics of Worldwide Stagflation* (Cambridge, Mass.: Harvard University Press).

Caves, R. and M. Uekusa (1976) *Industrial Organisation in Japan* (Washington DC: The Brookings Institution).

CEPG (Cambridge Economic Policy Group) (1979) *Economic Policy Review*, 5.

Chakravarty, S. and A. Singh (1988) *The Desirable Forms of Economic Openness in the South* (Helsinki: WIDER).

Chang, H.-J. (1994) *The Political Economy of Industrial Policy* (New York: St Martin's Press)

Chang, H.-J. and A. Singh (1993) 'Public enterprises in developing countries and economic efficiency – A critical examination of analytical, empirical and policy issues', *UNCTAD Review*, pp. 45–82.

Cosh, A., A. Hughes and A. Singh (1990) 'Takeovers and short-termism in the UK', *Industrial Policy Paper*, 3 (London: Institute for Public Policy Research).

Dertouzos, M., R. Lester and R. Solow (eds) (1980) *Made in America* (Cambridge, Mass.: The MIT Press).

Dore, R. (1985) 'Financial structures and the long term view', *Policy Studies*, 6(1): 10–29.

Dore, R. (1986) *Flexible Rigidities: Industrial Policy and Structural Adjustment in the Japanese Economy 1970–80* (London: Athlone).

Fanelli, J.M., R. Frenkel and L. Taylor (1993) 'The World Development Report 1991: a critical assessment', presented at the UN University/World Bank Symposium on Economic Reform in Developing Countries, 6 February 1993, Washington DC.

Fishlow, A. (1990) 'The Latin American state', *Journal of Economic Perspectives*, 4(3): 61–74.

Fishlow, A. (1991) 'Some reflection on comparative Latin American economic performance and policy', in T. Banuri (ed.) *Economic Liberalism: No Panacea* (Oxford University Press) pp. 149–70.

Gill, M.S. (1979) 'Punjab: what other states can learn from', *National Cooperative Development Corporation Bulletin*, 4–4 (August–October).

Glyn, A., A. Hughes, A. Lipietz and A. Singh (1990) 'The rise and fall of the Gold Age', in S. Marglin and J. Schor (eds) *The Golden Age of Capitalism* (Oxford: Clarendon) pp. 39–25.

Helpman, E. and P. Krugman (1989) *Trade Policy and Market Structure* (Cambridge, Mass.: The MIT Press).

Hughes, A. and A. Singh (1991) 'The world economic slowdown and the Asian and the Latin American economies', in T. Banuri (ed.) *Economic Liberalisation: No Panacea* (Oxford University Press) pp. 57–97.

Johnson, C. (1987) 'Political institutions and economic performance: the government-business relationship in Japan, South Korea and Taiwan', in F. Deyo (ed.) *The Political Economy of New Asian Industrialism* (Ithaca: Cornell University Press) pp. 136–64.

Kaldor, N. (1966) *Causes of the Slow Rate of Economic Growth in the United Kingdom*, Inaugural Lecture, University of Cambridge (Cambridge University Press).

Khan, M. and M. Knight (1988) 'Import compression and export performance in developing countries', *Review of Economics and Statistics*, **70**(2): 315–21.

Kindleberger, C.P. (1992) 'Why did the Golden Age Last So Long' in F. Cairncross and A. Cairncross (eds) *The Legacy of the Golden Age: The 1960s and their Economic Consequences* (London and New York: Routledge).

Krugman, P. (1987) 'Is free trade passé?', *Journal of Economic Perspectives* **1**(2): 131–44.

Lai, D. (1983) *The Poverty of Development Economics* (London: Institute of Economic Affairs).

Lockwood, W. (1965) 'Japan's "new capitalism"', in W. Lockwood (ed.) *The State and Economic Enterprise in Japan* (Princeton University Press) pp. 447–522.

Lucas, R. (1990) 'Review of *Trade Policy and Market Structure* By E. Helpman and P. Krugman', *Journal of Political Economy*, **98**(3): 664–7.

Maddison, A. (1982) *Phases of Capitalist Development* (Oxford University Press).

Maddison, A. (1985) *Two Crises: Latin America and Asia 1929–38 and 1973–83* (Paris: OECD).

Magaziner, I. and T. Hout (1980) *Japanese Industrial Policy* (London: Policy Studies Institute).

McCombie, J.S.L. (1987) 'Verdoorn's Law', in J. Eatwell, M. Milgate and P. Newman (eds) *The New Palgrave Dictionary of Economic Thought* (London and New York: Macmillan).

MIT Commission on Industrial Productivity (1989) *Made in America: Regaining the Productivity Edge* (Cambridge, Mass.: MIT Press).

Nelson, R. (1981) 'Research on productivity growth and productivity differences: Dead Ends and New Departures', *Journal of Economic Literature*, **19**(3): 1029–64.

Nino, K. (1973) 'On efficiency and equity problems in industrial policy – with special relation to the Japanese experience', *Kobe University Economic Review*, 19.

Odagiri, H. and T. Hase (1989) 'Are mergers and acquisitions going to be popular in Japan too? An empirical study', *International Journal of Industrial Organisation*, **7**(1): 49–72.

OECD (1972) *The Industrial Policy of Japan* (Paris: OECD).

Pack, H. (1988) 'Industrialisation and trade', *The Handbook of Development Economics* (Amsterdam: North-Holland).

Pesaran, M.H. and Smith, R. (1992) *Theory and Evidence in Economics*, Working Paper No. 9224, Department of Applied Economics, University of Cambridge.

Rao, C.H.H. (1992) 'Agriculture Policy and Performance', in Bimal Jalan (ed.) *The Indian Economy: Problems and Prospects* (New Delhi: Viking).

Rodrik, D. (1991) 'Closing the productivity gap: does trade liberalisation really help?', in G. Helleiner (ed.) *Trade Policy, Liberalisation, and Development: New Perspectives* (Oxford, Clarendon).

Rodrik, D. (1992) 'The limits of trade policy reform in developing countries', *Journal of Economic Perspectives*, 6(1): 87–105.

Ros, J. (1986) 'Mexico's stabilisation and adjustment policies (1982–85)', *Labour and Society*, 11(3): 335–60.

Ros, J. (1991) 'Foreign exchange and fiscal constraints on growth: a reconsideration of structuralist and macroeconomic approaches', paper presented at the Conference on New Directions in Analytical Political Economy, University of Notre Dame, 8–10 March 1991.

Sachs, J. (1985) 'External debt and macroeconomic performance in Latin America and East Asia', *Brookings Papers on Economic Activity*, 2, 523–64.

Sachs, J. (1987) 'Trade and exchange rate policies in growth-oriented adjustment programs', in V. Corbo, M. Khan and K. Goldstein (eds) *Growth-Oriented Structural Adjustment* (Washington D.C.: IMF and World Bank) pp. 291–325.

Scitovsky, T. (1986) 'Economic development in Taiwan and South Korea: 1965–81', in L.J. Lau (ed) *Models of Development: A Comparative Study of Economic Growth in South Korea and Taiwan* (San Francisco: Institute for Contemporary Studies) pp. 135–95.

Scott, B. (1991) 'Economic strategy and economic policy', A paper presented at the World Bank, 21 November 1991.

Short, R. (1984) 'The role of public enterprise: An international statistical comparison', in R. Floyd, C. Gary and R. Short (eds) *Public Enterprises in Mixed Economies: some Macroeconomic Aspects* (Washington DC: International Monetary Fund) pp. 110–95.

Singh, A. (1979) 'North Sea oil and the reconstruction of UK Industry', in F. Blackaby (ed.) *DeIndustrialisation* (London: Heinemann Educational) pp. 202–24.

Singh, A. (1984) 'The interrupted industrial revolution of the third world: prospects and policies for resumption', *Industry and Development* (June): 43–68.

Singh, A. (1985) *The World Economy and the Comparative Economic Performance of Large Semi-Industrial Countries* (Bangkok: ARTEP/ILO).

Singh, A. (1986) 'The great continental divide: the Asian and Latin American Countries in the World Economic crisis', *Labour and Society*, vol. 1, no. 3: pp. 277–93.

Singh, A. (1989) 'Third world competition and de-industrialisation in advanced countries', *Cambridge Journal of Economics*, 13(1): 103–20,

Singh, A. (1990) 'Southern competition, labor standards, and industrial development in the north and the south', in S. Herzenberg and J. Perez-Lopez (eds) *Labor Standards and Development in the Global Economy* (Washington DC: US Department of Labor).

Singh, A. (1992a) 'The actual crisis of economic development in the 1980s: an alternative policy perspective for the future', in A. Dutt and K. Jameson (eds) *New Directions in Development Economics* (Aldershot: Edward Elgar) pp. 81–116.

Singh, A. (1992b) 'Corporate takeovers', in *The New Palgrave Dictionary of Money and Finance* (London: Macmillan).

Singh, A. (1992c) 'The lost decade: the economic crisis of the third world in the 1980s', *Contention*, 1(3).

Singh, A. (1993a) 'The stock market and economic development; should developing countries encourage stock markets?', *UNCTAD Review*, 4, 1–28.

Singh, A. (1993b) 'Asian economic success and Latin American failure in the 1980s: new analyses and future policy implications', *International Review of Applied Economics*: 267–89.

Singh, A. (1993c) '"Close" vs "strategic" integration with the world economy and "market-friendly approach to development" vs an "industrial policy"', University of Duirbusg, INEF Report, Heft 4/1993.

Singh, A. (1994a) 'Global economic changes, skills and international competitiveness', *International Labour Review*, 133(2): 167–83.

Singh, A. (1994b) 'Growing independently of the World Economy: Asian economic development since 1980', *UNCTAD Review*: 91–106.

Singh, A. (1994c) 'Openness and the market friendly approach to development: learning the right lessons from development experience', *World Development*, 22(12): 1811–23.

Singh, A. (1994d) 'State intervention and the market friendly approach to development: a critical analysis of the World Bank Theses', in A. Dutt, K. Kim and A. Singh (eds), *The State, Markets and Development* (London: Edward Elgar) pp. 3–21.

Taylor, L. (1988) *Varieties and Stabilisation Experiences* (Oxford University Press).

Taylor, L. (1991) 'Foreign resource flows and developing country growth', WIDER Research for Action (Helsinki: WIDER).

Verdoorn, P. (1949) 'Fattori che regolano lo sviluppo della productivitá del lavaro', *L'Industria*, 1: pp. 2–10.

Wade, R. (1990) *Governing the Market* (Princeton University Press).

Williamson, O.E. (1985) 'Comment on Sachs', *Brooking Papers on Economic Activity*, No. 2: 565–70.

World Bank (1991) *World Development Report 1991: The Challenge of Development* (New York: Oxford University Press for the World Bank).

World Bank (1993) *The East Asian Miracle* (New York: Oxford University Press for the World Bank).

Yamamura, K. (1988) 'Caveat emptor: the industrial policy of Japan', in P. Krugman (ed.) *Strategic Trade Policy and the New International Economics* (Cambridge, Mass.: The MIT Press).

3 The Political Economy of the Current US Financial Crisis

L. Randall Wray

3.1 INTRODUCTION[1]

I will examine the causes of the financial crisis that unfolded in the USA during the 1980s. Other analyses have tended to focus on a very narrow range of factors that are purported to have caused the problems experienced by banks and thrifts (many of these, in fact, argue that it is an exaggeration to characterize these problems as a crisis; even among those that accept the crisis label, the view seems to be that the crisis is over). Some analyses focus on the contributing political factors: undue influence by politicians seeking political contributions (Adams, 1990; Waldman, 1990); excessive deregulation (Sherrill, 1990); or even excessive regulation (Kaufman, 1990). Others attribute the crisis to corruption, mismanagement and criminal involvement (Sherrill, 1990; Waldman, 1990; Pizzo, Fricker and Muolo, 1991). Non-orthodox analyses have also blamed monetarist policy of the Federal Reserve Bank (Greider 1989). On the other hand, most orthodox economists (Benston, 1990; Eisenbeis, 1990; Kane, 1990; Kaufman, 1990; Litan, 1990; Scott, 1990) have discounted these factors and blamed improper incentives (underpriced deposit insurance, regulatory forbearance); or have argued that at least in the case of thrifts, the very existence of these dinosaur institutions violates the norms of the market, thus, market forces are eliminating them. (Osterberg and Thomson, 1993)

Most of these analyses contain at least an element of truth, but none, as I have said before (Wray 1992a), can see the forest for the trees. What is needed is an analysis that recognizes the endogenous forces that generate instability in modern capitalist systems. This must include an analysis of the transformation of the financial structure over time. Rather than viewing the state as an exogenous force that interferes with stabilizing market forces, the political economy approach attributes to the state both stabilizing and destabilizing potential. To a great extent, the state *reacts to* economic processes – that is, state intervention is endogenous rather than exogenous. Finally, the analysis must take account of the international influences on the US financial system as well as the international repercussions and implications of the US financial crisis. In particular, monetary policy and, to a lesser extent, regulatory changes were driven by international considerations. Furthermore, the US experience has been repeated (but not duplicated because of different institutional arrangements) in other countries.[2]

This chapter presents a 'case study' that falls within the political economy tradition. This approach emphasizes 'the dynamic nature of capitalist economies, capital accumulation . . . conflict of interests . . . [and] cumulative causation' (Arestis and Sawyer, 1993, p. 1). While Arestis and Sawyer identified four strands of political economy, this chapter primarily will follow the institutionalist tradition that emphasizes the evolutionary nature of the economy while taking '[a]n interdisciplinary approach . . . along with a detailed and painstaking study of institutions' (ibid., p. 3). Like most political economists, I will argue that this evolution has been generated by forces within the system, and that it has proceeded along an unstable path – indeed, evolution over the post-war period has been from a relatively robust system to a fragile system. The analysis will draw heavily from the work of Minsky. Finally, this chapter will examine only the US case. It is hoped that this will spur similar analyses of the experience in other countries, as well as a comparative analysis.

3.2 THE INSTITUTIONAL SETTING

Because many readers will not be familiar with the institutional arrangements in the USA, I will briefly review them. In this section, I will summarize the post-war setting; in the next section, I will review the financial crises of the inter-war years that generated financial reforms that underlie the post-war arrangements.

The USA is unusual because of its complex, fractured, regulatory structure and because of the sheer number of financial institutions. The number of commercial banks peaked in 1921 at nearly 30 500 commercial banks, but during most of the post-war period, the USA had 15 000–16 000 commercial banks and 5000–6000 thrifts (savings and loan institutions). In addition, banks increasingly operate branches: in 1970, there were more than 21 000 branches of commercial banks; this number had risen to 53 744 by 1992 (Wheelock, 1993). On one hand, these numbers may not seem excessive given the size and population of the USA. However, the vast majority of the commercial banks are extremely small and a large proportion of these are located in the relatively less populated states throughout the midwest.[3] Their existence is usually attributed to restrictions on branching across state lines (and, in some states, even on branching within the state). These restrictions are due at least in part to fear of domination by large New York banks and to remnants of nineteenth-century popularism that feared branching would cause savings to flow from rural areas to cities. In any case, concentration of the financial sector in the USA is probably not much different from that of any modern capitalist country in spite of the number of banks and thrifts. In terms of assets, the largest dozen commercial banks are as large as the entire thrift sector, combined.[4] In 1987, the top 0.9 per cent of all banks held 59.3 per cent of all bank assets (Boyd and Graham, 1992).

Thrifts and commercial banks can have either a federal or a state charter (this is referred to as the dual banking system). Federally chartered banks are chartered, examined and supervised by the Comptroller of the Currency (the OCC, under the Treasury Department); the Federal Reserve Bank (Fed) is responsible for examining and supervising member (of the Federal Reserve System – FRS) state-chartered banks, which are also supervised by state agencies; the Federal Deposit Insurance Corporation (FDIC) insures deposits of member (of the FDIC) commercial banks through its Bank Insurance Fund (BIF), and charters, examines and supervises non-member (of the FRS) state banks; thrifts are chartered by either state agencies or by the Federal Home Loan Bank Board (FHLBB); and thrift deposits *were* insured by the Federal Saving and Loan Insurance Corporation (FSLIC).

The thrift counterpart to the FRS is the Federal Home Loan Bank (FHLB) System; just as the Fed provides reserves through its discount window to commercial banks, the FHLB would provide funding and liquidity to member thrifts – at below-market rates. However, while the FDIC is independent of the Fed, the FSLIC was put under the FHLBB. Another major difference between the FHLBB and the Fed was the explicit mandate of the FHLBB to actively promote the thrift sector – which it was also supposed to regulate. Because FSLIC went bankrupt during the thrift crisis, thrifts are now insured by the FDIC's Savings Association Insurance Fund (SAIF); the FHLBB was also replaced by the Office of Thrift Supervision (OTS) which, like the OCC, was placed under the Treasury. Finally, the Resolution Trust Corporation (RTC – under the OTS) was created to sell, merge, or liquidate insolvent thrifts; originally, the RTC could accept thrifts into receivership only until October 1993, but due to a backlog of thrift 'zombies', Congress extended its authority to January 1995, after which SAIF will deal with failing thrifts. In the meantime, insured deposits of failed thrifts are covered through a combination of RTC liquidations, taxpayer fund authorized by Congress (many of these are 'loans'), and funds raised through bond sales (for example, by Financing Corporation – FICO – created to deal with thrifts that failed before the RTC came into existence in 1989).

This may appear to be an inordinately complex institutional structure; recent proposals, including one apparently favoured by President Clinton, would attempt to consolidate the federal regulatory structure. The 'dual banking system' that gives financial institutions the option of either a federal or state charter has played an important role in encouraging competitive 'levelling down' of regulations because institutions could pursue the charter with the most favourable terms. However, it is unlikely that consolidation would eliminate the dual banking system.

One final point must be mentioned regarding the institutional setting: there is a very cosy (one might say incestuous) relationship among the regulated (banks and thrifts), the regulators, and politicians. Thrifts have always been viewed by politicians as favoured institutions, partly because they were generally local and because they promoted home ownership in the politician's district, but also because they have been important sources of campaign funding. Further, the politician's hometown thrift frequently was a source of funding for his/her own home or for various business projects. There is a natural and unavoidably tempting synergy involved: politicians need money and thrifts are able to create it on demand.[5] There is virtually a revolving door among the thrift trade association (the US League of Savings Institutions – USLSI), regulatory agencies, congressional staff, and political office. To a lesser extent, the same is true of the commercial banking sector. Of course, it is not uncommon for the regulated to capture the regulators, but the extremely small equity requirements and correspondingly large leverage ratios make banks and thrifts very appealing to those who need quick money. Politicians came to view banks and especially thrifts as their own personal piggy banks and are willing to go to extraordinary lengths to ensure that nothing hinders this relationship.[6]

Before turning to the reforms that generated the current US institutional structure, it may be useful to contrast that structure with the more typical structure found in Europe. The USA is unusual in three respects. First, the USA is the only major country without a true national banking system – as discussed, it operates with a dual banking system (both state and federal charters). Second, unlike European countries, it operates with a much more fragmented system (as does Japan), comprised of relatively rigid separation of institutions by function – although this is breaking down in the USA. In contrast, in Europe something approaching a 'universal' bank is more common (except in the UK), in which a wider range of activities is undertaken. In the USA, this functional segmentation generated maturity matching of assets and liabilities by institutional type. As will be discussed below, the European 'universal' banks maintain maturity matching within each institution. Finally, supervision is consolidated in Europe while it is highly fragmented in the USA. As mentioned above, US banks are supervised by state authorities, by the FDIC, by the Fed, and by the OCC depending on the type of charter held and by its membership in the FRS and FDIC. In contrast, most of the Group of Seven (as well as other major trading partners of the USA) place their financial regulators under a minister of finance or another single (national) government authority; prudential supervision is administered by a commissioned or incorporated agency. Interestingly, the FDIC is apparently the only insurer responsible for supervision of financial institutions.[7] (Bartholomew, 1989)

It is frequently claimed by US observers that the financial crisis has been generated by improper incentives provided by excessive safety nets and regulation; it is believed that if the United States were to rely to a greater extent on market forces, the risk of crisis would be reduced. Comparison with the practice of other countries, however, shows that the USA relies *more* on market forces, and that its safety net is *less* comprehensive than that of most other countries. All of the countries that signed the Basle Accord on capital standards have national deposit insurance – many of these insurance systems were established during the 1980s. Compared with other countries, the US deposit insurance system is at or near the top in terms of levels of coverage, premiums, government supervision, and percent of the industry insured. Some countries do not maintain a reserve fund, and many do not charge insurance premiums (CBO, 1990).

However, all of the European countries prevent important banks from failing; all protect depositors (whether insured or not) from loss; and most intervene to prevent failure even by non-bank financial institution (Corrigan, 1992). If anything, European regulators rely *less* upon market discipline than do US regulators – in most cases, there is no attempt to mimic a private insurance system by charging risk-based insurance premiums, nor is there an attempt to accumulate insurance reserves to cover projected losses. Instead, Europeans more readily accept treasury responsibility for financial bail-outs. This makes it unlikely that the much more severe financial crisis in the USA can be attributed to absence of market discipline.

It is possible that the worse experience of the USA is more apparent than real. European resolutions of troubled banks often take place through quiet, joint public and private efforts – which might be attributed to centralized supervision and smaller numbers of institutions. Recent revelations concerning BCCI indicate that other countries are not immune to the same sorts of problems experienced in the USA. During the 1980s, more than 25 governments were forced to intervene to help troubled financial institutions. Canada was forced to restructure its regulatory system after a number of banks and thrifts failed; Norway experienced troubles after depressed oil prices generated problem commercial and savings banks; the Philippines had to close more than 160 financial institutions; and Spain had to rescue 51 banks (holding 20 per cent of all deposits) between 1978 and 1983. However, in each of these cases, there 'were few signs of general panic or major public concern' due to the centralized regulatory systems and quick responses of the governments (Bartholomew, 1989, p. 20).

3.3 BACKGROUND TO THE CURRENT CRISIS

The current crisis of the US financial system is by no means the first; widespread crises occurred in 1873, 1884, 1893 and 1907. The

Federal Reserve System (FRS) evolved in response to the 1907 crisis, and the Federal Reserve Bank (Fed) was created specifically to act as a lender of last resort in order to prevent bank runs (See Dymski, 1991). However, this did not prevent another series of financial crises during the 1920s, when almost 6000 banks failed. Careful investigation has since revealed that a high proportion of these failures was due to insider abuse, overconcentration of loans in certain areas (particularly in real estate), developer-owner misuse of their banks for pet projects, and interference by politicians who protected bank owners and management from bank regulators (Adams, 1990). All of this may sound familiar.

The lender of last resort function was not designed to save unhealthy banks, thus the Fed did not feel obligated to bail-out the banks that failed during the 1920s. The Great Depression that followed lowered bank asset values so that most banks *became* unhealthy; again, the Fed let these fail because the lender of last resort function was designed to save healthy banks facing irrational runs. In 1930–1, nearly 4000 banks failed, about 9100 banks had failed by 1933, and a total of 9500 failed by 1940.[8] While the typical bank that failed in the 1920s had been small, the failures in the 1930s included large banks. Significantly, thrifts fared somewhat better because home mortgage loans dominated their portfolios, and mortgage loans are typically safer than commercial loans.[9]

In March 1933, during the dark days of the financial crisis. President Roosevelt called a banking 'holiday' (the day after his inauguration); banks were closed and were not allowed to reopen until they had proven they were not insolvent. The Reconstruction Finance Corporation (RFC), which was in charge of reopening banks, had been in operation since 1932. It would set up advisory committees which, with RFC agency managers and examiners, would decide whether a bank could be saved.[10] If so, loans would be made. By the time of the banking holiday, however, Jesse Jones of the RFC had come to the conclusion that loans were not the answer – loans provided 'liquidity' to meet withdrawals, but the problem was that bank net worth was negative because asset values had fallen below liabilities – what banks needed was an injection of capital. Five days after Roosevelt's inauguration, the RFC was authorized to purchase preferred stock in banks.

Banks were placed into three categories: 'A' banks were solvent and sufficiently capitalized; 'B' banks had no capital, but assets were equal to liabilities; 'C' banks had liabilities in excess of assets. The class A banks were immediately reopened; the class B banks were opened as soon as they were made sound; the class C banks were placed into the hands of conservators and either reorganized with RFC help, or ultimately liquidated. Reopenings began on 13 March 1933. Jones later admitted that perhaps as many as 4000 of the reopened banks were actually insolvent. However, the RFC planned to make them solvent. The RFC was very liberal in valuing assets – Jones believed that given sufficient time and guidance, most banks could survive. The RFC decided to purchase capital in banks which had assets at least equal to 90 per cent of the value of liabilities. In many cases, the RFC demanded that management of a bank receiving assistance be replaced. The RFC picked replacement management, or an RFC official was placed on the board of directors to keep an eye on management. The RFC at the same time demanded that bank owners take a loss on equity, and that large depositors convert deposits into equity shares. Eventually, the RFC put capital into almost half of all the banks, and Jones later claimed that probably only 20 of these really did not need the capital, indeed, most would have failed without it. All told, the RFC loaned and invested nearly $4 billion to rescue financial institutions, saved about 7000 banks, and eventually returned all the money it spent to the Treasury, with a profit. The long-term consequences included a stable financial sector led, for the most part, by conservative management.

In the aftermath of this final crisis, various financial system reforms were adopted. These included: separation of commercial banking from investment banking; other functional and geographic barriers to entry designed to reduce competition; deposit insurance corporations to guarantee deposits in a variety of institutional types;[11] deposit interest rate regulation (again to reduce competition but also to reduce the cost to financial institutions of issuing liabilities); capital requirements (banks and thrifts had to hold 5 per cent capital against assets); restrictions over the types of assets banks and thrifts could buy (for example, thrifts could not make consumer or commercial loans); ownership rules (all nationally chartered thrifts were mutuals – owned by depositors); and greater use of 'monetary policy' (open market operations, discount rate, and required reserve ratios) in an attempt to influence credit market conditions.

Perhaps the most important, even if unintended, results of these reforms were *de facto* maturity matching and limits on the ability of financial institutions to provide funds for speculation (see Kregel,

1992). Separation of commercial banking from investment banking, constraints on the type of assets banks and thrifts could buy, and other forms of market segmentation helped to create a financial system in which maturities of the assets and liabilities of financial institutions were more or less matched. Commercial banks primarily relied on short-term liabilities (demand deposits) and held short-term assets (commercial loans); thrifts relied on stable, essentially long-term passbook savings accounts and held long-term home mortgages; and investment banks underwrote long-term stock and bond issues which would be held by households as long-term savings (although secondary markets created liquidity for these long-term placements).[12] Furthermore, market segmentation also limited the ability of the financial system to finance a speculative explosion of asset prices – commercial banks were prohibited, for example, from financing speculation in the stock market. Various balance sheet constraints also made it difficult to finance even a real estate boom. Thus, the reforms helped to limit a run-up of asset prices that might occur in the presence of excessive optimism. Jesse Jones's conservative bank management also ensured that banker scepticism would keep speculation in check.

Were the reforms successful? From 1940 to 1980, banks and thrifts virtually never failed: the number of bank failures averaged six per year, and never exceeded more than 10 in any year (with the exception of the 1974–5 recession); thrift failures averaged about three per year.[13] There were no financial crises until 1966, and every financial crisis from 1966 until the thrift crisis of the early 1980s was successfully contained with quick, but relatively minimal, governmental intervention.[14] However, the crises have appeared with increasing frequency, and have become increasingly severe. The current crisis appears to be a crisis of the entire financial system. Indeed, it will eclipse any previous financial crisis in terms of its scope.

The annual number of thrift failures rose from 11 in 1980 to 223 by 1988.[15] By early 1992, the FSLIC and RTC had resolved 1141 thrifts, the RTC had already taken control of nearly 75 others that were in the process of being resolved, and the Office of Thrift Supervision estimated another 100 would need to be resolved by 1994.[16] Some observers have claimed that at least 600 and perhaps as many as 1600 still remain to be resolved. We have already lost about half of all thrifts (there were nearly 4000 thrifts in 1980, but approximately 2000 remained in mid-1992). And some say that at least half of the remaining thrifts are unhealthy.

Similarly, the number of bank failures also rose above 200 per year: between 1985 and 1990 more than 1000 banks failed. At the beginning of 1993, only 11 461 insured commercial banks remained – the lowest number this century. According to a recent study, approximately 1500 banks were in serious trouble at the end of 1991 with assets of approximately $1 trillion (Vaughn and Hill, 1992). Of these, 1150 banks were already insolvent if their assets were valued at market prices. In terms of potential costs to the Bank Insurance Fund (BIF), the problem was concentrated in 10 huge bank holding companies, all of which would have been massively insolvent if assets were marked to market.

As a result of thrift failures, the FSLIC itself become insolvent and was dissolved. Estimates of the negative net worth of the FDIC ran as high as $62 billion in the early 1990s. Estimates of the costs of the crisis range from the CBO estimate of nearly $500 billion as the present value of the costs of the thrift bail out, to an estimate by Vaughn and Hill (1992) of direct and indirect costs of $1 trillion already incurred by society due to bad banks and thrifts. In addition, they believe that the costs of dealing with problem banks will add another $174 to 279 billion over the next few years. Some have concluded that direct costs (including interest) for the thrift crisis alone would total $1.5 trillion over the next 40 years (Vaughn and Hill, 1992, pp. 24–7). Even though it is impossible to obtain a consensus regarding the ultimate costs, no one doubts that they are large, nor can anyone believe that the reserves of the FDIC will be sufficient should a reversal of the current tranquil period occur. In spite of this recognition, Congress has been reluctant to provide additional funds to the RTC beyond the $87 billion initially approved, a reluctance illustrated in 1993 when, after much debate, $18.3 billion was added to finish the RTC's cleanup.[17] It is hard to believe that Congress is prepared to provide several hundred billion more for a bail-out of banks. The crisis is by no means over. What went wrong?

3.4 CAUSES OF THE CURRENT CRISIS

I will argue that the causes of the current crisis include (in increasing order of importance): deregulation; monetarist policy; corruption; and the natural evolution to a fragile financial structure, as described in Minsky's 'Financial Instability Hypothesis' – the FIH. Of course, none of these should be considered as a separate cause, for the crisis is the result of the cumulative effects of interrelated causes.

Deregulation

Deregulation began in the 1960s for a number of reasons including the recognition that innovations were already subverting the reforms of the 1930s. For example, banks had been able to avoid the prohibition of interest on transactions deposits even in the 1950s by offering overnight repurchase agreements. This was supplemented by the invention of the negotiable certificate of deposit (CD) in 1961. After the Treasury Accord of 1951 (which freed the Fed from the obligation to keep interest rates on government debt low), the Fed began to use monetary policy to fight inflation. During the early 1960s, this would cause market interest rates to rise above ceiling rates on CDs, leading to 'disintermediation'. Between 1963 and 1966, the Fed was forced to raise the ceiling rates four times. In 1970, the Fed removed the ceiling on three-month jumbo CDs ($100 000 or more). And in 1973, all ceilings on jumbo CDs were removed (Dymski, 1991). After the creation of the money market mutual fund (in 1972 by Merrill Lynch), relatively small balances could earn rates near market rates. The Fed was forced to raise deposit rate ceilings in 1973, 1974, and 1977 and banks and thrifts were permitted to issue new kinds of deposits to compete with the money markets (Dymski, 1991). Thus, the deregulation that validated private innovation was forced by use of monetarist policy. As will be discussed below, this anti-inflation policy was dictated to some extent by fiscal policy and international considerations.

The reforms of the 1930s were further dismantled in 1974, when the FHLBB allowed thrifts to abandon the mutual form, incorporate, and issue stock. At first, each thrift had to have at least 40 owners, but restrictions were gradually relaxed until an individual could be the sole owner of a thrift (Mayer, 1990). This opened the thrift industry to the same sort of practices that caused widespread bank failures in the 1920s – insider abuse, including use of financial institutions by developers to finance their own projects.[18] The mutual form of ownership of thrifts gives the proper incentives to owners and management: as the depositors own the thrift, failure of the thrift means losses for both owners and depositors. This is not necessarily the case when, say, a developer owns a thrift. Developers need a source of working capital during the construction phase of a project. Once the project is complete, the developer receives profits up front. (The developer can always ensure sale of the project at a profit, as the buyer is given a loan on favourable terms through the developer's – or an associate's – thrift. Sometimes, the buyer is encouraged to renege on the loan, leaving the thrift with the – often worthless – development project.) Because owner equity in a typical thrift is very small in relation to its assets, the potential profits to be made in the development projects can dwarf the losses to the developer as owner of a failed thrift. Furthermore, a dishonest developer-owner has a number of practices at his disposal that ensure that profits will far exceed potential losses incurred when the thrift fails.[19] As states reduced barriers to entry beginning in the 1960s, the value of thrift charters fell – further reducing the value of the thrift to the developer.[20] By 1987, 80 per cent of all Texas thrifts were owned by developers and, not coincidentally, Texas is blessed with perhaps the most unhealthy financial sector of any state.[21]

In addition, bankruptcy laws were changed in 1978. Many observers, including the American Bankers Association, contend that the bankruptcy code now excessively favours debtors, making it difficult and costly to foreclose and recover property from defaulters.[22] Not only does this increase the potential losses to financial institutions that must force a debtor into bankruptcy proceedings, but it also makes it difficult for the government (either an insurer, such as FDIC, or the RTC) to recover losses in a bank or thrift resolution.

Deregulation continued with the Monetary Control Act of 1980, which phased out interest rate ceilings, raised deposit insurance limits so that 'hot money' jumbo CDs (issued in $100 000 denominations) were covered, overrode usury laws, and allowed thrifts to buy riskier assets. The Garn–St Germain[23] Act of 1982 further deregulated thrifts, allowing them to make 'direct investments' (purchase real estate for their own portfolios – inherently more risky than making real estate loans to others because only the value of the real estate backs up the loan). Just as thrifts were being deregulated so that riskiness was rising, capital requirements were reduced from 5 per cent to 3 per cent of assets; accounting procedures were changed from GAAP (generally accepted accounting principles) to RAP (regulatory accounting principles) – which had the effect of 'increasing' net worth by nearly one-fifth; and the Reagan administration cut the supervisory budget.[24]

The lower accounting standards allowed regulators to count 'goodwill' and 'net worth certificates' as equity. As Mayer explains, supervisory goodwill was created when one paid more for a thrift than it was worth on paper. The 'logic' behind this was that the purchased thrift must actually be worth more, as only the insane would pay in excess of nominal value. Thus, the excess worth was counted as equity. This meant that two demonstrably insolvent thrifts could merge and create enough 'goodwill' to become solvent. Thrifts could also count 'appraised equity capital' which was created when property owned by the thrift was reappraised at a higher value. This led to 'daisy chains'[25] in which thrifts would sell a piece of property back-and-forth at an escalating price, creating equity.[26] Finally, thrifts were essentially allowed to write their own equity through net worth certificates.[27] Thrifts could also use 'loss deferral' to create 'profits': they were encouraged to sell loans at a loss, take the loss for tax purposes and write down any profits from previous years, claim credit for overpayment of taxes, and continue to count the (sold) loan as an asset whose losses were slowly amortized for regulatory accounting purposes. If all of this sounds unbelievable, see Mayer (1990).

Many changes were made that allowed, even encouraged, speculation in real estate.[28] In 1978, pension funds and other institutional investors were allowed to increase the share of their portfolios in real estate. The Economic Recovery Tax Act of 1981 reduced the depreciation period for commercial and industrial real estate by more than half, making real estate development more profitable. When Garn–St Germain allowed thrifts and commercial banks to make more real estate loans, to take equity positions in the projects, and to make loans without margin limits (indeed, developers could borrow *more* than 100 per cent of the projected costs of a project), a real estate boom was created. Even as vacancies in non-residential real estate grew, fully two-thirds of the growth of bank lending in 1984 was for real estate. During the boom, builders built more than a third of all the commercial space that had been built since the founding of the nation. The tax reforms of 1986 lengthened the depreciation period for real estate, leading to a real estate slump that slowly moved around the country. By the end of 1991, bad real estate deals accounted for more than half of all nonperforming loans. In a study of the largest bank failure in Texas (First Republic Bank), it was found that of the 77 bad real estate loans that caused the failure, 75 would have been illegal before Garn–St Germain.

After Garn–St Germain, thrifts were allowed to offer interest-bearing NOW (negotiated orders of withdrawal – essentially interest-bearing cheque) accounts, to make commercial real estate loans (up to 40 per cent of their assets), to make consumer loans (up to 30 per cent of assets), to buy commercial paper and corporate bonds – including 'junk' – (up to 100 per cent of assets), and to make commercial and agricultural loans (up to 10 per cent of assets). Thrift holdings of such 'non-traditional' assets increased to nearly one-quarter of their assets by 1984. Not only did the composition of assets change, but the aggregate quantity of assets held by thrifts also grew rapidly. Between 1979 and 1983, the inflation-adjusted aggregate quantity of assets held by thrifts actually declined by five percentage points. But by 1988, the inflation-adjusted aggregate quantity of assets held by the thrift industry was 54 per cent higher than it had been in 1979 (Benston and Carhill 1992).

States also deregulated: the California Nolan[29] Act of 1983 has been called the most liberal banking law ever passed anywhere. Indeed, the California legislation eliminated all asset restrictions – thrift purchases were only limited by supervision by state regulators. Texas also deregulated – indeed, it is said that in order to buy a bank in Texas, one need only prove that one is not currently in jail (Mayer, 1990, ch. 9). In addition, pro-business regulators were appointed at both the federal and state level. Larry Taggart, head of the California Saving and Loan Commission spent only half of his supervisory budget – even though supervision provided the only constraint over the types of assets thrifts could purchase.[30]

'Regulators' deregulated by fiat – and this continues: Alan Greenspan, chairman of the Fed, has recently allowed several banks, including his former employer, J.P. Morgan's bank, to underwrite stock and bond issues in violation of the Glass–Steagall Act that separated commercial and investment banking (Pizzo, 1991). The Reagan administration appointed three successive heads of the FHLBB, Richard Pratt, Edward Gray, and Danny Wall. Two of these (Pratt and Wall – both of whom had worked for Senator Garn) were unapologetically 'pro-business' and prevented supervisors from doing their jobs. Gray (former employee of then-Governor Reagan, and of Taggart) was chosen because he was considered a patsy for big business, although he turned out to be a better regulator than anyone expected (for which he earned the eternal wrath of Donald Regan – Secretary of the Treasury in Reagan's first term, and then White House Chief of Staff).[31] Reagan also appointed

William Seidman to head the FDIC. Seidman announced to his staff: 'Bankers are our friends; the FDIC should be a friend of the industry', like a 'trade association' for the industry[32] (Mayer, 1990, p. 245).

In summary, deregulation legalized risky behaviour. It reduced market segmentation, thus increased maturity mismatching and enabled financial institutions to fuel speculative booms. And it gave improper incentives to developer-owners and others ('moral hazard' encouraged banks and thrifts to 'play with house money' – insured deposits). However, the crisis of the financial system would almost certainly have occurred even without deregulation because financial institutions were actively subverting the reforms of the 1930s – even before deregulation occurred – to exploit profit opportunities through innovations. Indeed, deregulation, by itself, cannot explain why financial institutions would have purposely engaged in risky behaviour merely because it became lawful – presumably most banks and thrifts would not want to dissipate their net worth nor the value of their charters through excessively risky behaviour. As I will argue, monetarist policy increased the incentive to 'grow fast' in order to restore profitability and net worth, and wide-scale corruption played an important part in increasing the scope of the crisis. But corruption itself is a corollary of Minsky's FIH, which is the most important element in an explanation of the innovative behaviour that led to corruption and crisis.

Monetarist Policy

Beginning in the late 1960s, and gaining dominance by the late 1970s, the monetarist religion spread inexorably throughout the economics profession, and converted policy makers. The Fed periodically implemented tight money policy as a remedy for inflation, and after 1966, in each case, tight money policy induced a financial crisis (Minsky, 1986; Wolfson, 1986; Wray 1993a). By 1979, Monetarist fundamentalism had become so widespread that President Carter appointed Paul Volcker to head the Fed. Volcker announced that he would bring the economy to its knees through tight money policy in order to eliminate inflation.[33] When the resulting recession actually led to higher inflation, Volcker tightened the screws until the worst recession since the Great Depression (that is, until the recession of the early 1990s) hit the US economy and spread throughout the capitalist world.

Kregel (1993) argues that the adoption of monetarist policies throughout the developed world since the 1960s can be attributed to two factors: first, to the reluctance to use fiscal policy to fight inflationary tendencies; but secondly, and more importantly to the failure of the international monetary system adopted at Bretton Woods. Kregel attributes this failure to the asymmetrical adjustment mechanism adopted at Bretton Woods, in which surplus countries are not expected to bear any of the costs of imbalanced trade – a result fully anticipated by Keynes in arguments for his bancor system. If only trade deficit nations are forced to adjust by adopting austerity and/or devaluing currencies, this exerts a depressionary influence on the world economy. Deficit countries are reluctant to use currency depreciation, for this will generate domestic inflation and are thus forced to choose between tight fiscal or monetary policy. Again, tight fiscal policy has generally been less feasible and most of the burden of adjustment has been placed on monetary policy. This prevents depreciation of the currency (in the case of the USA, rapid appreciation followed Volcker's announcement) and makes it difficult to move toward balanced trade. Only those countries that can successfully move toward export-led growth can avoid this dilemma. But export-led growth can work only if a portion of the globe runs commensurately large trade deficits. In the presence of austere monetary policy, large US government deficits have been necessary to act as the 'engine of growth' for the world economy as the USA moved toward large trade deficits in the early 1980s (Wray, 1993b).

In the USA, tight money policy drove interest rates to record heights, reversing the normal interest rate spread (loan rate less deposit rate) from which banks and thrifts receive profits. Thrifts were more seriously affected because their assets (such as home mortgage loans) were much longer term than their liabilities became in a regime of high market interest rates.[34] (Again, this mismatch of maturities can be partially attributed to deregulation and to extension of deposit insurance to hot money – which increased thrift reliance on volatile short-term jumbo CDs.) In 1979 (before Volcker), only 7 per cent of thrifts lost money.[35] In 1982, 85 per cent of thrifts were unprofitable, two-thirds of thrifts were insolvent, and the (market) net worth of the thrift industry was perhaps a negative $100 billion. In other words, the thrifts on average were massively insolvent (Kane, 1990). At this point, supervisors could have closed the insolvent thrifts but the FSLIC could not have endured losses of this magnitude. Thus, supervisors encouraged thrifts to try to 'grow to profitability'. If the average return on assets could be increased through rapid growth, then the interest rate spread could again become positive.[36] Paradoxically, the high interest rate caused by monetarist policy generated rapid growth of the money supply as banks and thrifts tried to restore profitability – although the tight money policy was purportedly adopted to slow the rate of growth of money in order to stop inflation (Wray, 1993a).

Rapid growth was facilitated by two factors: insured hot money; and relaxation of capital requirements. Any thrift could issue an essentially unlimited quantity of insured liabilities in the form of jumbo CDs through brokers such as Merrill Lynch (the former employer of deregulator Donald Regan, and by far the biggest supplier of hot money) (Adams, 1990, ch. 11). Purchasers of these jumbo CDs did not need to worry about the credit-worthiness of the insuer since insurance (and ultimately government guarantees) stood behind them. Because supervisors relaxed capital standards, thrifts could purchase assets almost without limit by issuing jumbo CDs. By 1981, a thrift with only $2 million in equity could issue $1.3 billion in 'hot money' through brokers in order to buy assets (Mayer, 1990, p. 66). This led to spectacular rates of growth for many thrifts: there were some 40 thrifts that attained a rate of growth of 1000 per cent or better in a single year (Sherrill, 1990, p. 599); the thrift industry deposits as a whole grew by more than 20 per cent in 1984; while the Texas thrift industry grew even faster – by nearly 38 per cent (Horvitz, 1990).

If the purchased assets had proven worthy, rapid growth might have worked. Unfortunately, the second wave of insolvency occurred when many of the assets proved worthless. As discussed above, half of all thrifts have already failed and the number of bank failures rose above 200 per year. At the end of 1991, half of remaining thrifts were said to be in trouble, along with perhaps 1500 banks. While it is true that the situation of banks improved during 1992 and 1993 as interest rates fell and the cost of bank funds plunged, there is still reason to believe that the worst is yet to come. At the end of 1992, banks had $90 billion in nonperforming real estate loans – three-fourths of these held by the 57 largest bank holding companies – and $439 billion in performing nonresidential real estate loans whose book values overstated market values by over $100 billion (Vaughn and Hill, 1992, p. 37). These problems will not be solved by low interest rates, rather they will require recovery of regional real estate markets.

In addition, the boost to profits created by easier monetary policy during 1993 is only temporary: as loans and mortgages are refinanced, the interest rate spread falls, lowering profitability. For more than a year, there was a rush to refinance home mortgages at rates as low as 6 per cent (in the USA, most home mortgages are still made at fixed rates.) Thus, banks and thrifts have been able to nearly duplicate the initial conditions of the thrifts in the late 1970s, when profitability required that rates on their liabilities remain low! In some ways, the position might appear even more delicate, first because the problem is not limited to thrifts (indeed, banks now hold more one – four-family mortgages[37] than do thrifts), and second, because there are no longer any constraints on rates paid on liabilities (indeed, the public is much more willing to seek higher market returns even if this means abandoning insured deposits).

Finally, should the current stagnation[38] end, the Fed will be tempted to push interest rates up sharply, causing the same sorts of problems we experienced in the early 1980s. Indeed, Greenspan has been quite open about his disappointment that inflation has not been completely eliminated and has been warning markets that he is preparing to raise short-term rates. While it is beyond the scope of this article, Greenspan has argued that the only way to bring long-term rates down is to push short-term rates sufficiently high to wring the last expectations of inflation out of the economy.[39] Thus, he started to push the discount rate up in February 1994. This led to an immediate rise of long term rates. Presumably, reports of falling profitability of banks and thrifts will be forthcoming soon.

Corruption

I must emphasize that there is nothing unusual about the recent corruption in the banking and thrift sectors – similar problems are encountered presently throughout all sectors of the economy, and were found in the banks during the 1920s. As Robert Sherrill of the Nation writes, 'thievery is what unregulated capitalism is all about.'[40] There is no doubt, however, that corruption played a major role in creating the current crisis, and that corruption played a role in virtually every bank or thrift failure. It must also be emphasized that although unregulated capitalism breeds thievery, corruption on the scale currently in evidence in the USA throughout the corporate and government sectors cannot be explained without reference to Minsky's FIH. This will be the topic of the next section.

Newspaper reporter Pete Brewton claims that the CIA and the mob are linked in at least 22 thrift failures: individuals involved in these thrifts were involved in gun running, drug smuggling, money laundering, and covert aid to the Contras (Sherrill, 1990, p. 615). The authors of *Inside Job* say that in nearly every thrift investigated, clear evidence of mob, Teamster, or organized crime involvement was found (Pizzo, Fricker and Muolo 1991, p. 20). Furthermore, they never once examined a thrift failure without encountering individuals they had come across in another failure. That is, there seems to be a network of failed thrifts and in many cases the mob went after easy thrift targets. The FBI believes that a crook named Herman Beebe was involved in at least a hundred thrift failures. William Sessions, director of the FBI, says fraud is pervasive, while Seidman claims it was involved in at least 60 per cent of failed thrifts.[41] The OCC argues that only 7 per cent of bank failures were due solely to the state of the economy – the rest had greed, fraud, or bad management as contributing factors. The US General Accounting Office (GAO) reviewed the worst thrift failures of 1985–7 and found fraud in every single case. In fact, it seems that everyone from Jimmy Carter to George Bush, and from Ollie North to Mother Teresa was involved in the corruption.[42]

As Litan (1990) argues, one must distinguish between the existence of fraud (or bad management) and the importance of fraud (or bad management) in *causing* failure. According to Day (1993), regulators estimate that fraud played *some* role in 75 per cent of thrift failures, but they certainly disagree over the extent of its importance. Litan argues that we do not know and probably will never know the extent of the damages caused by fraud, even though it appears that fraud was 'involved in many, if not most, of the thrift failures so far investigated'. (Litan, 1990, p. 29) Ultimately, according to Litan, it does not matter, because the important question is: 'Why would so much fraud occur in one particular industry during one short period of time?' (ibid., p. 29). He goes on, incorrectly in my view, to attribute the explosion of fraud to government policy that invited these activities. This simplistic explanation gets the timing wrong (much of the fraud was already widespread in the 1970s – before the policy changes he cites), it ignores the dialectical relation between business and government, and it fails to recognize the endogenous processes that cause a robust financial system to move toward fragility. We will first examine a few examples of the role played by corruption, and then will move on to the application of Minsky's FIH to the analysis of the crisis.

Charles Keating got his start as Richard Nixon's appointee to the President's Commission on Pornography, and, as we shall see, Keating has very high moral standards indeed. He was convicted of securities fraud, but that did not prevent Gray (head of the FHLBB) from approving his purchase of Lincoln Savings (a deal financed by the sale of junk bonds handled, of course, by Michael Milken).[43] He had previously handled John Connally's campaign for the presidency, and had been appointed by Reagan as ambassador to the Bahamas (a natural choice, but the deal fell through when Congress got wind of his prior felony). One of Keating's first deals as a thrift owner was to loan $70 million to Connally, who defaulted on the loan. He also loaned $134 million to his friend and lawyer, Lee Henkel, then got Donald Regan to lobby Reagan to appoint Henkel to the FHLBB (which supervised Keating's thrift). Henkel promptly wrote a new rule which his staff determined could benefit only one thrift in the country – guess which one. Henkel was forced to resign.

When supervisors in the San Francisco office of the FHLBB began finding irregularities at Lincoln, Keating tried to buy-off Gray with a job offer at $400 000 a year. The story of the publication of this allegation makes for interesting reading. Michael Binstein broke the story of Keating's job offer for a column he wrote with Jack Anderson (a well-known 'muck-raker'). Anderson first required that his lawyer, David Branson, look the story over to determine whether it might lead to a lawsuit. In spite of Branson's objections, Anderson published the story, although fear of lawsuits prevented him from publishing any more stories on corruption in the thrift industry. Later, Anderson found that Branson worked for a law firm that represented Keating even as he was giving advice about the story on Keating. When an Arizona newspaper republished the allegations, Keating sued – represented by Branson. Although the suit was later dropped, the newspaper spent $150 000 in its defense. Fear of such suits helped the crooks to keep similar revelations out of newspapers (Kurtz, 1992).

Keating donated $1.4 million to five senators (the 'Keating 5': Cranston, DeConcini, Glenn, McCain, and Riegle),[44] who continually hounded Gray on Keating's behalf. Gray was eventually replaced by Danny Wall (in 1987), who was more compliant. Wall transferred supervision of Lincoln from the FHLBB's San Francisco office (which was already recommending that Lincoln be closed) to the Washington DC office, and lifted rules on direct investment so that high flyers like Keating could grow quickly through questionable real estate deals. Seidman believes Wall delayed closing Lincoln in order to assuage Keating's feelings that had been damaged by Gray – Bush would need the campaign contributions that Keating might be persuaded to provide. During the twelve-month review undertaken by the Washington DC office, Lincoln speculated in real estate and lost badly, greatly increasing the eventual costs to the government.

Keating was able to purchase lots of friends. He paid Greenspan (current head of the Fed) a mere $40 000 to testify before Congress on his behalf.[45] Greenspan argued that Keating's thrift was performing as well as 17 other high flyers: within three years, 16 of the 17 were bankrupt. Economist George Benston claimed that Lincoln was doing as well as 34 other rapidly growing thrifts: by 1989, 32 of these were insolvent, many with evidence of corruption (Mayer, 1990, p. 140). Keating also hired President Ford to speak on his behalf. He hired Taggart (head of the California S&L Commission) and put him on the payroll even before Taggart left state employment. And he gave Mother Teresa $1.4 million, for which he received a crucifix and her undying devotion.[46] Even after his conviction (for milking the elderly), she wrote to his judge that Keating 'has always been kind and good to God's poor and always ready to help whenever there was a need . . . Mr. Keating has done much to help the poor' (Lynch, 1992, p. 1C). The Vatican also begged the judge for leniency in Keating's case, because Keating had always shown concern for the underprivileged. Keating's view of 'God's people' is evidenced in a memo written to his staff: 'always remember, the weak, meek, and ignorant are always good targets'.[47]

Keating was certainly not the only convicted felon who was allowed to buy a bank. James Fail, previously convicted of securities fraud, was allowed to buy a package of 15 failed thrifts for an investment of $1000 of his own money. In return, he receives a cheque from the government for $23 million every *month* to compensate for any risk he might face (Sherrill, 1990). The government, however, had already removed all bad assets from the books of these thrifts, so the risks are not great. Indeed, Fail merged the thrifts into Blue Bonnet, which became the most profitable thrift in the country – it was also one of the few thrifts in the country that had no bad assets. The deal was arranged by Vice President Bush's aide, Robert

Thompson, who was indebted to Fail in the amount of half a million dollars, and the deal was approved by Wall. When Wall was asked why he would give such a good deal to a convicted felon, he responded that Seidman (head of the FDIC) had already let Fail buy a commercial bank. Notably, William 'bankers are our friends' Seidman was in charge of the bail-out of the thrift industry until his recent retirement.

Wall made a series of similar, secret, deals in his infamous 'Southwest Plan' which resolved 87 thrifts in 1988. Under this plan, moderate and small thrifts would be merged into large ones, with FSLIC taking the bad assets and guaranteeing the rest. Purchasers of the thrifts were also given tax write-offs and paid subsidies by FSLIC. Under tax laws that would expire at the end of 1988, the purchasers would not be taxed on profit income that was guaranteed by FSLIC, while they could deduct from their income any losses that would be made up through subsidies made by FSLIC. Thus, they got both a tax write-off and payment for the losses (Mayer, 1990). Seidman argues that Wall's self-imposed deadline (all deals had to be completed by the end of 1988) led to a buyer's market. The original estimate of the cost of the Southwest Plan was $10–12 billion. By 1990, it was estimated at $40 billion of direct costs plus $8 billion in tax write-offs. Later estimates of the cost ran as high as $67 billion (Mayer, 1990; Waldman, 1990). The House Banking Committee estimated that buyers got $78 in assets for every $1 invested (Waldman, 1990). It was later disclosed that the investors had contributed at least $2.8 million to presidential and congressional candidates while Wall was negotiating the deals (Day, 1993).

Two of the largest winners were Ronald Perelman and Robert Bass. Each made illegal donations of $100 000 to the Bush campaign, and each is the recipient of millions of dollars of subsidies at taxpayer expense. Bass put up $350 million to purchase thrifts, and received $2 billion in subsidies; Perelman put up $315 million to obtain $7 billion in good assets, $5 billion in cash to cover possible losses, and $900 million in tax write-offs.[48] As Representative Walter Fauntroy asked Wall, 'I have just one question for you, Mr. Wall, why is it only white folks who get that kind of deal?' (Mayer, 1990, p. 259; Sherrill, 1990). A better question would be: why are we paying such subsidies at all?

Some of the crooks have been prosecuted and fined or jailed. Some misappropriated funds have been recovered. For example, Ernst & Young, auditor of more than 300 failed thrifts (including many of those run by the most notorious crooks, such as Keating and Don Dixon – it was also the auditor of Neil Bush's Silverado) recently agreed to pay $400 million.[49] However, most of the crooks will not be prosecuted, and only a very small portion of losses will be recovered. This result is guaranteed by the very legislation that created the thrift bail-out: when Congress established the RTC in 1989, it provided for a three year statute of limitations for investigation of negligent behaviour that might have led to failure of a thrift.[50] This means that the RTC is prohibited from investigating virtually any of the crooks that caused failures, since the statute of limitations has run out for most of the crooked deals.[51] Part of the reason that cases have moved so slowly is that Gray had decided to emphasize recovery over prosecution. However, even where fines and restitution have been ordered, collections have been insignificant: according to the GAO, by early 1992 only $365 000 had been paid on $84 million in fines and restitution ordered in 55 S&L cases.

According to testimony presented to the Senate Banking Committee by Jacqueline P. Taylor, head of the Denver division of the Professional Liability Section (PLS) of the RTC, officials of the RTC continually interfered with investigations of corruption.[52] Gerald Jacobs, the RTC's general counsel, gave the impression to PLS staff that they should be less aggressive in their pursuit of lawsuits. (It was later alleged that Jacobs had used his office to obstruct a lawsuit against a thrift under RTC control. Jacobs had been the lawyer for a development company that defaulted on a $40 million dollar loan, contributing to the failure of the thrift. Jacobs had also defaulted on a loan from the same thrift (McGrath, 1993)) Taylor also implicated President Bush in the interference, who met with an outside director of a thrift the PLS planned to sue – after the meeting, the case was dropped. Bruce Pederson, who oversaw the PLS western field offices, claims that the interventions were designed to slow the investigations of prominent supporters of Bush as he faced a difficult reelection (McGrath, 1993). Eventually, the RTC legal department was 'reorganized' in May 1992 in such a way as to strip the PLS of its independence. Experienced PLS lawyers quit or were fired (about half lost their positions) and replaced with inexperienced attorneys. This reduced the likelihood that strong cases could be reformulated before the statute of limitations runs out.

Minsky's Financial Instability Hypothesis

To paraphrase J.M. Keynes, thieves may do no harm as bubbles on a steady stream of enterprise; but the position becomes serious when enterprise becomes the bubble on a whirlpool of thievery. As the FIH predicts, enterprise is naturally replaced by speculation and corruption as the Michael Milkens temporarily emerge as heroes before 'becoming' crooks. That is to say, the innovative, speculative behaviour for which our heroes receive accolades today, is exactly the behaviour for which they will be prosecuted tomorrow as it becomes apparent that this behaviour has generated crisis if it becomes the norm.[53]

According to Minsky, a successful financial system gradually evolves a more fragile financial structure as success breeds risk taking (Minsky, 1986). As discussed above, President Roosevelt called a banking 'holiday' in 1933. At the RFC, Jones was in charge of approving bank reopenings, and he personally approved the management chosen to take charge of many of the rescued banks. He purposely favoured conservative management that was not likely to take risks. Conservative management plus memories of the Great Depression ensured that banking would be a conservative business even in the absence of the reforms of the 1930s. However, such memories gradually faded, and conservative management was replaced with a younger breed: business school-trained MBAs. As long as the economy grew rapidly and avoided any prolonged recessions, risk-taking was rewarded with greater profits. Nothing succeeds like success in encouraging greater risk taking. Banks and their customers continuallly expanded the range of activities and the leverage ratios deemed worthy of credit.

Minsky characterizes the early post-war period as Managerial Capitalism, in which big government and counter-cyclical deficits placed a floor on aggregate demand and, thus, on profits (as is shown in Kalecki's well-known equation).[54] Furthermore, the combination of Fed willingness to intervene as a lender of last resort, plus government guarantees of various asset prices (through various kinds of deposit insurance and government agency guarantees – such as FHA-guaranteed home mortgages) helped to set a floor to asset prices and eliminated the possibility of a Fisher-type debt deflation such as that experienced during the Great Depression. Furthermore, various other institutional arrangements helped to ensure high aggregate demand: the Marshall Plan (which created a demand for US exports); the social security program (which increased the income of the elderly and other groups); the development of the welfare system; promotion of the growth of labour unions; and rapid growth of state and local government spending (partially financed through grants from the federal government). Minsky believes that during this period there was something like a 'social contract' in which capitalists accepted rising living standards of workers on the understanding that this would increase markets. At the same time, government policy would ensure the rising aggregate demand that would be necessary to validate expensive, long-lived capital projects undertaken by firms, as well as the expensive, long term commitments made to workers (pensions and health care plans). 'It' (a debt deflation and depression) would not be allowed to happen again.

However, stability is destabilizing. Private firms emerged from the war with very liquid balance sheets (which led some to fear inflation – remember the Radcliffe Committee) that gradually would become less liquid as positions in assets were taken by issuing liabilities. In the case of banks, it is usually said that they financed the early post-war expansion by 'operating on assets' – that is, by reducing holdings of government bonds and excess reserves and replacing these with loans. After 1954, the Fed began to push interest rates higher (as a precursor to the monetarist experiments that would come later). Banks innovated to economize on reserves by developing first the use of repurchase agreements (to reduce average demand deposits held) and next the fed funds market (the overnight, interbank market in reserves). In 1957, Minsky predicted that 'financial changes will occur most frequently during periods of high or rising interest rates' (Minsky, 1957, p. 172) as banks innovated to get around Fed constraints. Soon, banks created the negotiable certificates of deposit, and expanded the Eurodollar market. Banks also formed BHCs so each could issue debt instruments through the BHC that would compete in money markets. The development of such 'wholesale' sources of funds allowed banks to shift from operating on assets to 'operating on liabilities', in which banks would finance positions in loans by issuing liabilities. Thus, the net effect of all these innovations was to reduce the liquidity of private balance sheets. As 'it' did not happen again, the innovations were validated and innovators were rewarded with profits. However, rising leverage ratios led to closer articulation of income flows from assets to payment commitments on liabilities.

Gradually, the economy moved from the Managerial stage to the stage Minsky calls Money Manager Capitalism. Because 'it' had not happened again and because the 'social contract' for workers had included pension plans and health plans, huge blocks of 'managed money' in search of short-term returns were available for leveraging prospective income flows. In an environment of fairly rapid economic growth, in which most projects were successful, owners or management that increased leverage ratios and reduced margins of safety were able to increase the market value of both financial institutions and their customers. Innovation bordering on revolution allowed the clever Michael Milkens to transform a greater portion of future earnings into current debt. Again, this increased fragility and made the economy increasingly vulnerable to crisis.

The first crises began in 1966, partially due to the Fed's attempt to fight inflation through tight money, and crises became increasingly severe and frequent afterward.[55] In every case, the government (usually the Fed) intervened to contain the crisis. As one example, over the late 1960s, banks continually lost market share as firms turned to commercial paper and other instruments to raise short-term working capital.[56] In 1970, the default by Penn Central on its commercial paper led to a crisis in the market; the Fed promised to support banks that would back-up commercial paper in order to stop the crisis. As a result, it became standard practice to issue commercial paper with a back-up line of bank credit.

Each time an innovation pushed things too far so that a crisis was generated, the Fed stepped in to validate the innovation. This encouraged even greater risk taking and generated an attitude that no risk is too great. Where did this lead us? To junk bonds, leveraged buy-outs, insider abuse, and outright criminal activity. This is a natural evolution even in the absence of government intervention. Success will generate risk taking and will lead to the development of a fragile financial structure. If financing costs rise, if the economy turns down, or if people panic, a crisis can degenerate to a full blown collapse of the financial system unless the government intervenes. In the days before government intervention, the 'hero' speculator would quickly become the despised 'goat' as a massive default would generate a 'mania', followed by a debt deflation. The deflation would eliminate the fragile financial system and create the base (or, new 'initial conditions') from which a robust financial system could evolve. Today, however, government intervention prevents the deflation – so the system becomes increasingly fragile, and a series of heroes-become-goats is paraded before us. Thus, government intervention is necessary to prevent debt deflations, but intervention rewards risk taking and allows an increasingly fragile financial structure to emerge.

The great experiment in monetarism, begun in 1979 by Chairman Volcker (and continued by Chairman Greenspan) used tight money policy to slow the economy in an attempt to fight inflation. This was combined with supply-side economics to cut taxes in an attempt to stimulate entrepreneurship, along with a military build-up to fight Communism. However, the net result of 'Reaganomics' was an immediate sharp contraction of the economy, with investment in capital assets plummeting and with massive losses by banks and thrifts (partially due to rapidly rising interest rates on liabilities but only slowly rising rates earned on assets).[57] On the other hand, the government deficit grew very rapidly due to the combination of tax cuts and increased spending (resulting from defence spending and from mandated increases of social spending – primarily for social security and health care).[58] At the same time, the US trade balance moved from surplus to deficit, at least in part due to appreciation of the dollar caused by high interest rates.[59] In summary, although fiscal policy was on balance stimulative, monetary policy reduced interest-sensitive spending and contributed to the creation of a trade deficit. Matters were made worse by similar reactions of other countries to inflation in the later 1970s and through the 1980s. Tight domestic monetary policy in these countries lowered world-wide aggregate demand and made it impossible for the USA to close its trade deficit.[60] Furthermore, countries that experienced trade deficits also adopted austerity, further lowering world-wide demand, as discussed above.

After 1983, the US economy began to recover. Unlike previous recoveries, however, unemployment remained high and investment in capital assets failed to recover.[61] As I have shown, between 1981 and 1988, growth of non-residential fixed investment accounted for only 6 per cent of quarterly growth of GNP. Indeed, I found that over this period, the Reagan government deficits were about 50 times more important in generating economic growth than was investment in capital assets (Wray, 1989). The Reagan recovery, therefore, was neither supply-side, nor monetarist: rather, it was a stereotypical (if somewhat perverse) 'Keynesian' deficit-led recovery. The US marginal propensity to import foreign goods is greater than the foreign marginal propensity to import US goods (for most other developed countries). Thus when it grew faster than most (with the notable exception of Japan), its trade deficit rose so that the USA acted as the engine of growth (Blecker, 1992).

In addition to the role played by government deficits in generating the Reagan recovery, there were also booms at various points during the 1980s in commercial real estate, the energy sector, the stock market, junk bonds, and leveraged buy-outs. These, in turn, were a function of changes in tax laws, deregulation of the financial sector, and innovations in financial practices. Each of these increased debt burdens relative to income and wealth. For example, the average household's ratio of total borrowings to yearly income rose from 78 per cent to 94 per cent during the 1980s (Alpert, 1991). Corporate borrowing reached record levels during the 1980s, even though by the end of 1987, they 'owned no more tangible assets or financial instruments than they did at year-end 1980' (Friedman, 1988, p. 100). This was primarily due to debt-for-equity swaps, which ensured that by 1987, the market-value of non-financial corporate debt equalled 75 per cent of the value of equity – close to the 78 per cent reached during the depths of the recession in 1982 (Friedman, 1988, p. 101). Even in the face of falling interest rates through 1987, increasing leverage ratios caused corporate debt service to rise rapidly: by 1986, 56 per cent of gross corporate profits went to interest payments, versus an average of only 16 per cent in the 1950s and 1960s (ibid., p. 100). As a result, even during the long Reagan expansion, both the number of bankruptcies and the volume of debt declared in default rose continuously to record levels through 1987 (ibid., p. 101). Of course, similar arguments apply to the growth of federal government debt and to the effect of tight money policy on the costs of servicing that debt: at the peak, 17 per cent of federal government spending went to debt service, an amount that was approximately equal to the total federal deficit.[62]

As Minsky argues, initial conditions matter. The Reagan expansion was not like the early post-war expansion because the initial conditions were much different. In particular, firms emerged from the Reagan recession with less liquidity and greater debt burdens. Furthermore, rather than having memories of the Great Depression to guide behaviour, behaviour was guided by memories of three decades of expansion during which each innovation was accepted and supported by government action. Finally, rather than experiencing an expansion driven by rising consumer demand, the Reagan expansion was driven by speculation and by a government military build-up, in the face of rising trade deficits and loss of US manufacturing. This is the setting in which financial institutions tried to 'grow their way to profitability'. The initial conditions did not include a robust financial system, conservative behaviour, or rising standards of living for most Americans.

Although it is beyond the scope of this paper, for reasons that defy logical analysis, the Fed decided in the late 1980s that the expansion had proceeded for too long and began to tighten monetary policy in an attempt to achieve a 'soft landing'. Rising interest rates raised the portion of cash flows that had to be committed to debt service (by households, firms, and the federal government). The corporate 'restructuring' undertaken in the euphoria of the mid-1980s could be successful only if cash flows did not decline and debt service did not rise; Greenspan's tight money policy that began in 1988 brought on a recession and resulted in both unfavourable events. In 1990, the assets of corporations filing for bankruptcy reached nearly $83 billion, or 50 times more than they had a decade earlier. Much of this was accounted for by a small number of huge corporations that had engaged in leveraged buy-outs during the 1980s – 'by themselves, the ten biggest companies that failed in 1990 accounted for more than 80% of the year's bankrupt assets' (Sherman, 1991, p. 123). Ironically, the bankrupt included Drexel Burnham Lambert, which had 'enticed U.S. corporations into issuing $200 billion of junk bonds' (ibid., p. 124).

As the US economy slowed in the late 1980s, leveraged firms were forced to retrench, first by cutting 'unnecessary' expenses like research and development, next by 'downsizing'. This, of course, only made matters worse by lowering aggregate demand and capitalist cash flows. It also *increased* the dominance of the short view and casino over the long view and economic development as the management must operate to maintain the value of debt by keeping the managed money happy: no firm can allow a run out of its liabilities to develop. In summary, firms are faced with excessive debt service, with excess capacity,[63] and with world-wide stagnant demand even as Greenspan worries about inflation. Although the government deficit remains high (which, with lender of last resort activity prevents an asset-price deflation) much of the stimulative effect of the government deficit leaks out of the economy in the form of a trade deficit. Rather than being poised for a new period of managerial capitalism, our current conditions are more likely to generate market incoherence should Greenspan make good on his threats.

Minsky (1992) argues that a market can become incoherent, generating signals that lead agents to behave in ways that increase the market's incoherency – and this is particularly true in the case of financial markets. For this reason there is no free market solution to incoherence in the financial sphere. Rather, as financial markets become incoherent, there must be some institution that does not react to produced signals in a 'rational' – that is, profit-seeking – manner. For example, if asset prices begin to fall, the rational agent will sell-out position to minimize losses. This rational reaction to market signals will only increase incoherence of the market – and a debt deflation is the likely outcome. Lender of last resort action – which cannot be based on narrow self-interest – by the central bank stops market prices from serving as the signals on which private agents will act. Thus, central bank actions can introduce coherence to the market. However, this intervention will change future behaviour as agents, quite rationally, take prospective central bank behaviour into account when plans are formalized.

In consequence, according to Minsky (1992), bankruptcy is as necessary as is property law to a capitalist society. A well-functioning capitalist economy must 'institutionalize' scepticism, that is, the belief that things can go wrong. When excessive optimism dominates, or, when a 'radical suspension of disbelief' occurs, crisis inevitably follows. Agents operate in an uncertain world in which the future cannot be known. Positions in assets must be taken, frequently on the basis of issuing liabilities. Naturally this is most true of financial institutions, but it is also true of non-financial firms and of households. All those who issue liabilities to buy assets must rely on subjectively established rules of thumb regarding acceptable liability structures – and because these are subjectively established, they are subject to rapid revision. If past decisions regarding acceptable liability structures are easily validated by profitable performance, this can cause revisions to rules of thumb such that riskier positions are taken. If they are not validated, revisions are made (in the opposite direction) as scepticism is reinforced. When an economy performs well, more agents find their positions are validated than those who do not. Leverage ratios are increased and scepticism disappears. Agents rely on more debt financing. Indebtedness increases faster than do profit flows. More of income becomes committed to making interest payments and less to dividends and the positions of agents become more vulnerable to disappointment. In the absence of lender of last resort intervention, disappointment and bankruptcy could lead to an asset price deflation, which would restore scepticism. Lender of last resort intervention plus other constraints on bankruptcy (laws that favour debtors and government deficits that explode to prevent profit flows from declining precipitously) can make it more difficult to restore healthy scepticism.

Even as we have successfully avoided a run-away debt deflation, however, scepticism has returned to the USA. Indeed, many fear that bankers have an unhealthy level of scepticism and blame the current stagnation on a 'credit crunch'. 'Disbelief' seems to have returned for several reasons. First, sluggishness in the US economy does not seem to be due solely to a normal business cycle slump. Rather, the slump has been variously, and aptly, called a 'contained depression' (the term used by Jay and David Levy) or 'silent depression' (the term favoured by Wallace Peterson). In summary, this is due to excessive debt burdens accumulated during the period of the 'radical suspension of disbelief' of the 1980s. It may also be due to: loss of US competitiveness in world markets, and to restrictive economic policies adopted in other countries; bank 'retrenchment' – there may be some truth to the claim that banks have retrenched as they try to work off bad real estate and third world loans, and as they try to restore capital–asset ratios; sluggish commercial real estate markets that might be attributed to over-building during the 1980s and that may require several decades to eliminate vacancies; and policies and other forces that redistributed income away from the lower income classes and may have reduced aggregate demand.

Thus, as we attempt to resolve the financial crisis and reform the financial system, this must be done with a recognition of the current state of the economy. In the USA we have a fragile financial system, massive excess capacity (in manufacturing as well as in the financial sector), scepticism regarding the future of US manufacturing, uncertainty over the level of aggregate demand that can be provided by the federal government, down-sizing by firms, chronic trade deficits, and threats by the Fed to fight non-existent inflation. Any significant rise of interest rates is sure to cause further bank and thrift failures. Declining aggregate demand will cause heavily indebted firms to default, lowering bank and thrift asset values. If regional real estate markets do not recover, further defaults and bank and thrift failures will occur. Finally, even in this environment, financial innovation continues at warp speed, the stock market continues to perform well, and wealth owners continue to increase the share of their portfolios in uninsured liabilities.

3.5 SOLUTIONS TO THE CRISIS

The current policy is to use a taxpayer-financed bail-out to greatly reduce the number of financial institutions and subsidize concentration throughout the financial sector, to engage in 'fire sales' of failed thrift assets, to extend deregulation to new areas, and to give lip service to the allocative efficiency of free markets. Every aspect of the policy is misguided, and each is likely to exacerbate the crisis. Use of tax revenue will crowd out social spending. Increased concentration only raises the costs associated with an institutional failure, and reduces the quality and quantity of services provided to smaller customers. Fire sales depress asset prices and generate further defaults. Further deregulation speeds the natural evolution to a fragile financial structure. And 'free markets' do not 'efficiently allocate' credit. Indeed, there are no natural market forces that guarantee that credit is provided to finance activities with any social value.[64] Neither is there any guarantee that free markets will send the sorts of signals that generate coherence.

The RTC, created to deal with insolvent thrifts, has become the largest owner of real estate and junk bonds in the USA, (Day 1993, p. 377) and probably in the world (Greider, 1989). It is the second largest financial institution in the world (only the Japanese postal savings system is larger). It has nationalized one-third of the nation's thrifts. And it has owned everything from a buffalo sperm bank to a kitty-litter mine, from a town in Florida and 40 per cent of the land in Colorado Springs to 70 per cent of thrift assets in Arizona and even part of the Dallas Cowboys (football team) (Sherrill, 1990; Waldman, 1990). It relies on outside contractors to dispose of assets – at first it tried to bar anyone who had contributed to the collapse of a thrift, but this disqualified nearly all the major accounting firms, appraisers, lawyers, and so on, so the rule was dropped (Waldman, 1990). Thus, the RTC contracts with those who caused the failures in order to liquidate thrifts and their assets. Salomon Brothers, which is said to have made 50–90 per cent of its profits in the mortgage business merely by taking the other side of thrift trades (Mayer, 1990) now boasts that 'One of our biggest clients is a relative' under a picture of Uncle Sam, with the claim that it has advised the RTC on disposal of $10 billion worth of assets (Day, 1993, p. 377). Ironically, the RTC must rely on the same 'hot money' deposits handled by Wall Street firms such as Merrill Lynch that contributed to the debacle to keep the nationalized thrifts financed

– interest rates paid normally exceed government borrowing costs (Day, 1993, p. 377).

Through September of 1992, the RTC had closed more than 650 failed thrifts and sold more than $287 billion of assets. As the RTC disposes of assets, it causes a slow depreciation of asset prices that was supposed to have been prevented by the bail-out, leading to a 'contained', primarily regional, debt deflation that reinforces scepticism even without generating a 1930s style debt deflation. The nationwide glut of real estate slows RTC sales and lowers recovery ratios.

There are numerous mainstream proposals to 'reform' the financial system. For the most part, the orthodox economists blame the current crisis on improperly priced deposit insurance premia (Scott, 1990), on use of book value rather than market value accounting (Benston, 1990), and on supervisory 'forbearance' which allowed insolvent thrifts to "bet the bank" as they used insured deposits to engage in risky behaviour in desperate attempts to restore net worth (Kaufman, 1990). Thus, the proposals tend to argue for risk-based insurance premia that would properly price risk (sending the correct signal to the financial institution) and would generate sufficient insurance reserves to cover losses (Eisenbeis, 1990; Scott, 1990); for marking assets to market (Benston, 1990); and for closing an insolvent institution before its market-valued net worth equals zero (at this point, assets could be sold at a price sufficient to cover liabilities so that liquidation costs would be minimal) (Eisenbeis, 1990). The most extreme proposals would simply unleash free market forces: private insurers would offer insurance and monitor risk; rating agencies would provide information on risk to depositors; bankruptcy would discipline those who engaged in excessively risky behaviour.

Two widely cited orthodox proposals for reform are the Brookings Blueprint (The Brookings Institution, 1989) and the proposal of the Shadow Financial Regulatory Committee (SFRC) (Kaufman, 1990). The Brookings Blueprint would end 'subsidies' from the FDIC to risk-taking institutions by charging risk-based insurance premia; it would ensure that uninsured depositors and creditors are not bailed-out in the event of failure; it would rely on market-based valuation of assets by continuously marking assets to market; it would promptly close institutions that are insolvent (based on market value); and it would increase efficiency by reducing (or eliminating) restraints on all but the weakest institutions. The Brookings

Blueprint would classify banks and thrifts according to four tranches, based on the (market valued) equity-to-asset ratio. As an institution moved down the tranches, supervision would be increased – those in the top tranche would not require much supervision. The SFRC similarly blames the current crisis on flat rate premiums and forbearance. It would use risk-based, market valued, capital requirements and prompt closure to protect the BIF. As in the Brookings Blueprint, the SFRC proposal would adopt the tranche approach to supervision and regulation; banks and thrifts in the highest tranche could do just about as they like. The SFRC would retain low, flat insurance premiums in the belief that the tranche system and prompt closure would eliminate most risk to the BIF (it would still be exposed to losses in the event of fraud or sudden movements of market value). Both proposals would encourage diversification to reduce 'risk' and would place greater reliance on market signals. Benston (one of the contributors to the SFRC proposal and former consultant to Keating), in particular, would allow commercial banks to sell securities – eliminating the separation of commercial and investment banking – and he argues that potential conflicts of interest would not be great (Wheelock, 1993).

All of these proposals miss the point. There is no alternative to a bail-out and it is obvious that neither FSLIC (which went bankrupt) nor FDIC (which was insolvent) could have dealt with a major financial crisis. Indeed, it is apparent that no insurance scheme can possibly protect depositors, in that insurance reserves can never be large enough to rescue depositors in the event that more than a few banks or thrifts fail. Thus, the financial system must be backed by guarantees of credit worthiness, rather than by insurance reserves. As discussed above, this is the approach taken in some European countries. There are two possible ways to protect depositors: taxpayer guarantees; or central bank guarantees. The current policy is to sell bonds guaranteed by taxpayers to raise the funds required to pay-off depositors, and to have the taxpayers pay the interest on these bonds.[65] The alternative would be to have the Fed substitute its liabilities for those of insolvent thrifts. That is, the Fed would make good on any *insured* deposits in excess of the value of assets of a failed thrift. The *owners* of failed thrifts and banks should lose at least part of their investment (and should be held liable for any losses due to illegal activity). The holders of *uninsured* liabilities might take some loss (often called a haircut), as they chose higher prospective interest rates rather than the safety of insured deposits. For example, they could be forced to accept a loss equal to twice the differential they earned by purchasing uninsured liabilities over what they could have earned on insured liabilities.

Of course, orthodox economists react in horror at the suggestion that Fed liabilities be substituted for the liabilities of failed thrifts and banks, as it would supposedly generate inflation. This is nonsense, for it is based on the supposition that depositors would run out and spend any deposits made good. In reality, this intervention by the Fed would merely validate deposits already in existence: there is no reason to suppose this would lead to a rush of spending (which, given the current state of the economy, would not be inflationary, anyway). If there *was* any inflationary impact, it occurred when the loans were originally made, which allowed speculation in real estate, junk bonds, foreign exchange futures, and so on. It would serve no purpose to try to compensate *now* for inflation that occurred in the past.

Virtually all orthodox prescriptions for reform include proposals to force institutions continually to 'mark to market' all assets – a current market value would be calculated for each asset, perhaps once each day, and institutions would then calculate solvency based on these market values. Marking assets to market would only enhance the inherent instability of financial markets. A financial institution would be induced to sell assets as soon as prices started to decline, ensuring that asset prices would plummet – again, this is an example of rational reaction to market signals leading to incoherent results.[66] Even worse, a speculative boom would generate market-valued net worth and reward destabilizing behaviour. Furthermore, determining a market price for bank assets is extremely difficult and open to abuse – many bank assets are not marketable, and even some that are (say, securitized home mortgages) became marketable because an implicit or explicit government guarantee was placed on them.

Indeed, part of the reason for the development of commercial banking was due to the customer relation required in commercial loan activity. Finally, closing banks and thrifts in a slump that causes asset prices to temporarily fall is precisely the wrong response as it would only make the recovery that much more difficult. Benston has advocated that institutions should be closed when their market-valued net worth is still a small, but positive, percent of assets (he has suggested a figure like 1–2 per cent). If his advice had been followed in the early 1980s, virtually every thrift in the country would have been closed! (Nakamura, 1992). The effects on all financial markets in the USA (and probably throughout the world) would have been disastrous as the government tried to liquidate nearly all thrift assets and as all those holding uninsured liabilities of commercial and investment banks, of money market funds, of insurance companies, and so on, tried to liquidate them to obtain insured deposits.

Rather than liquidation or subsidized merger of troubled institutions, the Fed should follow the practice established by the RFC. Banks and thrifts should be placed into three categories (as discussed above): Class A banks and thrifts do not need help; Class B banks and thrifts must be recapitalized; and Class C banks and thrifts will require substantial intervention because liabilities exceed assets. As Jones argued, however, the Fed should liberally value assets because many are depressed only because of the current state of the economy. Given time, many asset values will recover. As Jones argued before the House of Representatives in 1939, 'Things nearly always get better if you give them time. That is particularly true with collateral and properties and people'[67] (Jones, 1951, p. vi). The government would buy preferred stock in those banks it chooses to rescue. Owners of stock would be forced to take a reduction in the par value of their stock to reflect previous losses (with the reduction based on degree of insolvency). Uninsured depositors could also be forced to accept common stock in place of their deposits (again, with some loss, as described above). The government might also force owners and uninsured depositors to inject additional private capital into the bank (the RFC usually made this a prerequisite to obtaining RFC capital). The bank would pay interest or dividends on the government's shares, and would gradually retire these capital notes out of earnings and recoveries. Following Jones's example, there would be no hurry to retire this preferred stock: 'In carrying out our preferred stock program we held to the conviction that, given a stable banking system in which public confidence had been restored, the bank would earn the money to pay for and retire their preferred stock within twenty years without, meantime, depriving their common stockholders of dividends' (Jones, 1951, p. 60). Furthermore, the management of any rescued bank should be subject to the government's approval – anyone who had played a role in bringing down a financial institution should be barred.

One possible method of resolving an insolvent *thrift* would be as follows: the management would be dismissed and would be replaced with conservative, honest managers (admittedly, these will be difficult to find). The thrift would be reorganized as a mutual, with depositors as the owners. This is fair, as the previous owners had already lost their investment (this is why the thrift is insolvent). It also gives the proper incentives to management and it does not promote rising concentration in the financial sector. Developer-owners and other owners who had abused their thrift should lose all of their investment (and should be sued for damages wherever feasible). Other (innocent) owners would have part of their equity converted to shares in the mutual (again, they should take some loss in the conversion). Insured depositors would receive full shares in the reorganized thrift, while uninsured depositors would receive partial shares (and so incur small losses).

A plan such as this would eliminate the need to liquidate thrift assets, or to subsidize concentration through merger. Many of the assets on the books of thrifts are grossly undervalued due to the depressed national and regional economies. In a sense, all I am advocating is a change in the rules of the game. Double entry book-keeping is a human invention, and we may change accounting rules. The current rule states that if a thrift's assets fall below the value of its liabilities, someone must lose (the FDIC, taxpayers, or uninsured depositors). Under the scheme outlined above, no *further* losses are necessary (however, owners have *already* lost their equity, and there were many social losses incurred due to corruption, drug running, gun smuggling, and so on, undertaken in the *past*). The goal is to reorganize and recapitalize banks and thrifts in a manner that would prevent further social losses. The Bush plan will cost taxpayers as much as $1.5 trillion over the next 40 years. The plan I have outlined would probably (eventually) return profits to the Treasury, just as the RFC did in the aftermath of the recapitalization of banks in the 1930s. Furthermore, the Bush plan is fundamentally unjust: the expenditures of taxpayers help to finance huge subsidies going to wealthy individuals and corporations. (The strange case of Fail was discussed above.)

The bail-out cannot take place in the current environment, however, as the entire regulatory system must be reformed. Deposit interest rates must be reregulated to help thrifts retain deposits, to help keep market interest rates low by reducing the tendency for competition to lead to spiralling interest rates, to protect the normal interest rate differential (loan rate less deposit rate) on which banks and thrifts live, and to reduce the pressures to purchase high-earning but risky assets. In spite of the conventional wisdom about Regulation Q (deposit rate ceilings), the truth is that regulated interest rates were quite successful in stabilizing bank and thrift profits and in keeping interest rates low until misguided policy began to dismantle the Depression-era reforms and to periodically squeeze the economy with induced high interest rates. In the presence of Regulation Q, tight money policy led to a credit crunch because banks and thrifts were limited in their ability to issue liabilities that paid market rates. However, they would not lose core deposits to money markets so long as uninsured liabilities were seen as risky. Interest rate regulation will be successful as long as government guarantees are not inappropriately extended to liabilities excluded from regulation. In other words, all liabilities that are backed by an explicit or implicit government guarantee must be subject to interest rate regulation. A 'level playing field' can be obtained through extension of regulation, rather than through elimination of regulations.

Regulated banks and thrifts could be made more profitable (and more competitive with unregulated financial institutions) by eliminating reserve requirements and deposit insurance premia. As discussed above, it is not possible to build sufficient BIF reserves to deal with a crisis anyway, thus the only argument for charging insurance premia is to provide 'proper incentives'. However, there is little evidence that risk-based cost of funds reduces risky behaviour – the average failed thrift actually paid 100 basis points more on its liabilities than did those thrifts that did not fail.[68] The 'proper incentives' can be provided through close supervision of the asset side of the balance sheet. As insurance funds are necessarily doomed to failure, the FDIC should be dissolved, and replaced with government guarantees of credit-worthiness. There is no logical reason for the creation of reserve funds. Thus, rather than relying on a FDIC, a Federal Deposit Assurance Corporation (FDAC) should be created. In order to ensure that it can respond to a crisis in a timely manner, it will need a line of credit at the Treasury. Required reserve ratios are generally justified on the basis that reserves are safe assets, and that reserves give the central bank control over the money supply. While reserves may be safe assets, they are non-earning assets, but given the large quantity of government bonds issued as a result of the huge deficits run by the Reagan–Bush administrations, a safe, earning asset is available in sufficient quantities. As theory and experience show, central banks are not able to control the quantity of reserves, nor would control over these give the central bank control over the money supply.[69] Thus, there seems to be no justification for maintaining legally required reserves. Of course, even in the absence of required reserves, banks and thrifts will hold reserves for clearing purposes.

Rather than trying to use the quantity of reserves as a constraint on the quantity of bank liabilities issued, the Fed should use the discount window to influence the types of assets financial institutions purchase.[70] As Fed liabilities are used to clear accounts among private financial institutions, the Fed can influence behaviour through determining the conditions under which its liabilities will be supplied. For example, the Fed could extend its discount procedures to include certain private assets held by banks. These might include securitized home mortgages, commercial paper issued by firms with a specified credit rating, and certain corporate bonds. The discount rate charged by the Fed could vary, depending on the perceived riskiness of the assets to be discounted. Through this method, the Fed could reward banks and thrifts that purchased the sorts of assets it preferred.

Various orthodox economists have advocated reform of deposit insurance – most of these would reduce maximum coverage limits, require co-insurance (for example: only 90 per cent of a deposit would be covered be covered by government insurance), or limit insurance to one insured account per individual. These proposals are designed to reduce exposure of the insurance reserves and to provide incentives to depositors to supervise financial institutions. In practice, however, experience in the USA and in European countries shows that the government does not allow uninsured depositors (at least in the case of 'important' banks) to suffer losses. As Randall (1992) argues, depositors behave *as if* uninsured deposits *are* covered because in most cases, the risk premium over interest rates on insured deposits is quite small (except in the case of an institution that is widely perceived to be in trouble). Furthermore, depositors are not able to discipline banks and thrifts because they rarely have timely information that would allow them to do so. Randall's research indicates that markets are not able to identify problem banks until long after they have made the decisions that eventually cause them to fail. In light of these considerations, it is probably best to extend explicit *assurance* to all deposits of banks and thrifts. The assurer must then have access to detailed financial records and the power to withdraw assurance from an institution. The threat of withdrawing assurance would be provide very effective discipline, for it would essentially mean that the institution would be closed (as depositors would be given notice so they could move deposits to another institution). Even if assurance is not extended to all deposits, the assurer (for example, the FDAC) should make greater use of the threat of loss of assurance to discipline errant institutions.

All institutions that are permitted to issue liabilities guaranteed by the government must also be subject to regulations concerning the types of assets that may be purchased. In particular, the thrifts should be restricted to home mortgage loans and to other activity closely related to home ownership. Every industrialized, capitalist, country in the world has a specialized housing finance industry; so did the USA until recently, when deregulators encouraged them to compete toe-to-toe (or head-to-head) with the big guys (banks and other sophisticated financial institutions). One of the primary purposes of a specialized home mortgage sector is to protect homeowners from the interest rate cycle so that they don't lose their homes when interest rates rise. (This is even more important when monetarist policy is the primary means used to fight inflation.) In addition, banks and other types of financial institutions should again be constrained by geographic and functional barriers. The usual argument that we need to remove such barriers in order to expand the financial 'services' offered through enhanced competition simply holds no water. The USA already suffers from massive over-capacity in the financial sector. The proof of this is that growth in the financial sector could only proceed by accepting the liabilities of the non-credit-worthy.[71] This is exactly why we are currently facing a crisis. Deregulation will lead to greater concentration of power, to greater excesses as financial-industrial megacorps compete for market share, and to *reduced* credit availability to households and small firms.

Regulations can be used (again) to enforce maturity matching. As discussed at the beginning of this chapter, one of the most important results of the reforms of the 1930s was maturity matching of assets and liabilities: commercial loans were matched with transactions deposits, while home mortgage loans were matched with stable passbook savings. If monetary policy is biased toward maintenance of low interest rates, if deposit interest rates fall under regulation, and if thrifts are redirected toward home mortgages, then effective maturity matching will again be achieved.

When thrifts became insolvent in the early 1980s, the response of regulators was to keep them open by counting phoney capital. Owners and management were encouraged to grow to profitability by taking on greater risk. The conventional wisdom now is that those thrifts should have been closed immediately to prevent eventual bail-out costs from exploding. Owners had nothing to lose (their capital was already lost) and everything to gain through risky speculation. This might be the correct response given a deregulated environment, and given that many of the regulators appointed by the Reagan administration opposed regulation (in other words, they refused to do their jobs). However, there is a better response. As I have discussed above, insolvent thrifts and banks should be reorganized and kept open. Through injections of capital into troubled banks, some of the equity of owners would be restored, so they would have some interest in restoring profitability. In the case of thrifts, some of the previous owners would now have share accounts and thus would also have an interest in the long-run profitability of the thrift. This cannot be done in the absence of supervision and regulation, however.

In return for a bail-out of banks and thrifts, greater social control over credit would be demanded. As mentioned above, there are no free market forces that guide provision of credit to activities with social value. If is also inappropriate to speak of 'efficient allocation' of credit, for credit is not a resource in scarce supply. We may have as much, or as little, credit as we want: credit is created whenever we accept the liabilities of someone who desires more purchasing power. Some social control over where that purchasing power will be directed, and over who will receive the purchasing power, is appropriate. Several centuries of experience have proven that free markets do exceedingly poorly at choosing whose liabilities are acceptable. Through selective use of the discount window, the Fed could encourage lending for those activities deemed socially desirable.

In addition, it is appropriate to strengthen the Community Reinvestment Act (which is designed to ensure that banks provide services to their defined communities) to increase the flow of credit to underserved communities (Papadimitriou, Phillips, and Wray, 1993). It is also appropriate for state policy to encourage development of alternative, community-based, financial institutions that would increase payment, investment, and credit services in targeted (generally, low income) communities. President Clinton has called for the creation of a system of Community Development Financial Institutions along these lines. The Jerome Levy Economics Institute has developed a more ambitious proposal (Minsky, Papadimitriou, Phillips, and Wray, 1993). Again, there is no reason to suppose that 'free markets' will provide an 'efficient' level of services to all communities. Recent trends toward concentration and consolidation in the USA have reduced the services provided to small depositors and small borrowers.

Finally, the crooks should be jailed. While this is unlikely to discourage further criminal activity (it is success that generates corruption – today's financial heroes invariably become tomorrow's crooks), it does seem just. This means that many accountants, lawyers, thrift owners, and politicians will be behind bars. While the Justice Department is making some progress, the achievements thus far are entirely inadequate. Even where convictions are obtained, sentences are too light and collected restitution funds are too small. We must do better.[72]

3.6 CONCLUSION

This chapter has examined a range of causes of the current financial crisis in the USA with special focus on the evolution of the system in the post-war period from a robust system to a fragile system. This evolution, itself, can be traced to endogenous domestic and international forces that generate instability. Unlike orthodox accounts which view market forces as stabilizing and government intervention as destabilizing, I have identified some stabilizing government interventions as well as destabilizing interventions and have identified destabilizing market forces. The ultimate impact of any of these forces will depend on the 'initial conditions', including those associated with the fragility of the financial system. Finally, I examined possible reforms that might help to 'cure' the current crisis. These reforms take into account existing institutional arrangements, market forces, and other initial conditions. This chapter has examined only one specific 'case': the transformation of the US financial system since WWII. I hope this can serve as the basis for other case studies, including those that will examine the situation in other countries.

Notes

1. I would like to thank Jan Kregel and the editors for comments.
2. More than 25 governments were forced to assist their financial institutions during the 1980s; this assistance was provided through deposit insurance systems, central bank intervention, industry assistance, and direct or indirect general government assistance. (CBO, 1990, p. 136) Perhaps only Canada has faced problems nearly as serious as those found in the USA. During the 1980s, the Canada Deposit Insurance Corporation (CDIC) resolved 21 depository institutions; by the end of the 1980s, the CDIC had a deficit of nearly $1 billion (Canadian).
3. If a 'small' commercial bank is defined as one with assets totalling less than $50 million in 1984 or $66.28 million in 1992 (to account for inflation), then in 1984, small banks numbered 9217 (64 per cent of the total) and held 8.6 per cent of commercial banking assets; in 1992, small banks numbered 6692 (59 per cent of the total) and held 6.3 per cent of total assets. Source: adapted from Wheelock (1993).
4. In 1990, the top ten banks held 22 per cent of all banking assets; the top 25 held 38 per cent (Boyd and Graham 1992). Concentration is increasing as more banks become affiliated with bank holding companies (BHCs): in 1970 only 30 per cent of total commercial bank assets were held by affiliates of BHCs, but this had increased to 74 per cent by 1992. In 1992, 3501 or 31 per cent of all banks were affiliated with BHCs (Wheelock, 1993).
5. President Clinton is, of course, no exception to the rule as evidenced by the slowly emerging Whitewater scandal: Clinton and his wife, Hillary, were partners of developer James McDougal, who owned a thrift, Madison Guaranty Savings and Loan. As governor, Clinton appointed state officials that regulated Madison, which subsequently failed at a cost to taxpayers of $47 million. At one point, Hillary legally represented Madison. It is alleged that the developer improperly used thrift funds in a development project that generated profits for the Clintons, and that funds might have been illegally used to fund Clinton's 1984 gubernatorial campaign. There are allegations that Hillary had documents relating to Madison destroyed during the 1992 presidential campaign; a White House counsel who had worked with Hillary allegedly committed suicide (the case has been reopened as a possible murder case) and documents relating to the case were removed from his office. Reports indicate that other documents relating to the case have been destroyed and that the White House may have interfered with the investigation. The Clintons and 10 current and former White House and Treasury Department officials were subpoenaed to report to a grand jury; Clinton issued an edict that prohibits his staff from destroying any more documents (Kasindorf, 1994). As will be discussed below, Presidents Carter and Bush had their own thrift scandals.
6. A friend at the OCC tells me that P.J. O'Rourke's 'Piggy Banks' (1989) is the most accurate (and certainly the funniest) account of this relationship.
7. Most countries actually operate assurance systems rather than insurance

systems; in most cases, no attempt is made to accumulate insurance reserves (no country charges risk-based insurance premia and only a few rely on co-insurance); many countries follow the Czechoslovakian system in which assessments are made only after member institutions have failed (Bartholomew, 1989).

8. Thus, between 1921 and 1933, the total number of banks declined from about 30 000 to 14 207 (not all of these due to failure); the total then remained nearly constant until 1980. (Source: Board of Governors of the Federal Reserve System, and Wheelock, 1993.)

9. According to data supplied to me by Jan Kregel, between 1925 to 1932, the number of nationally chartered banks fell by 24 per cent, the number of state chartered banks fell by 38 per cent, and the number of mutual savings fell by 31 per cent (these figures include attrition of nonfailed institutions). However, while both state chartered and nationally chartered banks lost deposits over this period (total deposits fell by 21 per cent), deposits actually flowed into the thrifts (total deposits increased by 22 per cent) because they were seen as less risky.

10. For a fascinating account, see Jones (1951).

11. The FDIC insured commercial bank deposits, the FSLIC insured thrift deposits, and the National Credit Union Share Insurance Fund (NCUSIF) insured credit union shares. Originally, commercial bank deposits were insured up to a maximum deposit of $2500, but this was gradually raised so that by 1980, the maximum was $40 000. In addition to explicit deposit insurance, various Government Sponsored Enterprises (GSEs) have been created to guarantee (implicitly or explicitly) various types of private debt (for example, Fannie Mae guarantees mortgage loans while Sallie Mae guarantees student loans). Government *guarantees* have spread so that today, approximately one-third of all non-federal-government debt is insured or guaranteed. See Stanton (1991).

12. According to Kregel (1992), this maturity matching that is achieved in the USA through functional segmentation is achieved in Europe *on* the balance sheet of each 'universal' bank – that is, banks will issue short-term liabilities against the short-term assets they hold, while issuing long-term liabilities against the long term assets held. This matching is accomplished at least in part through supervisory pressure – Kregel does not believe that market forces alone are able to accomplish this.

13. See Barth and Bradley (1989).

14. See Wolfson (1986) and Minsky (1986) for discussions of recent financial crises and for analyses of government containment of each.

15. For data on bank and thrift failures and on FDIC insolvency, see Barth and Bradley (1989), Barth (1991), Eisenbeis (1990), Greider (1991), and Brumbaugh and Litan (1990).

16. Sources: Congressional Budget Office, and 'Legislative Update', The Jerome Levy Economics Institute, 21 November 1992.

17. According to Osterberg and Thomson (1993), funding for RTC has consistently been insufficient. As a result, troubled thrifts that should

have been handled by the RTC are being left for SAIF to resolve. Furthermore, SAIF will soon have to begin paying $772 million in annual interest due on $11 billion bonds issued by FICO to resolve thrifts that failed before the RTC was created. The only way that SAIF can meet these commitments is by maintaining (or even increasing) deposit insurance premia – which will lower thrift profitability and will diminish the ability of thrifts to compete with commercial banks, whose premia are scheduled to decline (because it is believed the BIF will soon be sufficiently capitalized).

18. Banks were not immune to insider deals during the 1980s. Failed banks had made, on average, three times as many insider loans compared with those that did not fail (Seballos and Thomson, 1992). An insider loan is one defined as involving anyone with fiduciary responsibility to the bank (this includes officers, directors, as well as their friends and relatives).

19. Such practices would include 'quid pro quo' loans, straw loans, recourse loans, loan swapping, 'cash for trash', land flips, and fictitious sales. See Mayer (1990) and Waldman (1990) for discussions of these practices.

20. The same was true for bank charters: the barriers to entry were reduced so much in Texas that fully one quarter of all new bank charters granted in the 1980s were in Texas. Not coincidentally, Texas accounted for one-third of all bank failures in the 1980s: in 1988, 175 Texas banks failed (Wheelock, 1993).

21. See Sherrill (1990, p. 600). Virtually all large thrifts in Texas have failed, and, according to William Sessions, Director of the Federal Bureau of Investigation, more than one-third of the FBI's S&L cases are in Texas. See Sessions (1990, pp. 57–8). Also see Mayer (1990, ch. 9) and Horvitz (1990). According to Waldman (1990), half of the Texas thrifts that failed through 1987 were run by those who entered the business after 1979 – and 80 per cent of these came from the real estate industry. Between 1980 and 1991, more than 21 per cent of the thrifts resolved by the FSLIC and RTC were Texas thrifts; this accounted for 39 per cent of total spending by the FSLIC and RTC for thrift resolutions (source: Congressional Budget Office).

22. See Hilzenrath and Singletary (1992) and Singletary (1992).

23. Fernand St Germain served as the chair of the House Banking, Finance, and Urban Affairs Committee from 1981–9; after becoming chair, his campaign donations immediately doubled – more than 99 per cent of the donations came from outside his state, and 81 per cent of his PAC (political action committee) funding came from industries under the jurisdiction of his committee. Banks found it very hard to refuse his requests for loans – he was able to buy $1.3 million worth of restaurants without putting up a dime of his own funds. He bought waterfront condominiums at bargain prices through insider deals arranged by thrifts. James Freeman, lobbyist for the USLSI spent up to $20 000 per year to provide food and alcohol to St. Germain. According to William Seidman (recent head of both the FDIC and RTC). St. Germain 'was reported to have carried and used at will a credit card furnished

by the U.S. League of Savings Institutions' (Seidman, 1993, p. 212). When St. Germain finally lost an election, he went to work as a lobbyist for the USLSI. Jake Garn, chair of the Senate Banking Committee was the top recipient of honoraria provided by the financial industry during the mid 1980s. He was the ninth highest recipient of thrift campaign contributions during the 1980s. He was known as a promoter of thrift purchases of junk bonds. Three of the top five thrift purchasers of junk bonds happen to be among the top contributors to his Garn Institute of Finance at the University of Utah. Charles Keating was another contributor. Two members of Garn's staff, Richard Pratt and Danny Wall, went on to head the FHLBB (it is said that Pratt actually wrote the Garn – St Germain Act). See Sherrill (1990), Mayer (1990), Waldmann (1990), and Day (1993).

24. See Benston and Carhill (1992) for effects of changes in accounting procedures. Seidman (1993, p. 210) notes that many government examiners preferred the acronym CRAP (Creative Regulatory Accounting Principles) over RAP. The Reagan administration cut the number of examiners in District 9, which included Texas, by two-thirds (Sherrill, 1990, p. 601). Examinations of FSLIC insured thrifts fell from a total of 3210 in 1980 to 2800 in 1982 and to 2131 in 1983; examinations per billion dollars of assets fell from 5.41 in 1980 to 2.62 by 1983 (Litan, 1990, p. 30).

25. In a daisy chain arrangement, representatives from several thrifts would make a series of deals in which a piece of property was sold from one to another repeatedly at escalating prices. There are stories in which a number of thrift representatives would sit along a table to facilitate this practice: a property would enter the 'market' at one end of the table and exit at the other end at a price many times higher as a result of a series of transactions. Often, these sales could take place within the same company. At each step, the thrift would obtain loan origination fees and points – enhancing the profitability. See Waldman (1990).

26. As one example, Empire Savings of Texas was accused of a series of 'land flips' that raised the value of a 117 acre plot from $5 million to $47 million in a few weeks. In another case, J. William Oldenburg bought 363 acres of land in California for $874 000 in 1977 (of which he put up less than 10 per cent), and had it reappraised for $32.5 million in 1979; he then purchased State Savings (a Utah thrift) for $10.5 million and sold his plot of land to it for $55 million (Sherrill 1990). As discussed below, for a sufficient fee, appraisers were willing to provide an appraisal that would suit the needs of the customer.

27. In 1980, thrift industry GAAP net worth was $32 billion, of which 100 per cent was tangible net worth (equity less goodwill); in 1982, GAAP net worth had fallen to $20 billion, of which $4 billion was tangible; and by 1987, GAAP net worth was $34 billion, of which $9 billion was tangible. Source: Congressional Budget Office.

28. This discussion follows that of Vaughn and Hill (1992).

29. See Adams (1990) for a discussion of the Nolan Act. California Assemblyman Pat Nolan led the fight to deregulate thrifts. He received

$154 000 in campaign contributions from S&Ls during the 1980s (including contributions from Keating's Lincoln Savings). In 1988 it was alleged that he had accepted money in an undercover FBI sting operation (Day, 1993, p. 393).

30. Taggart bragged 'I was pro-business', and later went to work for two of the most notorious S&L crooks, Charles Keating and Don Dixon. See Adams (1990, ch. 13) and Mayer (1990 p. 50).

31. Mayer (1990) calls Pratt the 'angel of death' for the thrifts, and claims that if you want to blame one individual for the thrift crisis, Pratt deserves the blame. He essentially wrote the Garn – St Germain Act and kept zombie thrifts open so that the eventual costs of the bailout exploded. After leaving the FHLBB, Pratt went to work for Merrill Lynch, Donald Regan's former employer and the largest seller of 'hot money'. See Mayer (1990, pp. 23 and 61) and Waldman (1990, p. 60). According to Seidman, 'Regan did not want to hear that brokered deposits were dangerous, since the packaging of these deposits with deposit insurance was one of Merrill Lynch's major and more lucrative activities' (Seidman, 1993, p. 214). Regan also refused Gray's requests for more supervisors. Gray began warning in early 1984 that without 'firm, decisive, and remedial action . . . massive infusions from the Treasury, and hence the taxpayers, could well be required . . .' (Seidman, 1993, p. 217). Gray's credibility was hurt later by an FBI investigation into allegations that he improperly used entertainment funds to redecorate his office and that he had accepted thousands of dollars from the thrift industry – he eventually apologized and repaid some of the funds (Kurtz, 1992, p. 26).

32. Seidman (1993) presents a plausible case that he is an honest man who was in the wrong place at the wrong time. He says 'the disaster of the Savings and Loan industry during the 1980s was caused by a series of policy mistakes of unprecedented proportions. . . . We at the FDIC had no direct responsibility for insuring or supervising the runaway S&L industry . . .' (Seidman, 1993, p. 208). He goes on to argue that deregulation of the thrifts at a time when most were insolvent threatened the integrity of the entire financial system.

33. Volcker announced 'the standard of living of the average American has to decline' (Sherrill, 1990, p. 592).

34. Between 1974 and 1979, the mortgage interest rate fluctuated around 9 per cent. After Volcker's adoption of tight policy the mortgage rate exploded to a peak of 16.4 per cent in November 1981 (Nakamura, 1992). As market rates on bank and thrift liabilities also rose, they found the mortgages they had purchased in the 1970s were unprofitable.

35. It is frequently claimed that the problem in the US financial sector began in the 1970s due to high inflation that caused negative real interest rates. Since 93 per cent of thrifts were still profitable when inflation was at its peak in 1979, this shows that the profitability problems could *not* have been caused by inflation – rather, it was pursuit of monetarist policy that eliminated the interest rate *spread* from which bank and thrift profits come.

36. As Mayer argues, when deposit rates rise above loan rates, supervisors have no choice but to encourage thrifts and banks to seek higher yields at greater risk (Mayer, 1990). However, some argue that the evidence points of a 'reverse causation' phenomenon: rapidly growing thrifts had high failure rates *because* they grew fast. See Benston and Carhill (1992).
37. These include almost all owner-occupied residences, because this category includes single family homes plus residences of up to four families.
38. There is debate over whether the US economy (as well as that of many developed nations) should be considered as stagnant – although its rate of GNP growth in 1994 indicated it was not in recession, its unemployment rate remained high. Some observers maintain that the US continues to suffer from a 'contained depression' (the term favoured by David and Jay Levy) or a 'silent depression' (the term favoured by Wallace Peterson).
39. His arguments as well as his justification for the choice of a *real* interest rate target are contained in his July 1993 testimony (Greenspan, 1993).
40. Sherrill (1990, p. 590). Of course, it is not a coincidence that corruption is occurring outside the bank and thrift industries: those same factors that generated crooked behaviour in the thrifts are generating similar behaviour elsewhere – in the government bond market, in the securities markets, in politics, in nonfinancial sectors and in foreign financial systems. According to Mark Green, the New York City Commissioner of Consumer Affairs, 'A 1983 Gallup Poll found that four in 10 businesspeople said a superior had asked them to do something unethical; one in 10 said he or she had been asked to do something illegal'. Furthermore, a sociology professor asked more than 700 students 'to write personal essays about their current or most recent job and the honesty of the firm for which they worked... 71 per cent reported that the firm they worked for cheated or deceived the public...' (Green, 1992, p. C-3). Green claims that 90 per cent of electronics stores in economically distressed areas sell used goods as new; one of six gas stations inspected sells regular gas as premium; 90 per cent of nanny placement agencies violated one or more provisions of the city's consumer protection laws; and so on.
41. Sherrill (1990, pp. 618, 621). See also Sessions (199). In contrast, the CBO cites much lower estimates for the contribution of fraud to *costs to the government* of resolving failed thrifts: in the range of 3–10 per cent as the 'low', or 20–5 per cent in the 'high' range of estimates (CBO, 1992).
42. Mother Teresa's connection will be explored below. Jimmy Carter's appointee to head the FDIC in the late 1970s and early 1980s was William Isaac who approved deals made by the notorious Tennessee bankers, the Butcher brothers. It is also claimed that he had questionable ties to individuals involved with the mob. Bert Lance was appointed by President Carter to the Office of Management and Budget, but was forced to resign after only one year due to a series of questionable dealings with a number of banks; he also had various connections to unsavoury characters involved in bank fraud, and was

involved in the BCCI scandal. President Carter worked closely with Agha Hasan Abedi (founder of BCCI) on a number of humanitarian projects throughout the world. In all likelihood, Carter never understood that Abedi was using him to gain access to profitable deals (See Adams, 1990, for a discussion of the exploits of Carter's appointees and Adams and Frantz, 1992, for an examination of the BCCI scandal). Vice President George Bush had chaired the task force under President Reagan that advocated deregulation of thrifts; his son, Neil, contributed to the failure of Silverado in Denver (See Mayer, 1990; Day, 1993, and Seidman, 1993). Palmer National Bank funnelled money to Ollie North's secret Swiss bank accounts; the bank was started by Harvey McLean, Jr with money loaned by Beebe. McLean went on to become a major player in a number of failed Texas thrifts. He also worked on Bush's failed 1980 presidential campaign (See Sherrill, 1990).

43. The discussion of Keating's exploits that follows is taken from Mayer (1990, chs 7 and 8), from Seidman (1993), from Adams (1990, ch. 13), and from Sherrill (1990).

44. Interestingly, only Senator Cranston was formally rebuked by the Senate; Senator Riegle continues as the Chair of the Senate Banking Committee. An indignant Cranston argued that his colleagues in the Senate engaged in actions similar to his every day, and warned 'You are in jeopardy if you ever do anything at any time to help a contributor' (Day, 1993, p. 392).

45. See Waldman (1990, p. 95). Later, as Chairman of the Fed, Greenspan allowed the Fed to lend $98 million to Lincoln in 1989 – an unusual step because the Fed does not normally lend to thrifts. Chairman Gonzalez of the House Banking Committee believed this was done to protect uninsured depositors (Day, 1993, p. 393).

46. Sherrill (1990, pp. 602–4). Other friends and recipients of Keating's generosity included Jack Kemp, Pete Wilson, Tony Coelho, Paul Laxalt, Jim Wright, and Tom Gaubert. The accounting firm of Arthur Young provided glowing reports of Keating's financial prowess.

47. Sherrill (1990, p. 619). Keating ran a 'bait and switch' operation in which senior citizens were enticed with promises of high-interest rates on insured deposits, then sold uninsured Lincoln bonds.

48. According to Seidman, Perelman got one of the 'sweetest' deals by coming in at the last minute and dictating the terms of the contract on the last day of the year (Seidman, 1993, p. 220).

49. This fine merely represents a slight slap on the wrist – the government had already accumulated claims of more than $1 billion against Ernst & Young. The insurers of Ernst & Young will pay $300 million of the fine, while the firm has four years to cover the remaining $100 million – out of annual revenues of approximately $2 billion. Previously, Ernst & Young had agreed to pay $40 million to the government for the part it played in the Lincoln Savings debacle. It also agreed to pay $63 million to bondholders in a civil suit (Day, 1993, p. 383).

50. Amazingly, the act that created the RTC to bailout thrifts also denies bank and thrift examiners 'whistle-blower' protection that is commonly

given to those who bring corrupt practices to light (Mayer, 1990).
51. The investigation of Clinton's Whitewater debacle almost ended due to the three year statute of limitations. Congress, however, recently extended the deadline for that case.
52. Jacqueline Taylor's testimony is published in Taylor (1992). Within the RTC there was also a difference of opinion over the type of case to pursue. The PLS preferred to pursue cases of negligence, in which directors and management would be sued for contributing to thrift failures. Others within the RTC preferred to bring high profile cases of fraud and racketeering under the Racketeering, Influence and Corrupt Organizations Act (RICO). While these cases could potentially result in much larger settlements, it is much more difficult to prove fraud than to prove negligence (McGrath, 1993).
53. In many cases, it is obvious even to the perpetrator that his/her behaviour is criminal. However, in many other cases, the financial manipulations are so complex that one suspects the perpetrators are truly surprised to find themselves convicted of crimes. Prosecutors invariably find cases of bank and thrift fraud extremely difficult to win because even after detailed expert testimony, juries are not able to determine whether the practices were illegal or just normal business practice. Milken has been able to come full circle: from hero to crook to hero again. However, the junk bond has not yet been resurrected in the eyes of the public.
54. See Minsky (1990, 1993) for a discussion of the evolution of the financial system. If big government spending rises when private spending falls, and if taxes fall as income falls, then a deficit will result that helps to stabilize aggregate demand. Conversely, if the deficit falls as private spending and income rise, then it will help to constrain aggregate demand. Similarly, as the Kalecki equation shows, government deficits add to gross capitalist profits. Thus, if deficits rise when private investment spending falls, deficits will help to maintain profits. If deficits fall when private investment spending rises, they will constrain the growth of profits. In addition, government deficits are financed through debt issue, which provides a safe asset for banks and wealth-holders. Minsky argues that the big deficits of the Second World War led to liquid private portfolios dominated by government bonds. This 'robust' financial sector (combined with steadily rising aggregate demand) induced the private sector to expand balance sheets during the post-war boom.
55. While monetarist policy hastens crisis, crises will naturally occur even in the absence of misguided policy as innovation generates defaults because leveraged positions cannot be validated. See Wolfson (1986), Minsky (1986) and Wray (1993a).
56. The commercial bank share of US financial assets held by all financial service firms fell from 51.2 per cent in 1950 to only 26.6 per cent by the third quarter of 1992. Over this same period, the share of assets held by private pension funds and government retirement funds rose from 4.1 per cent to 23.9 per cent (Source: Board of Governors, Federal Reserve System).

57. Non-residential net private fixed investment (in nominal dollars) fell from $99 billion in 1981 to $66 billion in 1982 and to only $46 billion in 1983. Although it recovered somewhat – to $102 billion in 1985 – it was only $75 billion in 1987. Source: Wray (1989, p. 990), derived from the *Economic Report of the President*, January 1989.

58. The deficit grew rapidly from $40 billion in 1979 to $79 billion in 1981 and to $208 billion in 1983. It then rose to $221 billion in 1986 before declining somewhat in the later 1980s. However, by 1992, the deficit surpassed $365 billion. Source: *Economic Report of the President*, February 1992.

59. The multilateral trade-weighted value of the dollar (with March 1973 = 100) rose from 88 in 1979 to 143 in 1985. At the same time, the balance on goods, services and income fell from $5.6 billion to a negative $107 billion. Between 1946 to 1982, this balance had been positive in all but two years. Since 1982, this balance has remained large and negative. Source: *Economic Report of the President*, February 1991. As Kalecki's equation shows, a positive trade balance adds to gross profits, while a trade deficit reduces profits. By 1987, the US trade deficit was equal to 40 per cent of gross profits – representing a massive leakage of gross capitalist income. In the same year, the trade deficit was 78 per cent of the government's deficit. This means that just over three-fourths of the government's contribution to gross profits (the deficit) was lost in the form of a trade deficit. Source: Wray (1989, p. 990).

60. Movement toward the European Monetary System and toward integration through the Maastricht Treaty imposes further deflationary pressures on the EEC countries. At the end of 1992, of the EC countries, only Luxembourg enjoyed a positive government budget balance. Italy and Greece had budget deficits equal to more than 10 per cent of their GDP. The UK had a budget deficit equal to 6.6 per cent of GDP, while even Germany had a deficit equal to 3.2 per cent of its GDP. Only one of the EC nations could have met the fiscal requirements of Maastricht in 1993. All of the major nations will require 'considerable fiscal retrenchments' to meet the requirements – an optimistic projection concludes that the total of fiscal adjustments required amounts to about 2.5 per cent of the combined GDP of the EEC. Source: United Nations Conference on Trade and Development, *Trade and Development Report 1993*, pp. 75–84.

61. Data for investment have been presented above. The unemployment rate for civilian workers reached 9.7 per cent in 1982. It was still 7 per cent in 1986 after three years of recovery, and reached a trough of 5.3 per cent in 1989 before rising again in the most recent recession. In contrast, the unemployment rate fell as low as 3.5 per cent during the expansion of the 1960s. Source: *Economic Report of the President*, February 1991.

62. Unlike the case of firms, however, the federal government cannot go bankrupt, and its spending decisions are apparently much more independent of its income flows than are those of firms or households.

63. The capacity utilization rate for industry averaged only 80.4 per cent during the 1980s, and peaked at 84.2 per cent in 1989. By December

of 1990, it had fallen back to 80.4 per cent. Source: *Economic Report of the President*, February 1991.

64. The experience of the 1980s provides empirical support of this claim. See Wray (1993c) for theoretical arguments.
65. Interest payments on the bonds represent most of the cost of the thrift bail-out.
66. Thus, financial institutions would fail every time market valuations of assets fell. While we do not have time to go into theory here, part of the reason bank liabilities are widely accepted is because they cannot fall below par. This requires that floors must be placed on the value of their assets or they will default. (This is done in two ways: first, financial institutions are allowed to ignore market values because GAAP records assets at book value; second, as discussed above, the central bank intervenes directly and indirectly to prevent market values from going into a free-fall). That is, stability of the financial system requires the absence of market valuation of bank and thrift assets. Requiring that banks and thrifts hold only marketable assets against insured liabilities would not increase stability. Rather, contagious sales of assets would cause general asset price deflation. Furthermore, a proposal that would allow uninsured depositors to lose when a bank or thrift fails must presume that this would not carry through to the value of assets held by financial institutions. It is far more likely that losses by uninsured depositors would force at least some of these to default on their liabilities, causing asset values of financial institutions to plummet – leading to a debt deflation.
67. The conventional wisdom claims that regulatory forbearance caused the bail-out costs to explode as insolvent thrifts gambled with 'house money'. It is said that costs would have been minimal if regulators had moved quickly to close insolvent thrifts. However, some evidence seems to indicate that forbearance actually reduced bail-out costs because some thrifts that were insolvent managed to restore at least some equity. See Benston and Carhill (1992).
68. Keating paid a 398 basis point commission plus as much as a 200 basis point risk premium to obtain hot money from Prudential-Bache. The highest risk-adjusted insurance premium proposed by orthodox economists is 25 basis points – insufficient to change any behaviour (Mayer, 1990). Furthermore, the higher the premium paid to obtain deposits, the greater the return required on assets. Thus, risk-adjusted premia may actually encourage risk-taking.
69. See Wray (1990). Legally required reserve ratios have been reduced while balances required for clearing purposes have risen quickly (partially due to explosion of financial transactions) so that legal reserves are not binding for many institutions.
70. See Minsky (1986) for a discussion of this proposal.
71. Orthodox economists frequently justify proposals to deregulate financial institutions on the basis that this would increase the supply of credit and other services, arguing that financial institutions are constrained by regulations. However, deregulation of financial institutions in the 1980s increased the supply of credit primarily by allowing them to

lower standards so they could 'lend' in areas previously forbidden. As discussed above, in many cases this later led to rising default rates. This indicates the problem was lack of demand by the credit-worthy, rather than lack of supply of credit that led to rationing of the credit-worthy.

72. The average sentence for the convicted S&L crooks has been 1.9 years. The average sentence for a common bank robber is 9.4 years (Waldman, 1990, ch. 6). Dixon and his associates alone are accused of stealing $40 million from his thrift – more than the total take of all conventional bank robbers in a typical year (Sherrill, 1990, p. 602). Clearly, common criminals are rather unsuccessful thieves when compared to thrift owners, and the like, and are treated unusually harshly as compared with the treatment of crooked owners. As a thrift examiner told Mayer, 'What's wrong with this industry is that the people who own these institutions are *slime*' (Mayer, 1990, p. 55).

References

Adams, J.R. (1990) *The Big Fix: Inside the S&L Scandal* (New York: Wiley).
Adams, J.R. and D. Frantz (1992) *A Full Service Bank: How BCCI Stole Billions Around the World* (New York: Pocket Books).
Alpert, M. (1991) 'Personal Bankruptcy's Cheap Chic', *Fortune* (3 June) p. 132.
Arestis, P. and M. Sawyer (1993) 'Political economy: an editorial manifesto', *International Papers in Political Economy*, **1**(1).
Barth, J.R. (1991) *The Great Savings and Loan Debacle* (Washington DC: AEI Press).
Barth, J.R. and M.G. Bradley (1989) 'The ailing S&Ls: causes and cures', *Challenge* (March–April): 30–8.
Bartholomew, P.F. (1989) 'How some nations regulate depository institutions', *Office of Thrift Supervision Journal*, **19**(10): 20–3.
Benston, G.J. (1990) 'Market-value accounting by banks: benefits, costs and incentives', in G. Kaufman (ed.) *Restructuring the American Financial System* (Boston: Kluwer) pp. 35–55.
Benston, G.J. and M. Carhill (1992) 'The thrift disaster: tests of the moral-hazard, deregulation, and other hypotheses', manuscript, 7 September.
Blecker, R.A. (1992) *Beyond the Twin Deficits: A Trade Strategy for the 1990s* (Armonk, NY: M.E. Sharpe).
Boyd, J.H. and S.L. Graham (1992) 'Investigating the banking consolidation trend', in R.W. Kolb (ed.) *The Commercial Bank Management Reader* (Miami: Kolb) pp. 69–81.
The Brookings Institution (1989) *Blueprint for Restructuring America's Financial Institutions: Report of a Task Force* (Washington DC).
Brumbaugh, R.D. Jr and R. Litan (1990) 'The banks are worse off than you think', *Challenge* (January–February): 4–12.
CBO (Congressional Budget Office) (1990) *Reforming Federal Deposit Insurance* (The Congress of the United States, September).

CBO (Congressional Budget Office) (1992) *The Economic Effects of the Savings and Loan Crisis* (The Congress of the United States, January).

Corrigan, E.G. (1992) 'Reforming the US financial system: an international perspective', in R.W. Kolb (ed.) *The Commercial Bank Management Reader* (Miami: Kolb) pp. 47–60.

Day, K. (1993) *S&L Hell: The People and the Politics Behind the $1 Trillion Savings and Loan Scandal* (New York and London: W.W. Norton).

Dymski, G. (1991) 'From Schumpeterian credit flows to Minskyian fragility: the transformation of the US banking system, 1927–1990', unpublished manuscript, February.

Eisenbeis, R. (1990) 'Restructuring banking', *Challenge* (January–February).

Friedman, B.J. (1988) *Day of Reckoning: The Consequences of American Economic Policy Under Reagan and After* (New York: Random House).

Green, M. (1992) 'Crime in the suites: why Christmas shoppers should beware', *The Washington Post* (29 November).

Greenspan, A. (1993) *1993 Monetary Policy Objectives: Midyear Review of the Federal Reserve Board*, 20 July (Washington DC: Publication Services, Federal Reserve Board).

Greider, W. (1989) *The Trouble with Money: A Prescription for America's Financial Fever* (Whittle Direct Books).

Greider, W. (1991) 'The next bank robbery', *New York Times* (28 May).

Hilzenrath, D.S. and M. Singletary (1992) 'Trump went broke, but stayed on top', *Washington Post* (29 November).

Horvitz, P. (1990) 'The collapse of the Texas thrift industry: causes of the problem and implications for reform', in G. Kaufman (ed.) *Restructuring the American Financial System* (Boston: Kluwer) pp. 95–116.

Jones, J. with Edward Angly (1951) *Fifty Billion Dollars: My Thirteen Years with the RFC* (New York: Macmillan).

Kane, E. (1990) 'The need for timely and accurate measures of federal deposit insurers' net reserve position', in G. Kaufman (ed.) *Restructuring the American Financial System* (Boston: Kluwer) pp. 129–133.

Kasindorf, M. (1994) 'Clinton stands by his wife', *Denver Post* (8 March).

Kaufman, G. (ed.) (1990) *Restructuring the American Financial System* (Boston: Kluwer).

Keynes, J.M. (1979) *The Collected Writings of John Maynard Keynes*, vol. XXIX (ed.) Donald Moggridge (London: Macmillan).

Kregel, J.A. (1992) 'Financial fragility and the structure of financial markets', manuscript (November).

Kregel, J.A. (1993) 'A post Keynesian explanation for the causes of the current stagnation', mimeo.

Kurtz, H. (1992) 'Asleep at the wheel', *Washington Post Magazine* (29 November).

Litan, R.E. (1990) 'Remedy for S&Ls: operation "clean sweep"', *Challenge* (November–December).

Lynch, R. (1992) 'Keating seeks leniency; Mother Teresa on his side', *Denver Post* (2 April).

Mayer, M. (1990) *The Greatest Ever Bank Robbery: The Collapse of the Savings and Loan Industry* (New York: Charles Scribner).

McGrath, M. (1993) 'A matter of trust', *Westword*, 20–6 January.

Minsky, H.P. (1957) 'Central banking and money market changes', *Quarterly Journal of Economics*, **71**: 171.

Minsky, H.P. (1986) *Stabilizing an Unstable Economy* (New Haven and London: Yale University Press).

Minsky, H.P. (1990) 'Schumpeter: finance and evolution', in A. Heertje and M. Perlman (eds) *Evolving Technology and Market Structure: Studies in Schumpeterian Economics* (Ann Arbor: University of Michigan Press) pp. 51–74.

Minsky, H.P. (1992) 'The structure of financial institutions and the dynamic behaviour of the economy', manuscript (August).

Minsky, H.P. (1993) 'Schumpeter and finance', in S. Biasco, A. Roncaglia and M. Salvati (eds) *Markets and Institutions in Economic Development: Essays in Honour of Paolo Sylos Labini* (New York: St Martin's Press) pp. 103–15.

Minsky, H.P., D.P. Papadimitriou, R.J. Phillips and L.R. Wray (1993) 'A proposal to establish a nationwide system of community development banks', *Public Policy Brief*, 3 (The Jerome Levy Economics Institute).

Nakamura, L.I. (1992) 'Closing troubled financial institutions: what are the issues?', in R.W. Kolb (ed.) *The Commercial Bank Management Reader* (Miami: Kolb) pp. 488–97.

O'Rourke, P.J. (1989) 'Piggy banks', *Rolling Stone*, 24 August.

Osterberg, W.P. and J.B. Thomson (1993) 'Making the SAIF safe for taxpayers', *Economic Commentary, Federal Reserve Bank of Cleveland* (1 November).

Papadimitriou, D.P., R.J. Phillips and L.R. Wray (1993) 'A path to community development: the Community Reinvestment Act, lending discrimination, and the role of community development banks', *Public Policy Brief*, 6 (The Jerome Levy Economics Institute).

Pizzo, S. (1991) 'The trillion dollars question: will the banks go bust, too?', *Mother Jones* (September/October): 56–59.

Pizzo, S., M. Fricker and P. Muolo (1991) *Inside Job: The Looting of America's Savings and Loans* (New York: Harper Perennial).

Randall, R.E. (1992) 'The need to protect depositors of large banks, and the implications for bank powers and ownership', in R.W. Kolb (ed.) *The Commercial Bank Management Reader* (Miami: Kolb) pp. 501–13.

Scott, K.E. (1990) 'Never again: the S&L bailout bill', in G. Kaufman (ed.) *Restructuring the American Financial System* (Boston: Kluwer) pp. 71–94.

Seballos, L.D. and J.B. Thomson (1992) 'Underlying causes of commercial bank failures in the 1980s', in R.W. Kolb (ed.) *The Commercial Bank Management Reader* (Miami: Kolb) pp. 484–7.

Seidman, L.W. (1993) *Full Faith and Credit: The Great S&L Debacle and Other Washington Sagas* (Times Books, Random House).

Sessions, W. (1990) 'The FBI's war on bank fraud: facts and figures', *Challenge* (July–August): 57–8.

Sherman, S.P. (1991) 'Bankruptcy's spreading blight', *Fortune*, 3 June.

Sherrill, R. (1990) 'S&Ls, big banks and other triumphs of capitalism', *The Nation*, 25 (19 November).

Singletary, M. (1992) 'Critics urge bankruptcy law reform', *Washington Post* (29 November).

Stanton, T. (1991) *A State of Risk: Will Government-Sponsored Enterprises be the Next Financial Crisis?* (New York: Harper Business).

Taylor, J. (1992) 'A Second S&L Scandal', *Harper's* (November).

Vaughn, R.J. and E.W. Hill (1992) *Banking on the Brink: The Troubled Future of American Finance* (Washington DC: Washington Post Company Briefing Books).

Waldman, M. (1990) *Who Robbed America? A Citizen's Guide to the S&L Scandal* (New York: Random House).

Wheelock, D.C. (1993) 'Is the banking industry in decline? recent trends and future prospects from a historical perspective', *Federal Reserve Bank of St. Louis Review*, **75**(5): 3–22.

Wolfson, M. (1986) *Financial Crises: Understanding the Postwar U.S. Experience* (Armonk, New York: M.E. Sharpe).

Wray, L.R. (1989) 'A Keynesian presentation of the relations among government deficits, investment, saving, and growth', *Journal of Economic Issues*, **23**(4): 977.

Wray, L.R. (1990) *Money and Credit in Capitalist Economies: The Endogenous Money Approach* (Aldershot: Edward Elgar).

Wray, L.R. (1992a) 'The greatest-ever bank robbery: a state of risk: a review article', *Journal of Economic Issues*, **26**(1): 275–84.

Wray, L.R. (1992b) 'Alternative theories of the rate of interest', *Cambridge Journal of Economics*, **16**: 69–89.

Wray, L.R. (1993a) 'Money, interest rates, and monetarist policy: some more unpleasant monetarist arithmetic?', *Journal of Post Keynesian Economics*, **15**(4): 541–70.

Wray, L.R. (1993b) 'Government deficits, liquidity preference, and Schumpeterian innovation', Jerome Levy Economics Institute Working Paper.

Wray, L.R. (1993c) 'The development and reform of the modern international financial system', manuscript.

4 Financial Structures and Egalitarian Economic Policy

Robert Pollin

4.1 INTRODUCTION[1]

This chapter pursues a new approach to egalitarian economic policy. It is concerned with methods of bringing dramatic increases in the democratic control over financial markets and the allocation of credit, without sacrificing the basic sources of micro efficiency and macro co-ordination and stability that are necessary for any viable economic strategy. The focus here on financial issues is not meant to suggest that there is less need for comparable policy measures in other economic spheres, in particular the labour market and related institutions. Nevertheless, the premise of this paper is that policies focused on financial institutions and activities must be a central feature of any renewed egalitarian policy project.

There are several reasons why this is so. To begin with, it has been clear for some time that even the most mildly progressive governments face formidable opposition to their programmes from powerful interests within financial markets. Some well-known examples of this recurring phenomenon include the Labour governments in Britain in the 1930s, 1960s and 1970s; the Mitterand government in France in the 1980s; and, most recently, the Clinton Presidency in the USA.[2] Third World governments regularly confront even stronger pressures, especially since the 1980s, as the IMF and World Bank have imposed deflationary structural adjustment programmes on terms established by the international financial community.

But even assuming such political forces could be neutralized, the tendency of financial markets toward speculation and instability have also weakened the capacity of governments to implement egalitarian macroeconomic policies successfully. The primary instruments for conducting macro policy – deficit spending and central bank monetary interventions – are both financial mechanisms, and thus their ability to operate effectively depends on how well policy initiatives can be transmitted through the financial system. Financial market instability has increased substantially since the early 1970s relative to the first phase of the post-war period, including such period-defining events as the collapse of the Bretton Woods system in the early 1970s, the Latin American debt crisis in the early 1980s, and the merger and takeover wave in the USA and UK in the latter part of the 1980s. This rise of financial instability has weakened the transmission mechanism from policy instruments to policy targets.

Given these considerations, it follows that egalitarian movements will have to confront financial market pressures through explicit programmatic measures. But, unlike the situation with labour market issues, the left has for the most part failed even to consider the types of policies that might be effective in addressing both the political and structural problems deriving from financial markets.

There are also more positive reasons for egalitarians to give new attention to policies focused on the financial system. Finance is the conduit for all economic activity in market economies. Because nothing happens unless it is financed, exerting control over the financial system is an efficient way to influence the widest possible range of activity with a set of relatively small and simple policy tools.

Moreover, many researchers have now observed that there are considerable differences in the financial systems operating within the various capitalist economies. What has emerged from this research is that some financial systems – in particular what are often called the 'bank-based' systems – have been more successful than others – the 'capital market-based' systems – in promoting long-term growth and financial stability. The basis for the success of the bank-based systems is their reliance on non-market arrangements in organizing financial institutions. These non-market arrangements continue to operate, moreover, despite the wave of financial market globalization and liberalization that has been gaining momentum at least since the collapse of Bretton Woods. While these bank-based systems have not been constructed to advance egalitarian aims, the principle argument of the paper is that they can be successfully adapted for that purpose once their central operating mechanisms are understood and appropriately redeployed.

Following this introduction, the paper is organized into three main sections. Section 4.2 surveys the literature on bank-based and capital-market based financial systems. In general, this literature finds that bank-based systems, such as those in Japan, France,

Germany and South Korea have been more successful than capital market-based systems, such as in the USA and UK, in solving the incentive, co-ordination and informational problems inherent in capitalist economies, and indeed in all complex economic systems. Because of this, bank-based systems are better equipped to promote longer time horizons and a stable financial environment. Their structures also create more favourable conditions for activist government policy interventions, including both traditional macro policies and public credit allocation policies.

At the same time, the bank-based systems generally operate through highly undemocratic public and private bureaucracies, which are clearly inimical to any egalitarian policy project. The challenge then is to develop policy approaches which can combine the efficiency-promoting aspects of bank-based systems with a degree of democratic participation in the financial system not yet attempted in existing models.

Section 4.3 takes up this challenge. The angle through which it approaches this issue is to re-examine the different financial systems according to the exit/voice analytic framework developed by Hirschman (1970). In this framework, exit is the withdrawal from a relationship with a person or organization when one becomes dissatisfied with that relationship. Voice means directly expressing one's dissatisfaction to the relevant person or organization. In capitalist societies, the exercise of exit is pervasive within market relationships, while the political and bureaucratic spheres are dominated by the exercise of voice.

Within this framework, the fundamental distinction between financial systems can be seen as not whether they are bank-based or capital market-based, but rather whether they are dominated by exit or voice mechanisms. The bank-based systems are voice-led, and therefore provide more effective channels for political interventions in financial markets than do the exit-led capital market systems. Working from this point, the principal concern in formulating egalitarian policies can be recast: the issue is not the specific bank or capital market institutions prevailing in a financial system, but rather how all systems can be restructured to provide an effective basis for the democratic exercise of voice.

Posing the question in this way then enables us to consider various means of creating 'democratic voice' mechanisms that also retain the efficiency and stability promoting aspects of the existing bank-based financial structures, that is, the 'elite voice' systems.

Drawing primarily from recent literature on the US economy, I consider proposals in the areas of corporate governance, community reinvestment, pension fund management, and central bank policy. However, I also stress here that such democratic credit policies can be effective within a range of institutional frameworks and political environments. Indeed, the adaptability of this policy approach is one of its most important strengths.

In section 4.4, I then pose the following more general question: can the features of a voice-led model that promote stability and efficiency be sustained once we move from an elite to a democratic voice system? I approach the issue via the new model of 'bank-centric' market socialism developed by Bardhan and Roemer (1992). Working from their discussion provides a bridge for engaging the literature on market socialism to explore our central concerns about the efficacy of a democratic voice model.

The brief concluding section pulls together the main arguments in support of such democratic voice financial policies as a foundation for renewing egalitarian economic policies. In passing, this section notes that globalization and liberalization of financial markets pose new challenges to the viability of any bank-based or voice-led financial system. At the same time, experiences thus far suggest ways that the essential features of a voice system can be retained without having to resist all aspects of globalization.

4.2 ALTERNATIVE CAPITALIST FINANCIAL SYSTEMS

Bank-Based and Capital Market-Based Systems

Beginning with Gerschenkron's classic essay (1962), there has been a small but by now rapidly growing body of economic analysis which has attached significance to differences in the financial systems of capitalist countries. Gerschenkron, in particular, contrasted the financial development of Britain and Germany. He argued that because Britain's industrialization was early and gradual, businesses were financed primarily through reinvesting retained earnings. Large pools of intermediated saving had not yet formed, making it impractical for firms to rely on external sources for long-term financing. As a result, in the British tradition, non-financial firms did not develop close ties with financial institutions. When large financial institutions did begin to develop later, they were independent entities, with no special attachment to firms. The arm's length relationship between Britain's non-financial and financial sectors established the foundation for the country's highly developed and independent capital market.

Gerschenkron contrasts this pattern with that of Germany. Industrialization started later there, and as a result, firms were confronted with the problem of appropriating rapidly the capital technologies and production systems, such as those for steel, that the British had already developed. The firms were unable to finance these projects on their own, and as a result, large universal banks developed. They provided firms with both long-term funding as well as managerial direction. The universal banks were also able to coordinate the investment plans for the clusters of firms with which they were associated. Within this development path, opportunities were far more limited than in Britain for the formation of an independent capital market.[3]

As Jacobs (1994a, b) points out, Gerschenkron's account does not attempt to explain why the differences in the British and German systems were sustained long after Germany attained a comparable level of development to that of Britain. Nor did he pass judgement on the relative merits of either system as a foundation for future development. However, in roughly the last decade, a substantial literature has developed which has examined just these questions.[4] This literature has examined a wider set of countries than those considered by Gerschenkron, including the USA, Japan and France among the core group, and others as well, depending on the questions that a given study is pursuing.

This recent literature has continued to find useful the fundamental distinctions established by Gerschenkron, between what we are calling 'bank-based' and 'capital market-based' financial systems. Most generally, the capital market-based systems are characterized by highly developed capital markets, with widely dispersed ownership of equity and debt instruments, and relatively low involvement of large banks in either the allocation of funds or the ownership of financial assets. The bank-based systems, by contrast, are characterized by a small number of universal banks that are actively involved in the long-term financing of investment activity of the non-financial firms. The banks are the primary source of long-term funds and they retain ownership for the long term of their debt instruments. In these economies, there is relatively little secondary trading of financial assets.

Beyond this, Zysman's seminal contribution (1983) added a third dimension to the distinction between these systems: the nature of government involvement within them. Zysman found strong differences in the role of government within Japan, France, Germany, the UK and USA, the five countries he studied. In particular, he found that the government played a more limited role in the US and UK capital market-based systems. France and Japan, by contrast, were bank-based systems in which the government participates actively in allocating credit to private firms, both on the basis of price and quantity controls. Zysman then argues that Germany is unique as a bank-based system in which the government does not play an active role in administering prices or quantities.

In contrasting the systems below, I do not mean to convey that actual financial operations of the various countries have, over the period considered, become frozen in place. At various points, and in particular the conclusion, I discuss some of the ways that these systems have recently evolved. Nor am I suggesting that differences in financial systems can themselves explain overall differences in economic performance. The Japanese or South Korean growth 'miracles', for example, were crucially dependent on, among other things, initial support from the US economy (through spending on the Korean and Vietnam wars and other factors) docile labour movements, well-specified export strategies, and strong commitments to spending on education.[5] Nevertheless, by focusing here on the issue of financial structure, I am clearly assigning considerable significance to its relative importance as a determinant of overall economic performance.

Effects of Alternative Systems

Why do these features of countries financial systems matter? The answer first depends on the theoretical perspective from which one examines the question. From the neoclassical 'irrelevance' propositions developed by Modigliani and Miller (1958), financial structure should not matter at all in determining either the valuation of firms or, more generally, the pattern of investment. This is because, in perfectly competitive markets, the same product (a firm) will be priced equally in separate markets (debt and equity markets). Therefore, there can be no advantage to firms or their asset holders derived from the firm's capital structure.

Because the Modigliani–Miller thesis assumes the existence of perfectly competitive markets, it follows that what Shaw (1973) initially termed 'financial deepening' – the development of sophisticated financial markets through which the transaction costs of reaching ones optimal risk/reward profile are low – will enhance efficiency.

From this perspective, then, one would conclude that the Anglo-Saxon capital market-based model of deep and liberalized financial markets would attain superior results to the bank-based systems such as France, Japan or Germany. In fact, most of the literature has found the contrary to be the case: over a range of measures, the bank-based systems have out-performed the capital market-based systems. What are the reasons for this?

The literature here builds from a range of perspectives. Some of it, within the Gerschenkron tradition, is primarily historical and descriptive (for example, Zysman, Cox). More explicit theoretical approaches are motivated by: new-Keynesian and New Institutionalist concerns with problems of information and principal/agent relationships; Post-Keynesian ideas on uncertainty and financial fragility; and from what is increasingly termed the 'organizational capabilities' view of the firm.[6]

Perhaps the single most influential idea underlying this literature is traceable to the classic 1932 study by Berle and Means of the development of US corporations. They argued that the growth of the corporate form of organization would encourage a divergence in the interests of managers and owners – what is now termed a principal/agent problem. The problem, more specifically, is that managers, as agents of a dispersed and unorganized set of owners within a capital market-based financial system, will act in behalf of their own interests. Their interests, moreover, are not necessarily identical to, nor even compatible with, those of the firms' owners. Managers, for example, may seek to maximize their own salary, security, power and perquisites, rather than the shareholder's value. Such objectives would constitute a classic instance of an incentive incompatibility between principal and agent.

But at least equally problematic is that even if the Berle and Means-type incentive incompatibilities were resolved satisfactorily, this in itself is still not likely to promote the long-term viability of the firm.

The reasons for this stem from the related problems of asymmetric information between owners and managers, incentive incompatibilities between owners and the firms workers, and the uncertainty that dominates the operations of financial markets. To begin with, the information to which the shareholders will tend to respond will be short-term financial indicators. These are not necessarily congruent with the firm's ability to produce desired products at competitive costs, the basic determinant of the firms' long-term viability.

On the one hand, shareholders will recognize straightforward cost-reducing measures, such as wage cuts or layoffs, and will respond favourably to these. But other sources of long-term viability, such as the firm's capacity to innovate technically and its ability to create a productive environment for its workers, are likely to be unrewarded or even denigrated by shareholders. This is in part a problem of asymmetric information, in that shareholders are not adequately informed about the firm's operations. But there is also the perhaps more basic problem of incentive incompatibilities, or, straightforwardly here, class conflict. That is, because these longer-term sources of productive viability may not reduce costs in the short term, the benefits of them will not flow to shareholders who are most interested in the short-term capital gains stemming from rising asset prices. On the other hand, the benefits of maintaining competitiveness through creating a productive work environment rather than wage-cutting and layoffs is clearly in the interest of the firm's workers.

Finally, as post-Keynesians have long argued, asset prices in deep capital markets are heavily influenced if not entirely dominated by the activities of speculators, whose only concern is to outguess the market, not evaluate a firm's productive potential. Thus, far from enhancing the flow of useful information between owners and managers, a deep and freely functioning financial market is more likely to encourage chronic bouts of speculative financial excess – that is, pervasive 'co-ordination failures' in contemporary terminology.

The argument within the literature is that the bank-based systems resolve these problems of asymmetric information, uncertainty and co-ordination failure as well as class conflict and other incentive incompatibilities more successfully than the capital market-based systems. As a result, the bank-based systems achieved superior performance in three crucial areas: promoting longer time horizons; encouraging financial stability; and providing a framework for the successful implementation of government policy.

Time Horizons and Financial Stability

The most basic reason given in the literature for the superior performance of the bank-based systems is that they foster long-term time horizons, which in turn promote long-term productive investment. By contrast, the capital market-based systems foster shorter time horizons, in that firms' managers are primarily concerned with achieving the performance standards defined by the transactions-orientated capital markets.

It will be useful now to consider Porter's terminology, in which the two systems are distinguished according to whether they are 'fluid' or 'dedicated' capital systems. In the 'fluid' capital systems, firms' relationships with capital suppliers are at arms length, and thus, shareholders have limited information or direct influence on managerial actions. Shareholders and bondholders' decisions are made on the basis of simple corporate financial ratios and stock prices. Moreover, their interventions in the corporate governance process are primarily *ex post*, as through the sale of shares or the deterioration in bond ratings. Within this arrangement, managers are forced to follow the same standard financial measures of performance.

In 'dedicated' capital systems, by contrast, the capital suppliers have major stakes and long-term relationships with the non-financial firms. This enables the capital suppliers to share a focus with managers on technical expertise and building market positions. Capital suppliers are thus able to exert *ex ante* influence. The firms, in turn, benefit from what Lazonick (1990) calls 'financial commitment', which he defines as a situation in which claimants to the firms' revenues 'will not enforce these claims in ways that undermine the development and utilisation of the firms' organisational capabilities' (p. 51). Because of this type of financial commitment associated with dedicated capital systems, the factors that are conducive to high performance among workers – including less hierarchical work structures and long-term employment security – have a far greater opportunity to develop.

In addition, the *ex ante* flow of information and control in dedicated capital systems induces a greater tolerance on the part of the lenders/investors for higher leverage ratios. At the same time, the capital market-based systems are more susceptible to financial instability than the bank-based systems. Why is this so?

The underlying source of financial instability, at the simplest level of accounting, must be that debt commitments are systematically outstripping the income flows necessary to service them. In turn, the basic explanation for the systematic deviation between debt commitments and income flows is that borrowed funds are used disproportionately to finance activities that do not yield an adequate return flow of income. The types of financial activities that are most likely to create such a debt trap are speculative and compensatory spending, that is, borrowing to purchase existing assets with the expectation of capital gain and to compensate for declining income streams or other internally generated funds. Put another way, instability results when debt is used insufficiently to finance productive spending; that is, spending that raises incomes by enhancing the productive capacity of firms and individuals. When credit is extended for speculative and compensatory spending to a disproportionate degree relative to productive spending, the likely result will be income streams inadequate to finance the growth of debt.[7]

Note here that the basic source of difficulties is not the rise of debt *per se*, nor even the rise of debt relative to income or assets. High leverage ratios are therefore sustainable as long as, over time, a return flow of revenue is generated to service them.

As a general model, the bank-based systems are better designed to avoid mismatches between debt commitments and income flows. This is because the thrust towards speculative finance is reduced inasmuch as finance is dedicated to a greater degree to long-term productive projects. Moreover, the commitment to long-term projects means that the projects will have a longer grace period before they have to generate returns to their lenders.

Evidence on Time Horizons and Financial Stability

Time Horizons, Cost of Capital and Investment

A wide range of research has accumulated in recent years supporting the view that the bank-based systems have promoted longer time horizons and greater financial stability.

To begin with, survey evidence of corporate CEOs in the USA, Japan and Europe developed by Poterba and Summers (1992) found that US CEOs believe that their time horizons are shorter than those for their counterparts in Europe and Japan. According to the US CEOs, their relatively short horizons derive to a significant extent from the financial market environment in which they operate.

These managers contend that US equity markets undervalue long-term investments. Were the firms valued more in accordance with the perceptions of managers, the managers believe that their long-term investments would increase, on average, by perhaps as much as 20 per cent.

The survey also found that for the US CEOs, the minimum expected rate of return that would induce them to commit to a new investment project – that is, the 'hurdle rate' – is substantially higher than standard cost-of-capital analysis would suggest. On average, US CEOs reported that their hurdle rate was 12.2 per cent. This compares with an average real return over the past 50 years of less than 2 per cent on corporate bonds and around 7 per cent for equities.

Moreover, as Porter (1992) reports, this difference in time frames and hurdle rates is associated with a striking difference in managerial goals: US managers rank return on investment and higher stock prices as their top two corporate objectives, whereas Japanese managers rank improving existing and introducing new products, and increasing market share as their two highest priorities. Higher stock prices is ranked last by Japanese managers among the eight objectives included in the study.

These survey findings are also consistent with evidence from corporations' actual operations. Porter (1992) found that the share of investment going to research and development, intangibles (especially investment in 'corporate training and human resources') and plant and equipment is lower in the USA than in Germany and Japan. In addition, the proportion of total research and development expenditures going to long-term projects is lower in the USA. In the USA, 22.6 per cent of total R&D budgets were allocated to such projects, while in Japan and Europe, the figures were 46.8 per cent and 60.5 per cent respectively.

Related to this, recent studies also find that short-term financial market pressures have created formidable obstacles to developing 'high-performance' work environments, despite the increasingly widespread recognition of the long-term gains that are achievable through a more secure and less hierarchical workplace. Thus, Appelbaum and Berg (1996) report on the results of a 1995 survey of senior line and human resource executives at mid-sized and large US companies. The survey found that 98 per cent of respondents agreed that improving employee performance would significantly improve business results and that 73 per cent said that their company's most important investment was in people. Still, when asked to rank a number of business priorities, the respondents put performance of people and investment in people near the end of the list, well below standard measures of financial performance.

Considering more direct financial indicators, at least over the 1970s and 1980s, various studies have found that the real after-tax cost-of-capital was higher in the USA than in Japan and Germany, and that differences in these countries financial systems are seen as a major contributing factor. McCauley and Zimmer (1989), for example, write that greater integration of industry and finance has permitted higher leverage without raising bankruptcy risks equivalently, and also greatly reduced liquidity risks of non-financial firms. Moreover, according to McCauley and Zimmer, the Japanese and German governments are more actively involved in mitigating the direct costs associated with non-financial firms' periods of financial distress.

Mergers, Takeovers and Speculation

It is consistent with these general findings that the bank-based systems almost fully avoided the corporate mergers, buyouts and takeovers that were pervasive within the USA and the UK in the 1980s. Indeed, according to the work of Jensen (for example, 1988), the most influential mainstream analyst of the 1980s merger and buyout wave, the US/UK merger wave represented precisely an effort to resolve the principal/agent problems resulting from the Anglo-American financial system. This effort was almost entirely salutary in Jensen's view.

Jensen argues that the market for corporate control, and the corporate restructurings it has forced, remedies the incentive, co-ordination and informational problems due to the Anglo-American corporate form through straightforward means: by limiting the prerogatives of managers and increasing the control of owners. Managers are forced to face constant threats to their power and position, and are therefore much more responsive to shareholders' interests. This view also holds that the substitution of debt for equity is a powerful tool for reducing management authority over unutilized cash flow because, unlike with dividend payments to equity owners, managers are legally bonded to distribute interest payments on their debt.

Following this perspective, one would expect that the enormous investment in corporate takeovers in the 1980s would have generated comparably large net benefits to the US and UK economies. And while considerable controversy exists over evaluating the experience, a careful survey by Crotty and Goldstein (1993) of the US experience found that the overall social costs have far exceeded its benefits:

> The evidence is mounting that the costs of creating and allocating credit through the deregulated financial markets of the 1980s are likely to be significant and persistent. In many cases, employees in merged firms suffered a direct loss of security, income and/or jobs. The spillovers from these losses have been substantial; communities have suffered, and workers' commitment to productivity growth has been badly shaken. Productivity is threatened also by the constraining effects of debt on investment and R&D expenditures. And finally, the financial stability and flexibility of industrial and commercial companies and financial institutions throughout the economy has been impaired. (p. 276)

This is not to say that speculative finance is absent in the bank-based systems. The 1980s inflation of the Japanese stock market and its crash in 1989 provide dramatic evidence of volatility there comparable to that in the USA and UK (Goldstein, 1995). But the crucial point is that, because of the close relationship between financial and non-financial firms in bank-based systems, speculative financial behaviour does not exert significant influence on real economic activity. In Japan itself, for example, controlling blocks of many firms' shares are held among strategic partners within Keiretsu, the bank-industry clusters. Yet roughly 40 per cent of corporate stock is held by non-allied shareholders. This segment of the Japanese market is even more engaged in short-term trading than the US market, with the net result being that overall trading volume and turnover are very similar in the two countries. Goldstein describes the Japanese financial market as strongly bifurcated into fluid and dedicated segments, with the dedicated segment still exercising predominant influence.

Economic Policy under Alternative Systems

Broadly speaking, bank-based systems are structured more suitably than capital market-based systems for achieving favourable results from two primary policy tools – expansionary policy and industrial strategy. The basic source of the advantages inherent in bank-based systems is the greater integration between non-financial and financial firms, which engenders a commonality of purpose that is absent in capital market-based systems.

Expansionary Macro Policy

In bank-based systems, since banks hold equity positions and are active in the management of firms, the banks, along with the nonfinancial firms, will be more favourably disposed toward expansionary macro policies. In the Anglo-American system, where financial firms are not directly linked to industry, the financial firms are more likely to favour restrictive policies. The value of outstanding financial assets are more important to the Anglo-American financial firms than the growth prospects of non-financial firms, and as such, they are more concerned about the threat of inflation than comparable institutions in bank-based systems.[8]

Related to this, in the US/UK model, the independence of the financial system has lead to a strong international orientation for its financial sector. In both cases, the domestic currency is used extensively for international transactions, and a formidable industry has developed around international finance. Maintenance of confidence in the currency is therefore given greater priority than in bank-based systems (see Fine and Harris, 1985, pp. 61–2, and Epstein and Schor, 1990).

It also appears that the negative collateral effects of expansionary policy tend to be stronger in the Anglo-American than the bank-based systems, though more research is needed to establish this point. The most general problem is that expansionary policy in capital market-based systems are more likely to engender an allocation of credit toward speculative finance, such as mergers, buyouts, and real estate investments. Again, the bank-based systems have high degrees of speculation as well. But at the core of the credit market systems are institutional provisions for productive finance.

Industrial Strategy[9], Financial Markets and Government Planning

The advantage of bank-based systems here is that they are more amenable to public credit allocation policies as a central focus of industrial strategy. Public credit allocation policies, in turn, are regarded in much of the literature as an effective instrument of industrial strategy. At the same time, in considering the historical experience – particularly that of the USA, which has pursued extensive public credit policies – the actual causal relationships between a country's financial structure, its degree of public credit allocation, and its efforts and attainments in the area of industrial strategy, is not clear cut.

That is, while it may appear that countries with bank-based systems are more successful at implementing credit policies and industrial strategy, this appearance may primarily result from the fact that the same countries are more actively engaged in both credit allocation and industrial strategy. Relatedly, the historical record is not clear on the extent to which countries with capital market systems can deploy credit policies to compensate for the capital market's distortions – that is, engaging credit policies to replicate the desirable features of a bank-based system within the existing capital market institutional framework. We return to these questions in section 4.3. As a prelude to that discussion, I now briefly review the experiences of various countries with credit policies and industrial strategies.

Zysman (1983), for one, argues emphatically that public credit allocation policies are necessary – indeed are the one essential tool – for successfully implementing industrial strategies. He says there are two reasons for this. The first is that:

> business decisions are hard to control or influence through administrative or regulatory rules. Those same decisions may, however, be influenced by negotiation in which the payment for services rendered is unambiguously calculated in monetary terms. Discretionary influence in industrial finance permits the government to deal within the framework of business decisions and to affect the balance sheet directly. (pp. 76–7)

In addition, Zysman argues that public credit allocation is a universally applicable policy instrument. As such, it 'eliminates the need to find specific authority to influence specific decisions or to control an agency that has formal authority over a specific policy instrument.' By comparison, Zysman contends that tax policy is not nearly as effective a policy tool. Taxes tend to operate on gross profits from earnings, and thus are an *ex post* rather than *ex ante* incentive to pursue the priorities of the industrial strategy. Tax policy is also less flexible. It can be used reasonably well to target categories of activity but not specific industrial ends.[10]

Despite differences in details, there appear to be three basic common elements to public credit allocation policies among the countries that have used such policies for financing an industrial strategy. To begin with, the national government is the major initial recipient of the economy's saving supply. This is achieved through various mechanisms. In Japan, it is done through the postal saving system, in France and Taiwan through the public ownership of banks. In South Korea, public bank ownership was supplemented by the government running persistent budget surpluses. Through all these mechanisms, the state has power to act as the economy's principal financial intermediary.[11]

From here, the state is then able to utilize the disbursement of credit as a policy tool. This can be done either by disbursing to private intermediaries, as is done in the Japanese system, or by the state making direct loans to non-financial firms, as is done in France or Korea.[12] Finally, powerful state agencies – such as MITI in Japan and the Tresor in France – are in a position easily to monitor the process of their industrial strategy via their oversight over the return flow of debt servicing by the borrowing units.

Experiences in the USA and UK

The USA and UK have had divergent experiences with respect to public credit allocation and industrial strategy. Since the 1930s, the USA has had considerable experience with public credit allocation policies. Indeed, considering all forms of credit allocation (direct loans, guaranteed loans and government-sponsored enterprise loans) the federal government is the largest creditor in the US financial market, lending or underwriting on an annual basis between about 15 per cent and 30 per cent of all loans. Major recipients of funds have been the housing sector, agriculture and education. These programmes, moreover, have achieved considerable success relative to their stated goals. For example, they have contributed substantially to the unprecedented access to homeownership enjoyed by a high proportion of the non-wealthy in the USA.[13]

The extent and success of these programmes demonstrate that credit policies can be implemented effectively within a capital market-based financial system. At the same time, while these policies have been crucial to the development of targeted sectors, they have not been used in the USA to guide an overall industrial strategy. It is therefore difficult to gauge the extent to which a broader-based set of credit/industrial policies might be frustrated by the structure of US financial markets. But the success of these programmes on their own terms suggests, contrary to Zysman, that the ability to implement credit allocation policies successfully may not depend significantly on whether a country's financial system operates as a bank or capital market-based system.

As for the UK, the Labour party governments in the 1960 and 1970s did attempt to pursue industrial strategies. But they did not pursue public credit allocation policies as part of that effort. The private capital market financial system thus acted as a barrier to the successful attainment of industrial policy (see Zysman, 1983, p. 82; and Fine and Harris, 1985, pp. 123–4).

Objectionable Aspects of Bank-Based Systems

Despite the many successful features of bank-based systems, these systems also have serious deficiencies, in particular from the perspective of constructing an egalitarian economic programme. The close interlocking relationships between major firms, banks and government bureaucracies create opportunities for clientism in credit allocation.[14]

But even more objectionable from the perspective of constructing an egalitarian programme is the fact that public credit allocation policies have been most successfully implemented in countries such as Japan, South Korea and Taiwan, where the government planners were completely independent from democratic decision-making processes. In France, similar to the East Asian economies, government credit policies were independently established within the elite Tresor unit of the Treasury. But these policies were still subject to some democratic pressures within the framework of the French polity. But for just this reason, Cox (1986) argues that public credit allocation policies in France were less successful than those in Japan: that is, the French were forced to a far greater degree to use these policies simply to subsidize ailing industrial firms, avoiding the social costs of closing the plants. Regardless of the accuracy of Cox's assessment, the point he raises is important. He is suggesting that the more the state is a site of political conflict, the greater the likelihood that credit allocation policies will become an instrument for competing, rent-seeking constituencies. Such observations raise questions as to the idea that public credit allocation policies can be successfully implemented within a democratic framework – much less, as we are proposing, that such policies be the instrument for substantially extending democracy as well as improving economic performance. This is the basic question that we consider in the next section.

4.3 DEMOCRATIC FINANCE AND EGALITARIANISM

Exit and Voice in Financial Systems

Hirschman's exit/voice framework is important for this discussion because it provides a vehicle for exploring the extent to which financial systems can be used to increase equality as well as efficiency. Within this framework, the Anglo/American system is one dominated by exit as a means of exercising influence. Thus, dissatisfied shareholders or bondholders of a firm will typically express displeasure by selling their claims to the firm. A voice mechanism is incorporated into the US system through its extensive system of public credit allocation. But again, these programmes were designed with limited goals in mind, and as such, the voice mechanism is correspondingly limited.

By contrast, the bank-based financial systems are premised on the exercise of influence by voice. Major financial institutions and state agencies are actively involved in charting a non-financial firm's long-term plans and then committing themselves to the process of implementing those plans. At the same time, as we have noted, the exercise of voice in these economies is almost entirely confined to an elite grouping of capitalists, political leaders and high-level bureaucrats.

We pursue two specific questions here. The first is how the exercise of voice might operate within a democratic institutional framework while still retaining the capacity that exists with existing bank-based/voice systems effectively to solve incentive, co-ordination, and informational problems. Such a democratic extension of the voice mechanism would necessarily depend upon the development of collective organizations seeking to influence public credit allocation policies. These, in turn, could provide a foundation for building what Cohen and Rodgers (1993) call 'associative democracy', that is, the attainment of 'egalitarian aims by improving the kinds and extent of collective organizations available to citizens' (1993, p. 236). The second question, which we take up in the next section, is whether voice-dominated financial systems could be extended still further in an egalitarian direction, specifically to serve, in a manner suggested by Bardhan and Roemer (1992, 1993), as a foundation for market socialist economies.

Problems with Exit-Dominated Systems

Hirschman himself discussed the Anglo-American financial model as an example of an exit-dominated system, and recognized the costs associated with such as a system. While Hirschman's argument points towards the benefits of a strong voice option, he also recognizes that the most favourable situation is one that achieves an appropriate balance between exit and voice. Reaching such a balance, however, is difficult.

To begin with, voice can atrophy in situations when both options are available but exist is highly accessible. Consider, for example, an important case in which a voice mechanism was injected into the exit-dominated US financial system. This is the experience since 1977 with the Community Reinvestment Act (CRA). Under the terms of the CRA, banks are obligated to provide funds for the communities in which they operate. However, this regulation exists within a highly unfavourable environment. The banks, in dealing with small-scale borrowers, generally seek to package standardized loans into marketable securities for the national and global market. But almost by definition, loans that bring new opportunities to poor communities will tend not to meet the conditions of the standardized loans. In addition, local communities have no institutional means of monitoring bank compliance with the law. Not surprisingly, the CRA has had little impact on bank lending practices.[15]

It follows that exit options must be limited in order that voice be effective. But it is also true that an environment which lacks a credible exit option is also not viable. Without the exit option, the sanctions one can threaten in expressing dissatisfaction will carry little credibility. Considering financial markets, the bifurcated Japanese market offers a useful model. There, as we have seen, controlling blocks of firms are closely held within Keiretsu, who manage their interlocking companies through the exercise of voice. At the same time, the roughly 40 per cent of financial assets that are publicly traded provides a viable exit option and also transmits the public market's assessment of a firm's performance. This does also create wide opportunities for speculative finance, but they generally do not diminish the 'financial commitment' (referring again to Lazonick's term) of the Keiretsu to the long-term operations of a firm.

Political Power and the Exercise of Voice

Of course, giving priority to voice over exit does not at all address the issue of whose voice is being empowered. In existing bank-based systems, as we have discussed, the extension of the voice option is quite limited. Can voice-dominant financial systems be viable when the voice option is substantially extended?

In considering this question, it will be useful to consider a formulation by Banfield (1961) to which Hirschman refers: 'The effort an interested party makes to put its case before the decisionmaker will be in proportion to the advantage to be gained from a favourable outcome multiplied by the probability of influencing the decision' (cited in Hirschman, 1970, p. 39).

Drawing from this framework, the challenge can be defined as developing institutions through which there is both advantage to be gained through exercising voice and a good probability that advantage will be so gained. In capitalist societies, of course, the wealthy have far greater means to organize effective voice mechanisms. Indeed, a legitimate criticism of efforts to extend the voice option is that this will merely generate new vehicles for rent-seeking (and attaining) by the wealthy. This is why means to strengthen associative democracy are crucial components of strengthening the voice option, especially, as Cohen and Rodgers write, 'efforts to promote the organized representation of excluded interests' (1993, p. 238). How can this be done within financial systems?

A dramatic intervention in this direction would be to nationalize a substantial proportion of a country's financial institutions. We put aside whether such a strategy is politically feasible. However, an even more basic concern is whether a nationalization strategy, on its own, is likely to change the structure of a country's financial institutions in any significant way, and specifically whether it is likely to promote the extension of voice.

The French experience is instructive. Roughly half of the French banking system has been nationalized since the 1940s and the Mitterand government nationalized another 30 per cent after coming to power in 1981. Nevertheless, as Lipietz (1988), among others, has written, the financial system operated in a manner essentially indistinguishable from private banks, both before and after 1981.

Moreover, the Mitterand government's decision to nationalize was never linked to a broader strategy of financial market democratization or even experimentation. Quite the contrary: the government's first major policy decision was to defend financial orthodoxy with respect to the exchange rate, a position it maintained consistently thereafter.[16]

A nationalization policy thus begs the question of how to promote a democratic voice within financial institutions. More to the point are a range of proposals that have been developed recently which, given existing property relations, focus on specific methods of extending the voice mechanism. For illustration, I will cite some that have been developed primarily within the US context, but the general approach advanced is generalizable beyond this one case. I consider these proposals in terms of both of Banfield's criteria for evaluating voice mechanisms: whether they provide means of increasing the probability of influencing decisions and whether they increase the advantage to be gained from favourable decisions.

Influencing Decisions through Democratic Voice

In terms of this first criterion, Block (1992) has developed a proposal for changing the laws of corporate governance. He suggests that the boards of directors of public corporations consist of, for example, 35 per cent employers, 35 per cent asset holders, and 30 per cent others, perhaps including consumers or community representatives. This would be a direct means of increasing the decision-making authority of corporate stakeholders relative to shareholders.

Considering workers' pension funds – the largest saving vehicle in the USA, incorporating one-third of the economy's financial assets – Barber and Ghilarducci (1993) propose substantially increasing the rights of the fund contributors. They would mandate participants representation on corporate pension fund boards. Under current US practice, pension fund managers are required to treat their fiduciary responsibility as equivalent to that for incompetent heirs. That is, all authority rests with the managers, none with the fund participants.

A variety of proposals have also been advanced to bringing greater accountability to the Federal Reserve, and thereby weakening its independence from democratic political pressures. One proposal is to institute direct elections of the Boards of Directors of the Federal Reserve Banks in each Bank region. At present, the regional bank boards are selected by officers of private member banks of the system.[17]

Gaining Advantage Through Democratic Voice

However useful on their own terms, none of these proposals to increase democratic voice mechanisms directly address Banfield's other criteria of increasing the advantages to be gained by favourable outcomes. In countries that already have extensive public credit allocation systems or, as with Germany, a voice-dominated private system, democratizing these existing voice mechanisms may itself bring more favourable outcomes. However, within private capital market-based systems such as in the USA and UK, such democratic interventions would have little impact unless a broad system of public credit allocation were introduced concurrently.

Here again, some basic ideas for extending public credit allocation have been sketched. For example, returning to the US Community Reinvestment Act, one major problem with the act is that it applies only to banks. The banks legitimately claim that they are placed at a competitive disadvantage relative to other intermediaries. A simple but dramatic means of strengthening the Act would be to extend its requirements to all intermediaries – that is, to 'level the playing field upward' for all financial institutions.[18] In addition, the procedures for democratizing the central bank at the regional level would then also provide the means for greatly improving compliance with the Act.

With pension funds, Barber and Ghilarducci (1993) argue that fiduciaries are currently obligated to obtain risk-adjusted maximum rates of return in capital markets that are assumed to be free and efficient. As a result, pension fund managers and regulators have not taken account of how the allocation of pension funds affects employment, community development, and long-term investment. Indeed, pension funds were major financiers of the 1980s merger movement and other speculative excesses in those years. Barber and Ghilarducci support programmes for 'economically targeted investment' of pension funds, which entails including employment and community effects in calculating the social rate of return of pension fund investments. They acknowledge that many initial efforts in the 1970s at economically targeted pension funds investing in the USA were flawed. Increasingly, however, evidence is building that this is becoming a successful method of public credit allocation.

It would of course become more effective still if such policies operated within an overall financial structure that discouraged speculation and subsidized investment activities that yield high social rates of return.[19]

With respect to the Federal Reserve, it is equally important that, along with policies to increase its democratic accountability, further measures need to be taken to create a public allocation mechanism targeted toward long-term productive investment. At present, open-market operations and discount window policy are exclusively concerned with short-run movements of interest rates and credit aggregates, and their ability even to achieve their short-run targets is questionable.[20] Pollin (1993), for example, proposes two relatively simple mechanisms to increase the Fed's long-term allocational role.

1. The first is to increase the role of discount-window reserve creative relative to open market operations. This will give the system's district banks, each of which operates its own discount window, more direct regulatory authority over the lending activities of private intermediaries, enabling them to promote longer time horizons and financial stability. It will also redistribute downward Federal Reserve decision-making power, creating more effective channels for accountability.
2. The second suggestion is to establish differential asset reserve requirements for all US intermediaries. Preferred uses of credit – those that generate high social rates of return and would be supported through an expanded Community Reinvestment Act or Economically Targeted pension fund investing – would then receive subsidies relative to non-preferred uses of funds, such as mergers and real estate speculation.

Finally, a securities transaction excise tax would also be a useful tool for discouraging speculative finance. The aim of such a tax would be to reduce speculative financial activity by raising the costs of trading financial assets. This would be done by subjecting all financial assets trades to a small tax. The tax rate would be low enough that it would be negligible in cases where assets were purchased and held for lengthy periods. The burden of the tax would only be felt among those who are frequent traders.

One of the advantages of this proposal is that, even if it failed significantly to reduce speculative trading, it then would become formidable source of government revenue, which could in turn finance, for example, a public investment programme. Baker, Pollin and Schaberg (1995) estimate that, given the level of trading in the current US securities markets, a tax of 0.5 per cent on equities which was then scaled down appropriately for all bonds and derivative instruments, would raise roughly $30 billion a year in revenue even if trading volume fell by one-half.

Of course, such a tax would operate more effectively in conjunction with a similar tax, as proposed by James Tobin, on foreign exchange trading in which all countries co-operate.[21] But experiences with purely domestic versions of the tax make clear that they can function effectively within this more narrow context, especially in a country such as the USA with a deep market for domestic securities.

Are These Proposals Utopian?

The specific policy ideas sketched here are drawn entirely from programmes that have been used or at least seriously considered in the US or other advanced capitalist economies. Considered in technical terms, they are therefore feasible in that they do not represent a serious departure from existing institutional or policy arrangements. They also are adaptable to whatever are the existing political realities in a country, in that they could be implemented in stages, beginning, again, with the institutional configuration already in place.

At the same time, considered as a whole, there is no doubt that such extensions of democratic voice would entail a substantial shift downward in economic power, and would therefore be resisted by the political and economic elite. In particular, one would expect elite groups persistently to seek to undermine the effectiveness of any such policies once they were enacted into law, as has been done in the USA with the CRA. This raises the issue posed by Coakley and Harris (1983) for the UK and Lipietz (1988) for France: whether public ownership of financial institutions remains an imperative, not as an end in itself, but as the means of implementing the types of egalitarian reforms outlined here.

We will once again leave aside the political dimensions of that question, though they are obviously of fundamental importance, and turn instead to the implied economic issue: how a voice-dominated financial system would operate under public ownership.

4.4   PUBLIC OWNERSHIP AND CREDIT POLICIES

The Bardhan – Roemer Model of Market Socialism

Bardhan and Roemer (1992) have argued that what I am calling a voice-led public credit allocation system can be used as the central organizing institution for a workable market socialist economy. Their proposal incorporates levels of public ownership beyond that of the financial sector, to include large-scale nonfinancial enterprises as well. But the general thrust of their proposal brings into focus issues relevant for various types of nationalization strategies. More generally, as I discuss below, their approach can be viewed as one strategy within a range of alternatives for developing a framework of democratic voice of financial systems.

Bardhan and Roemer argue that a market socialist economy is one in which the economy's large-scale productive assets are publicly owned in some fashion. In this way, the profits from these enterprises are distributed equally among the public. The fundamental challenge for such an economy is the same as that which was never successfully resolved in the former Communist economies: how to resolve the principal/agent problem between managers as agents and the widely dispersed firm owners – that is, the state and ultimately the citizenry – as principals.

Because Bardhan and Roemer view this problem as equivalent to that between owners and managers in corporate capitalism, they argue that its most efficient resolution will emulate the successful resolutions that have occurred in capitalist economies – that is, through a set of voice-led financial institutions with a competitive managerial labour market and clear standards for managerial success. They further argue that resolving the system's incentive problems will establish strong safeguards against what Kornai (for example, 1993) has termed 'soft budget constraints' – the means through which governments will deviate from established budgetary, tax and pricing policies to bail out inefficient firms rather than allow them to fail. Bardhan and Roemer devote less attention to the ways in which voice-led financial systems might also effectively resolve co-ordination and information problems, though as I discuss below, particularly as these problems have macroeconomic ramifications, these features of a voice-led system should also be transferable to economies dominated by public ownership.

They have outlined a set of financial institutions which draw heavily

from the Japanese Keiretsu system and other existing voice-dominated systems. For example, in their model that is most closely
akin to a Keiretsu system, firms are organized as joint stock companies – owned by their workers, other public companies within
their group and the main investment bank which finances the group
and observes these activities. There could also be other subsidiary
owners, including pension funds and insurance companies. The state
would be the major owner of the banks, pension funds, and insurance companies. In this case there would be several monitors of
the firms' activities: the worker-owners; the workers and managers
of the other firms in the same industrial group; the managers of
the pension funds and insurance companies; and most importantly,
the managers of the main bank. As the primary suppliers of funds
for the non-financial firms, the bank managers would have responsibility for financing the individual group and maintaining its level
of performance. In particular, the shares of the large firms can be
sold to the main bank. The main bank will therefore receive information on firm performance based on their own evaluations as well
as those of other institutions.

The primary source of external finance in this arrangement would
be the banks, and the banks are themselves publicly owned. Funds
could thus be readily channelled from the state, via the public banks,
to the firms. How then could these systems avoid the problem of
soft budget constraints? Bardhan and Roemer point to three main
safeguards. The most important is the incentive system for managers. Bank managers who are forced to plead with the state for
bailout funds will have damaged their reputation in the process.
Moreover, the state would have to make credible pre-commitments
to performance standards, and be prepared to liquidate businesses
which fail to meet them. Finally, the economy would be open to
international competition.[22] This would create an external source
of accountability for the firms and the system as a whole.

Exit/Voice Finance and Alternative Property Relations

The Bardhan-Roemer proposals, then, are essentially a means of
stretching the egalitarian possibilities of voice-dominated financial
systems by combining the democratic features of a voice system
with an egalitarian redistribution of property rights. The relationship between this proposal and the others we have surveyed is summarized in Table 4.1. The rows of the matrix characterize the three

Table 4.1   Financial systems and forms of property

Predominant financial institutional framework	Predominant ownership form		
	Private	Mixed	Public
Exit	US UK – 1980s	UK 1960s–70s (primary public ownership of non-financial firms)	—
Elite Voice	Japan, Germany	France, South Korea (primary public ownership of financial firms)	Former USSR
Democratic Voice	Proposals for USA on community reinvestment, pension funds, Federal Reserve, security transaction taxes	Coakley – Harris Proposal	Bardhan– Roemer Proposal

types of financial system: exit-dominated, elite voice-dominated, and democratic voice systems. The columns characterize predominant property arrangements: private, mixed, and public. We locate various historical and existing systems along the first two rows, distinguishing between them according to whether they are exit or elite voice-dominated and by their predominant system of property ownership. The various proposals we considered are along the bottom row, since all include a democratic voice mechanism, but are distinguished by their predominant system of property ownership.

It becomes clear from this figure that the one change for which there is no equivalent experience is the southward movement toward a democratic voice mechanism. This raises the question of whether the successes of the elite voice systems are transferable to democratic voice systems. At the same time, the proposals represented in the southwest cell, which combine democratic voice with predominantly private ownership, are designed to be implemented incrementally as a reformist programme within existing capitalist systems located in the more northerly cells of the matrix. South-eastern movements toward the Bardhan-Roemer proposals would entail a more substantial transformation relative to the existing capitalist economies, though not necessarily to the former Soviet-type economies. In any case, movements south-eastward pose the additional issue of whether combining democratic voice with public ownership would further erode the benefits of the elite voice systems. These are the issue to which we now turn.

Democratic Finance, Public Ownership and Critique of Market Socialism

The question of whether democratic financial systems can retain the efficiency features of the elite-dominated voice systems can be evaluated within a broader and more venerable debate: whether a market economy's sources of efficiency can be replicated within any egalitarian economic arrangement.

This question has received considerable attention within debates over the viability of market socialism. Oscar Lange (1936) was of course the first to offer a model showing that a market socialist economy could function efficiently. He demonstrated that in an economy with free consumer choice but where the means of production are publicly owned, the price mechanism could still be deployed for solving the informational problem associated with price formation and resource allocation.

But Lange was attacked by Hayek (1940, 1988), who held that Lange's model, while internally consistent, nevertheless overlooked the fundamental source of capitalism's efficiency. This was not its ability to allocate resources through competitive price formation, but rather the nature of its property rights system. In particular, Hayek held that the system of private property associated with capitalism encourages technical progress, and that technical progress, in turn, was the source of capitalism's dynamism.

It has been recently argued, moreover, most carefully by Howard and King (1994), that this Hayekian critique of market socialism in fact parallels Marx's own understanding of the sources of capitalism's dynamism. Howard and King write that

> Disregarding the difference in language, Marx and Hayek are in agreement on two fundamental matters concerning the nature of capitalist social relations. First the strength of capitalism lies in its dynamic transformative power, not its ability to engender

allocations which satisfy static utilitarian welfare criteria. Second, capitalism is especially effective in raising productivity. (p. 143).

From this perspective, capitalism engenders efficiency because its system of property relations provides freedom to capitalists to develop new methods of production and discard existing techniques, and, similarly, to deploy and discard employees as needed. Moreover, the system has a powerful incentive structure for the capitalist, by holding out formidable material rewards for those who succeed in raising productivity through innovation and severe punishments for those who fail.

For Howard and King, it is clear that a market socialist economy cannot allow private individuals this degree of freedom in choosing methods of production and especially in hiring and firing workers. It cannot therefore replicate the basic source of capitalism's efficiency, and will thus inevitably be outcompeted by an economy with capitalist private property relations.

Howard and King argue that if a market socialist economy were able to compete with a capitalist economy in terms of innovation and productivity, then such competitive socialist forms of organizations would have been making embryonic appearances within contemporary capitalism.

How Would a Democratic Voice System Fare?

The departure point of the various democratic financial arrangements is that they are not relying on the market as a mere computer analogue (as Patnaik, 1991 uses the term), guiding price formation and resource allocation. Rather, they are centred around a set of institutional relationships for solving the incentive, co-ordination and informational problems that result within large-scale enterprises and, more broadly, within modern economies at the macro level, regardless of the property forms around which these economies are organized. As such, these voice dominated systems are able to transcend the criticisms of Lange-type market socialist schemes.

First, as we have seen, the existing elite voice-dominated financial systems are more efficient than the exit systems in promoting long-term productivity growth, and – focusing primarily now at the macro level which Bardhan and Roemer did not address – in supporting productive investment, reducing financial fragility and mitigating the effects of speculation. That is, elite voice-led systems do indeed outperform the exit-led systems according to Howard and King's yardstick of productivity and innovation.[23]

In addition, because voice-dominated systems have functioned well in various institutional settings, it is fair to say that they have met Howard and King's more stringent test: they have emerged within the interstices of capitalism, and have survived and grown precisely because they outperform exit-dominated financial systems.

It is true that part of the basis for their success has been the willingness of the elite class to pursue longer-term 'organizational capabilities' strategies to high performance, thereby forgoing a shorter-term route to rewards through following financial market indicators. This suggests that if the elite classes perceived the short-term gains of a financial market strategy were rising significantly in relative terms, it might become increasingly difficult to maintain an elite consensus around a voice system. On the other hand, were the elite voice systems to be substantially democratized, one of the premises behind such a transformation would have to be to create a new political coalition committed to nurturing the long-term advantages of a voice model.

Could a democratic voice model function without relying upon unemployment and allied punishments as a source of efficiency? Several points are relevant here. First, to the extent that the purpose of unemployment is to preserve the capitalists relative bargaining power in labour markets, any significant extension of public ownership and democratic voice should reduce that source of pressure for unemployment.

Second, to the extent that unemployment is associated with macroeconomic fluctuations independent of labour market imperatives, we have seen that the voice-dominated financial systems perform better at maintaining a stable macro environment. Moreover, because they are able to create a more stable macro environment, these systems also are better able effectively to utilize the traditional tools of fiscal and monetary policy.

But could the democratic voice systems also maintain the set of micro-incentives available to an elite-voice system? Bardhan and Roemer suggest that they could, as long as the economy is open to international competition, the government is committed to maintaining clear performance standards and hard budget constraints, and, most importantly, there exists a competitive managerial labour market. However Roland and Sekkat (1993) contend that the managerial labour market will not be efficient within a Bardhan–Roemer type public ownership framework, and their points raise concerns about all democratic voice systems. Their argument is that any system dominated by public ownership will have foreclosed the exit option for managers dissatisfied with a career in the public sector. Predominant public ownership will put the state in the position of a monopsonist relative to the managerial labour market, giving the government 'hold-up' power over the careers of managers.

This is indeed a serious problem, but it fully applies only to a system with complete public ownership, one in the extreme southeast corner of the matrix in Table 4.1. What their position points toward is the relative merits of arrangements somewhere in the middle cell of the last row of Table 4.1 – that is, a democratic voice financial dominated system with both public and private ownership of corporations. This is likely to provide both a favourable environment for innovations in voice-dominated finance while also preventing the state from becoming a monopsonist in the managerial labour market.

4.5   CONCLUSION

Democratic voice-led financial systems offer a highly promising foundation on which to reconstruct an egalitarian economic policy agenda. Such an approach, first of all, is premised on what Patnaik argues is the fundamental requirement for an egalitarian economy, 'the creation of appropriate institutions for the active participation of the working class in economic and political life' (1991, p. 33). In addition, this approach is highly flexible. It can be developed on the basis of existing institutional arrangements within capitalist economies, and thus, depending on political circumstances, can be implemented in varying increments on the foundation of the existing institutions. Moreover, this policy apparatus can be effectively adapted to diverse property ownership systems, ranging from private ownership economies such as the contemporary USA to predominantly public ownership systems such as still exist in most of Eastern Europe or as envisaged by Bardhan and Roemer.

Of course, capitalists and their political allies will resist any serious encroachments on their prerogatives in financial markets. Democratic voice systems will not be implemented on the basis of their compelling logic alone. This is why we would go along with Coakley and Harris's suggestion that public ownership of major financial institutions may be necessary, not as an end in itself, but as the basis for implementing effective democratic credit policies. Even still, in countries such as the USA where public ownership of the financial system is not politically feasible, important elements of a democratic voice agenda are still possible. Programmes such as community reinvestment, the targeting of pension fund investments and changing both the operating goals and degree of accountability of the central bank are politically feasible even within the existing US economy and should be primary concerns of progressive movements. In addition, by working to build such policy initiatives within private financial systems, we gain experience and understanding about the limits of reform under private financial systems.

Much, if not most, economic activity within any version of the democratic voice model would still be conducted through markets. However, the democratic voice model is not vulnerable to the legitimate critique of the Langeian market socialist model – that is, that such a model employs markets as a mere computer analogue, neglecting the social relationships underlying them. At the same time, to the extent that the democratic voice model operates effectively, it should also be able to utilize traditional macro policy tools – indeed, it should be better positioned to use them than more free market-orientated economies – to minimize unemployment. More importantly, it should be well positioned to trade off the efficiency 'benefits' of unemployment with alternative sources of efficiency.

Are voice-dominated financial systems viable within increasingly globalized markets?[24] It is true that advanced capitalist economies with bank-based systems, such as Japan, France, and Germany, have followed the worldwide trend since the 1970s in liberalizing their financial systems (see Swary and Topf, 1992, *passim* and World Bank, 1993, pp. 339–41).

At the same time, fundamental elements of the bank-based systems have, until the present, remained intact. For example, close bank–industry relationships, such as the Japanese Keiretsu system, have not eroded despite security market liberalization. In addition, state involvement in credit allocation remains strong in the bank-based systems (with the exception of Germany, which has never relied on this mechanism). The governments of bank-based systems continue to receive a substantial proportion, if not the majority, of their economies' saving through postal saving systems and similar forms of public intermediation. Given this source of funds, the governments are able to retain considerable influence in credit allocation decisions, which they exercise through their respective planning agencies (Grabel, 1996). The fact that, over the late 1980s, active markets for corporate control did not develop in the traditional bank-based financial systems indicates that liberalization has not subverted these countries 'dedicated capital' financial relationships.

It is not clear whether these voice-dominated institutional forms will surrender to the pressures of global financial markets over time. For this to happen would require that the continued financial deepening generated through globalization would create ever greater – and finally irresistible – profit opportunities through 'fluid' investment strategies.

In short, we leave as an open question the extent to which globalization represents a threat to the future viability of existing bank-based systems, to say nothing of democratic voice policies. Nevertheless, the existing Japanese model of a bifurcated system – with an open segment that is free to pursue all market opportunities and a controlled 'dedicated capital' sector – appears to offer the outlines of a solution that is viable both for the existing bank-based systems, and, more importantly, for the development of democratic voice policies that a progressive movement would want to pursue. Beyond this, the issue must be evaluated in political terms. If globalization is indeed destructive of egalitarianism, then progressive political movements will have in develop economic programmes that can neutralize these destructive forces while simultaneously advancing egalitarian economic arrangements that promote both micro efficiency and macro stability. My surmise is that an approach guided by democratic voice financial policies can provide the foundation for such an economic programme.

Notes

1. I wish to thank the following people for their stimulating comments on this work: Philip Arestis, Dean Baker, Fred Block, Bob Brenner, Jerry Epstein, Andrew Glyn, Ilene Grabel, John Grahl, Marty Hart-Landsberg. Michael Howard, Makoto Itoh, John King, seminar participants at the Universities of Vermont, Cambridge, and California-Riverside, and participants at the September 1994 Conference on

'Demand Rehabilitation: Finance, Trade and Technology' sponsored by Pantheon Sorbonne Paris 1 and SOAS, University of London. I am also grateful to my graduate students at UC-Riverside for moving with me into this topic.

2. The Clinton administration's abdication before financial market pressures is chronicled in great detail in Woodward (1994). Woodward portrays Clinton himself as well as the relatively progressive members of his administration as truly stunned by the power of financial markets to override his electoral mandate. Clinton, for example, at one point declares. 'You mean to tell me that the success of the program and my reelection hinges on the Federal Reserve and a bunch of fucking bond traders?' (p. 84). He later concludes. 'Here we help the bond market and we hurt the people who voted us in' (p. 91).

3. Gershenkron's historical account of the German experience conforms to the contemporaneous observations of Hilferding (1981 [1891]). However, Hilferding's analytic approach was mistaken for having regarded the German universal banking model as a more advanced and essentially inevitable stage through which capitalist economies would proceed. This perspective underestimated the durability of the British-type capital market model, as well as the evolution of banking enterprises themselves. Harris (1988) provides a good discussion of these issues.

4. Some of the leading studies in this literature include Zysman (1983), Rybczynski (1984), Cox (1986), Mayer (for example, 1988). Berglof (1990) and Porter (for example, 1992). Hutton (1995) is an excellent journalistic discussion of these issues, particularly as they relate to the contemporary British economy. Recent studies examining these questions from political economy perspectives, and from which I have benefited substantially are Goldstein (1995), Grabel (1996) and Jacobs (1994a, 1994b).

5. For fuller treatments on Japan and South Korea, see Itoh (1990) on Japan and Amsden (1989), Hart-Landsberg (1993) and Chang (1994) on South Korea.

6. Stiglitz (for example, 1992) is a background reference on new-Keynesian perspectives on informational problems and financial structure. Crotty (1994) discusses post-Keynesian perspectives on uncertainty and financial fragility. Porter (1990) and Lazonick (1990, 1992) present different versions of an 'organizational capabilities' view.

7. The most influential contemporary perspective on financial instability has been developed by Minsky (for example, 1986). For various perspectives on and developments from the Minsky approach, see Fazzari and Papadimitriou (1992) and Dymski and Pollin (1994).

8. This argument is developed theoretically and empirically in Epstein and Schor (1990).

9. Following Sawyer (1994). I use the term 'industrial strategy' rather than 'industrial policy'. Sawyer draws a distinction between a broad notion that government 'can play a positive enabling role in the economy and that institutions ... can have a beneficial influence on the workings of the economy,' associated with 'industrial strategy,' and the concept of 'industrial policy' as equivalent to 'competition policy' and the as-

sociated idea that the role of policy is to eliminate market imperfections (p. 177).

10. Working with US data, Karier (1994) for example finds that tax credits to stimulate private investment are highly inefficient: only 12 per cent of the credits are actually spent on new investment. The other 82 per cent are used to pay higher dividends, buy stocks or bonds, or otherwise reduce reliance on external sources of funds. On the other hand, Stiglitz (1993, p. 5) raises concerns about credit subsidy programs because the costs are diffuse and difficult to calculate.

11. Note that the state collection of private saving also enables the state to provide deposit insurance without facing the moral hazard problem – that is, encouraging excessively risky lending practices by private intermediaries carrying government guaranteed deposits – that exists with a public deposit insurance/private intermediation system such as that in the USA. It was precisely this problem in the USA that was the proximate cause of the Savings and Loan fiasco. See Wolfson (1993).

12. Chang (1994) discusses how a combination of quantity rationing and interest rate subsidies were used in South Korea to promote the domestic machinery industry. He writes that credits were usually refused to those who wanted to import domestically available machines, and instead subsidized credits, which sometimes amounted to 90 per cent of the product value, were provided to the purchasers of domestic machinery (p. 102).

13. Bosworth, Carron and Rhyne (1987) is a basic reference on the development of federal credit programs in the USA.

14. Considering the East Asian economies, small and medium-sized firms were clearly discriminated against in their access to subsidized credit. Yet these firms did still benefit from the public credit policies as suppliers to the larger, directly subsidized firms. Moreover, in Japan and more recently in South Korea, the government also allowed small and medium-sized firms to take shelter behind legislation allowing them to cartelize. See Amsden (1989), pp. 180–4.

15. See Campen's (1993) discussion of the Community Reinvestment Act.

16. Halmi, Michie, and Milne (1994) discuss the development of the Socialists thinking on this issue from their campaign platform through the early period of the Mitterand government.

17. A range of proposals is discussed in Dymski, Epstein and Pollin (1993). The proposal to directly elect Directors of Federal Reserve Banks is developed in Pollin (1993).

18. The proposal to 'level the playing field upward' for all financial institutions is presented in D'Arista and Schlesinger (1993). Further background on the evolution of the financial regulatory structure is presented in D'Arista's (1994) extensive and important study.

19. Contrasting perspectives on the viability of comparable strategies in the UK are given by Murray (1988) and Minns (1988). The experience in Sweden since 1976 with the wage-earner fund proposed by the union economist Rudolph Meidner also offers interesting perspectives on the progressive management of pension funds. However, Meidner's

plan was an effort to extend worker ownership and control over the operations of the firm (paralleling the Block proposal in this latter aspect), in addition to influencing the broader composition of investment, the primary concern of social investment strategies in the US. See Pontusson (1994) on the political issues aroused by Meidner's proposal.

20. See, for example, Friedman (1988) on the limited capacity of standard monetary policy tools to achieve their goals.
21. Felix (1995) develops the basic arguments on behalf of 'Tobin' foreign exchange trading tax, including the position that its revenues be directed at financing the United Nations.
22. Though Bardhan and Roemer are not clear on this point, opening an economy to international competition should not be interpreted to imply an endorsement of unfettered free trade. Considering an extreme example, we would not expect an economy operating under socialist precepts to open its markets to goods produced by prison labour.
23. There is no presumption here as to which route to high productivity is more appropriate for either a technological leader or follower, though it is true that historically, voice-led systems have been associated with late developers, such as Germany, Japan, and South Korea, while the exit-led systems. in the USA and the UK, began as technological leaders. Chang (1994, esp. ch. 3) presents several reasons as to why a state-led industrial policy can be at least as effective in promoting endogenous technical innovation and long-term dynamic efficiencies. Perhaps a more fundamental issue here is that the discussion assumes that productivity gains, without reference to the composition of output, are themselves necessarily desirable. While this not the case, there is little doubt that what Nell (1992) terms a 'transformational growth path' – that is, a change in output composition that incorporates the environmental effects of production on social rates of return – is desirable, and that the means to attaining that will entail sustaining both relatively high levels and an efficient allocation of investment resources.
24. This discussion has benefited greatly from preliminary work on this question by Ilene Grabel.

References

Amsden, A. (1989) *Asia's Next Giant* (New York: Oxford University Press).
Appelbaum, E. and P. Berg (1996) 'Financial market constraints and business strategy in the U.S.', in J. Michie and J. Grieve Smith (eds) *Restoring Full Employment: Rebuilding Industrial Capacity* (Oxford University Press).
Baker, D., R. Pollin and M. Schaberg (1995) 'The case for a securities transaction excise tax', manuscript, Department of Economics, University of California-riverside.
Banfield, E. (1961) *Political Influence* (New York: Free Press).
Barber, R. and T. Ghilarducci (1993) 'Pension funds, capital market, and

the economic future', in G. Dymski, G. Epstein and R. Pollin (eds) *Transforming the U.S. Financial System: Equity and Efficiency for the 21st Century* (Armonk, NY: M.E. Sharpe) pp. 287–320.

Bardhan, P. and J. Roemer (1992) 'Market socialism: a case for rejuvenation', *Journal of Economic Perspectives*, **6**: 101–16.

Bardhan, P. and J. Roemer (eds) (1993) *Market Socialism: The Current Debate* (New York: Oxford University Press).

Berglof, E. (1990) 'Capital structure as a mechanism of control: a comparison of financial systems', in M. Aoki, B. Gustafsson and O.E. Williamson (eds) *The Firm as a Nexus of Treaties* (London: Sage) pp. 237–62.

Berle, A.A. and G.C. Means (1932) *The Modern Corporation and Private Property* (New York: Harcourt, Brace and World).

Block, F. (1992) 'Capitalism without class power', *Politics and Society*, **20**: 277–303.

Bosworth, B.P., A.S. Carron and E.H. Rhyne (1987) *The Economics of Federal Credit Programs* (Washington DC: The Brookings Institution).

Campen, J.T. (1993) 'Banks, communities and public policy', in G. Dymski, G. Epstein and R. Pollin (eds) *Transforming the U.S. Financial System: Equity and Efficiency for the 21st Century* (Armonk, NY: M.E. Sharpe) pp. 22–52.

Chang, H-J. (1994) *The Political Economy of Industrial Policy* (New York: St Martins).

Coakley, J. and L. Harris (1983) *The City of Capital: London's Role as a Financial Centre* (Oxford: Blackwell).

Cohen, J. and J. Rodgers (1993) 'Associative democracy', in P. Bardhan and J. Roemer (eds) *Market Socialism: The Current Debate* (New York: Oxford University Press) pp. 236–52.

Cox, A. (1986) 'The state, finance and industry relationship in comparative perspective', in A. Cox (ed.) *The State, Finance and Industry* (Sussex: Wheatsheaf) pp. 1–59.

Crotty, J. (1994) 'Are Keynesian uncertainty and macrotheory compatible? conventional decision making, institutional structures and conditional stability in Keynesian macromodels', in G. Dymski and R. Pollin (eds) *New Perspective in Monetary Macroeconomics: Explorations in the Tradition of Hyman P. Minsky* (Ann Arbor: University of Michigan Press).

Crotty, J. and D. Goldstein (1993) 'Do US financial markets allocate credit efficiently? The case of corporate restructuring in the 1980s', in G. Dymski, G. Epstein and R. Pollin (eds) *Transforming the U.S. Financial System: Equity and Efficiency for the 21st Century* (Armonk, NY: M.E. Sharpe) pp. 253–86.

D'Arista, J.W. (1994) *The Evolution of U.S. Finance, Vol. II* (Armonk, NY: M.E. Sharpe).

D'Arista, J.W. and T. Schlesinger (1993) 'The parallel banking system', in G. Dymski, G. Epstein and R. Pollin (eds) *Transforming the U.S. Financial System: Equity and Efficiency for the 21st Century* (Armonk, NY: M.E. Sharpe) pp. 157–200.

Dymski, G., G. Epstein and R. Pollin (eds) (1993) *Transforming the U.S. Financial System: Equity and Efficiency for the 21st Century* (Armonk, NY: M.E. Sharpe).

Dymski, G. and R. Pollin (eds) (1994) *New Perspectives in Monetary Macro-economics: Explorations in the Tradition of Hyman P. Minsky* (Ann Arbor: University of Michigan Press).

Epstein, G. and J. Schor (1990) 'Macropolicy in the rise and fall of the Golden Age', in S. Marglin and J. Schor (eds) *The Golden Age of Capitalism: Reinterpreting the Postwar Experience* (New York: Oxford University Press) pp. 126–52.

Fazzari, S. and D.P. Papadimitriou (eds) (1992) *Financial Conditions and Macroeconomic Performance: Essays in Honor of Hyman P. Minsky* (Armonk, NY: M.E. Sharpe).

Felix, D. (1995) 'The Tobin tax proposal: background, issues, and prospects', *Futures*, **27**(2): 195–208.

Fine, B. and L. Harris (1985) *The Peculiarities of the British Economy* (London: Lawrence & Wishart).

Friedman, B. (1988) 'Lessons of monetary policy from the 1980s', *Journal of Economic Perspectives*, **3**: 51–72.

Gerschenkron, A. (1962) *Economic Backwardness in Historical Perspective* (Cambridge, Mass.: Harvard University Press).

Goldstein, D. (1995) 'Financial structure and corporate behavior in Japan and the US: insulation vs. integration with speculative pressure', manuscript, Department of Economics, Allegheny College.

Grabel, I. (1996) 'Saving and the financing of productive investment: the importance of national financial complexes', in R. Pollin (ed.) *The Macroeconomics of Finance, Saving and Investment* (Ann Arbor: University of Michigan Press).

Halmi, S., J. Michie and S. Milne (1994) 'The Mitterrand experience', in J. Michie and J. Grieve Smith (eds) *Unemployment in Europe* (London: Academic) pp. 97–115.

Harris, L. (1988) 'Alternative perspective on the financial system', in L. Harris, J. Coakley, M. Croasdale and T. Evans (eds) *New Perspectives on the Financial System* (New York: Croom Helm) pp. 7–38.

Hayek, F.A. (1940) 'Socialist calculation: the competitive "solution"', *Economica*, **7**: 125–49.

Hayek, F.A. (1988) *The Fatal Conceit* (University of Chicago Press).

Hart-Landsberg, M. (1993) *The Rush to Development: Economic Change and Political Struggle in South Korea* (New York: Monthly Review Press).

Hilferding, R. (1981) *Finance Capital: A Study of the Latest Phase of Capitalist Development* (London: Routledge & Kegan Paul).

Hirschman, A.O. (1970) *Exit, Voice and Loyalty: Responses to Decline in Firms, Organizations and States* (Cambridge, Mass.: Harvard University Press).

Howard, M. and J.E. King (1994) 'Is socialism feasible? an analysis in terms of historical materialism', *Review of Political Economy*, **6**(2): 133–52.

Hutton, W. (1995) *The State We're In* (London: Cape).

Itoh, M. (1990) *The World Economic Crisis and Japanese Capitalism* (New York: St Martins).

Jacobs, M.P. (1994a) 'National financial systems, aggregate investment, and the cost of Capital', manuscript, Department of Economics, New School for Social Research.

Jacobs, M.P. (1994b) 'A cluster analysis of twelve countries' financial systems', Essay I. PhD Dissertation, New School for Social Research.

Jensen, M. (1988) 'The takeover controversy: analysis and evidence', in J. Coffee, Jr., L. Lowenstein and S. Rose-Ackerman (eds) *Knights, Raiders and Targets: The Impact of the Hostile Takeover* (New York: Oxford University Press) pp. 314–54.

Karier, J. (1994) 'Investment tax credit reconsidered: business tax incentives and investment', *Public Policy Brief No. 13*, The Jerome Levy Economics Institute of Bard College.

Kornai, J. (1993) 'Market socialism revisited', in P. Bardhan and J. Roemer (eds) *Market Socialism: The Current Debate* (New York: Oxford University Press) pp. 42–68.

Lange, O. [(1936) 1956] 'On the economic theory of socialism', in B. Lippincott (ed.) *On the Economic Theory of Socialism* (Minneapolis: University of Minnesota Press).

Lazonick, W. (1990) 'Organizational capabilities in American industry: the rise and decline of managerial capitalism', *Business and Economic History* (2nd Series) **19**: 35–54.

Lazonick, W. (1992) 'Controlling the market for corporate control: the historical significance of managerial capitalism', *Industrial and Corporate Change*, **1**(3): 445–88.

Lipietz, A. (1988) 'The limits of bank nationalization in France', in L. Harris, J. Coakley, M. Croasdale and T. Evans (eds) *New Perspectives on the Financial System* (New York: Croom Helm) pp. 389–402.

Marglin, S. and J. Schor (eds) (1990) *The Golden Age of Capitalism: Reinterpreting the Postwar Experience* (New York: Oxford University Press).

Mayer, C. (1988) 'New issues in corporate finance', *European Economic Review*, **32**: 1167–89.

McCauley, R.N. and S.A. Zimmer (1989) 'Explaining international differences in the cost of capital', *New York Federal Reserve Bank Quarterly Review* (Summer) 7–28.

Minns, R. (1988) 'Pension funds: an alternative view, in France', in L. Harris, J. Coakley, M. Croasdale and T. Evans (eds) *New Perspectives on the Financial System* (New York: Croom Helm) pp. 325–44.

Minsky, H.P. (1986) *Stabilizing an Unstable Economy* (New Haven, CT: Yale University Press).

Modigliani, F. and M. Miller (1958) 'The cost of capital, corporation finance, and the theory of investment', *American Economic Review* (June): 261–95.

Murray, R. (1988) 'Pension funds and local authority investment', in L. Harris, J. Coakley, M. Croasdale and T. Evans (eds) *New Perspectives on the Financial System* (New York: Croom Helm) pp. 306–24.

Nell, E. (1992) *Transformational Growth and Effective Demand* (London: Macmillan).

Patnaik, P. (1991) *Economics and Egalitarianism* (New Delhi: Oxford University Press).

Pollin, R. (1992) 'Destabilizing finance worsened this recession', *Challenge*, **35**(2): 17–24.

Pollin, R. (1993) 'Public credit allocation through the Federal Reserve:

why it is needed; how it should be done', in G. Dymski, G. Epstein and R. Pollin (eds) *Transforming the U.S. Financial System: Equity and Efficiency for the 21st Century* (Armonk, NY: M.E. Sharpe) pp. 321–54.

Pontusson, J. (1994) 'Sweden: after the Golden Age', in P. Anderson and P. Camiller (eds) *Mapping the West European Left* (London: Verso) pp. 23–53.

Porter, M. (1990) *The Competitive Advantage of Nations* (New York: Free Press).

Porter, M. (1992) *Capital Choice: Changing the Way America Invests in Industry* (Washington, DC: Council on Competitiveness).

Poterba, J. and L. Summers (1992) 'Time horizons of American firms: new evidence from a survey of CEOs', manuscript, Department of Economics, Massachusetts Institute of Technology.

Roemer, J.E. (1994) *A Future for Socialism* (Cambridge, Mass.: Harvard University Press).

Roland, G. and K. Sekkat (1993) 'Market socialism and the managerial labour market', in P. Bardhan and J. Roemer (eds) *Market Socialism: The Current Debate* (New York: Oxford University Press) pp. 204–18.

Rybczynski, T.M. (1984) 'Industrial finance systems in Europe, US and Japan', *Journal of Economic Behavior and Organization*, 5(3–4): 275–86.

Sawyer, M. (1994) 'Industrial strategy and employment in Europe', in J. Michie and J. Grieve Smith (eds) *Unemployment in Europe* (London: Academic) pp. 177–87.

Shaw, E.S. (1973) *Financial Deepening in Economic Development* (New York: Oxford University Press).

Stiglitz, J.E. (1992) 'Banks vs. markets as mechanisms for allocating and coordinating investment', in J.A. Roumasset and S. Barr (eds) *The Economics of Cooperation: East Asian Development and the Case for Pro-Market Intervention* (Boulder, Colo.: Westview) pp. 15–38.

Stiglitz, J.E. (1993) 'The role of the state in financial markets', manuscript, Department of Economics, Stanford University.

Swary, I. and B. Topf (1992) *Global Financial Deregulation: Commercial Banking at the Crossroads* (Cambridge, Mass.: Blackwell).

Wolfson, M.H. (1993) 'The evolution of the financial system and the possibilities for reform', in G. Dymski, G. Epstein and R. Pollin (eds) *Transforming the U.S. Financial System: Equity and Efficiency for the 21st Century* (Armonk, NY: M.E. Sharpe) pp. 133–56.

Woodward, R. (1994) *The Agenda* (New York: Simon & Schuster).

World Bank (1993) *The East Asian Miracle: Economic Growth and Public Policy* (New York: Oxford University Press).

Zysman, J. (1983) *Government, Markets and Growth: Financial Systems and the Politics of Industrial Change* (Ithaca, NY: Cornell University Press).

5 Financial Markets, the State and Economic Development: Controversies within Theory and Policy

Ilene Grabel

5.1 INTRODUCTION[1]

One of the most significant global economic developments of the past 20 years has been the liberalization of financial markets. Many developed countries, like the USA and the UK, undertook policy reform in the 1980s to free financial markets from what were seen to be onerous government regulations. But the most dramatic liberalization programmes have occurred in developing countries. Financial liberalization swept first through the Southern Cone countries of South America in the mid-to-late 1970s, then to Central American, East Asian and Southern European countries, and even more recently to former socialist countries. The recent promotion of stock markets exemplifies the trend toward continued adoption of market-mediated financial systems in developing and former socialist countries.

The theoretical foundations of this kind of reform were laid in 1973 by the complementary works of McKinnon and Shaw. What became known as the 'McKinnon–Shaw hypothesis' proved to be immediately and immensely influential. By the early 1980s market-led financial systems had supplanted state-led systems in many developing countries. The results of these experiments were dramatic. Within five years of their initial liberalization measures, countries in the Southern Cone of South America experienced severe financial and macroeconomic difficulties. With soaring interest rates, waves of bank failures and other bankruptcies, extreme asset price volatility and extensive loan defaults, the real sector entered deep and prolonged recessions. Widespread loan defaults and bank distress necessitated massive bailouts of struggling financial institutions (see Diaz-Alejandro, 1985; Ramos, 1986a; Gonzales-Arrieta, 1988; Cho and Khatkhate, 1989; McKinnon, 1989). While these events seemed to call into question the liberalization prescription, orthodox theorists remained committed to it. Rather, in what will be called 'neoclassical revisionism', these theorists modified the original thesis to take account of what they now recognized as troublesome attributes of developing country economies (see McKinnon, 1973, 1988, 1989, 1991; see also Balassa, 1990–1: Kapur, 1992; Galbis, 1993). These attributes were seen to require careful sequencing of policy reform, and careful attention to the broader macroeconomic environment within which they were to be undertaken. Through these *post hoc* theoretical extensions, the liberalization prescription was seen to be defended against the disappointing empirical record.

Financial liberalization has not been uncontested, however. In the wake of economic crisis, neostructuralists began to interrogate the central conclusions of the orthodoxy (see, for example, Taylor, 1983, 1991).[2] Neostructuralists argue that financial liberalization can induce stagflation and a reduction in available credit.

Is the neoclassical or the neostructuralist account of the macroeconomic consequences of financial liberalization in general, and the calamitous record of countries that undertook these policies in particular sufficient? And does either approach provide a compelling theoretical foundation for the continued pursuit of market-led financial arrangements in developing and former socialist countries today?

This chapter argues that these two approaches fail on both accounts. It provides an alternative approach, informed by post-Keynesian theory, that better captures the macroeconomic dynamics associated with financial liberalization. It will be shown that the latter introduces new opportunities for disruptive speculative financial activity, and intense pressures that ensure that these opportunities will be exploited. These practices are likely to introduce just the kinds of macroeconomic effects that have been in evidence in many of the countries that have undertaken liberalization. The central contention of this chapter is that the present orthodox direction of financial policy in developing and former socialist countries is misguided when judged against the developmental imperatives facing these countries.

These matters will be approached in the following manner. Sections 5.2 and 5.3 investigate in some detail the orthodox and neostructuralists positions *vis-à-vis* financial liberalization in developing countries. Two themes will emerge in this discussion. The first is that neither neoclassical nor neostructuralist theory develops an adequate theoretical or empirical basis for a defence or critique (respectively) of financial liberalization programmes in developing countries. This failure extends as well to the more recent discussions of stock markets. The second theme is that both neoclassical and neostructuralist theories are marked by an ambivalence concerning the degree to which the financial sector should be insulated from state interventions via regulation.[3] Section 5.4 will develop a post-Keynesian account that incorporates central Keynesian insights regarding the contradictions of market-based financial mediation.

The final section (section 5.5) will present some thoughts about the kinds of alternative policy prescriptions that are consistent with this theoretical approach. Notably, these prescriptions will run counter to the market mentality that has come to inform theory and policy in recent decades.

5.2   ORTHODOX REVISIONISM: MAINTAINING THE MARKET'S PRIMACY

Financial reformers in the early 1970s called for a complete and immediate liberalization of developing country financial markets. Financially repressive policies had been widely adopted as part of import-substitution industrialization strategies of the 1950s and 1960s. Financial repression generally involved some combination of controls on interest and foreign exchange rates and credit allocation, state imposition of non-interest bearing reserve requirements, various legislative obstacles to the development of financial markets (such as equity markets), and controls on inward and outward capital movements.

These policies were seen by neoclassical theorists to have a number of adverse consequences. First, financial repression retarded savings, forcing the self-financing of investment. Low savings also discouraged financial intermediation, encouraged capital flight, and induced a bias in favour of current consumption. All of these impeded economic growth. Second, financial repression induced a fragmentation of domestic financial markets and undermined their allocative efficiency. Politically connected borrowers gained access to low-cost credit in formal regulated markets, while disenfranchised borrowers were squeezed into unregulated 'curb' markets at high interest rates.

Early Reform Efforts

If these were the problems, the solution followed directly – financial markets were to be liberalized. A comprehensive financial liberalization programme would include abolishing interest rate ceilings, deepening financial markets and diversifying available instruments, eliminating the reserve requirement tax, fixed exchange rates and capital controls, unifying capital markets, and ensuring that conditions of competitiveness and free entry prevailed in the financial system (Fry, 1995). Although the term 'financial liberalization' is used to refer to a multi-faceted reform programme, the literature in the 1970s to early 1980s focuses on but one issue, namely the salutary effects of allowing interest rates on loans and deposits to rise to their competitive free-market rate.

The seminal works of McKinnon (1973) and Shaw (1973) were bold programmatic statements calling for nothing less than immediate and complete financial liberalization.[4] Liberalized competitive financial markets are seen as a necessary condition for the efficient allocation of funds across diverse investment projects (McKinnon, 1991; Rybczynski, 1984). Liberalized competitive financial markets entail an arms-length relationship between lenders, financial intermediaries and borrowers – that is, one that is strictly mediated by the market rather than by extra-market institutional linkages (see Lazonick, 1991). Profit-seeking behaviour in such markets encourages financial innovation associated with a proliferation of financial instruments (and markets and instruments to trade them). In this way, innovation perfects the market, inducing financial deepening by providing participants with a growing array of products and opportunities for risk-diversification. The resulting liquidity of these markets also implies a rapid (approaching instantaneous) price adjustment mechanism, so that these markets approximate the Walrasian ideal in a way that sluggish goods markets generally do not.

The Experiment

Under the banner of the new free-market orthodoxy, the campaign to liberate developing country financial markets gathered momentum. These prescriptions were adopted quite readily, and guided financial policy in many developing countries from the mid-1970s through the early-1980s.

The most ambitious and widely assessed financial liberalization experiments were carried out in the Southern Cone countries of Uruguay (1973–83), Chile (1974/5–83), and Argentina (1976/7–83).[5] Implementation differed across countries with respect to the sequence of liberalization. For example, Chile liberalized trade prior to finance, while Uruguay liberalized in the reverse order. In each of these cases, however, full financial liberalization occurred swiftly, ranging from several months to less than two years. Rarely are social scientists afforded a laboratory in which to test their hypotheses. But in a space of 10 years, McKinnon–Shaw witnessed several thorough practical tests of the financial liberalization hypothesis.

Unfortunately for the reformers, the Southern Cone financial liberalization experiments of the 1970s and early 1980s largely failed to deliver the rewards promised by their proponents (see Akyüz, 1983: Fischer and Reisen, 1993; Foxley, 1983: de Melo and Tybout, 1986, p. 581; Diaz-Alejandro, 1985; Ramos, 1986a). The financial liberalization experiments did indeed induce structural shifts in saving and investment behaviour, but not in the manner predicted by McKinnon–Shaw. This period was marked by extremely high real interest rates (Balassa, 1990–1; Galbis, 1993). Ramos (1986b) reports that real deposit rates peaked at 9, 29 and 27 per cent in Chile, Argentina, and Uruguay, respectively, while real lending rates in these countries peaked at 27, 127, and 40 per cent. These data presented new theoretical questions: did these interest rates simply reflect the incredible surfeit of profitable opportunities in Southern Cone nations?[6] And if so, were they the harbinger of an incipient economic miracle?

Several theoretical attempts to explain this trend in interest rates emerged. On the demand side, some have argued that regulated financial markets repressed borrowing and not saving (Ramos, 1986b, p. 18). Thus, financial liberalization unleashed a massive pent-up demand for credit by households and firms that was not offset by a comparable increase in the savings rate. Loan rates rose as households used credit to finance the purchase of consumer durables,

and firms plunged into speculative investment with the assurance
that government bail-outs would prevent bank distress in the event
of defaults (Akyüz, 1993; Ffrench-Davis, 1993; Diaz-Alejandro, 1985,
p. 16; Ramos, 1986b). On the supply side, extremely high loan and
default rates were attributed to the practices of banks under conditions of financial liberalization. As the number of non-perform-
ing loans increased, banks increased the deposit rate in order to
attract new funds (Akyüz, 1993; Corbo, de Melo, and Tybout, 1986,
p. 629). Lending rates, in turn, were raised in step with increases
in deposit rates. In the absence of any supervision of lending practices, banks were able to increase deposit and loan rates in efforts
to compensate for losses attributable to loan defaults (Ramos, 1986a).

In contrast to the McKinnon–Shaw prescription, high real interest
rates failed to act as a magnet for domestic savings or a boon to
investment (Akyüz, 1993). Total private domestic savings and
investment (as a proportion of GNP) actually fell during this period
(Diaz-Alejandro, 1985; Ramos, 1986a, 1986b). The only type of
'savings' that did increase sharply was foreign savings (that is,
external debt) (de Melo and Tybout, 1986, p. 569; Ramos, 1986b,
p. 8).[7] Of course, neoliberal policy-makers were not surprised by
the dramatic increase in foreign savings brought about by the adoption
of 'appropriate' macroeconomic policies. These capital inflows were
expected to promote economic growth. In reality, though, foreign
savings proved to be a Trojan horse. Opening the economy to foreign
savings inflows appears to have amplified the dependence on this
source of funds rather than ensure the long-run viability of the
experiment. Liberalized economies became more vulnerable to external interest rate shocks given that the majority of external loans
were at variable rates (Ramos, 1986a, p. 101). As external debt-
service obligations grew, the groundwork was laid for the debt crisis
of the 1980s and 1990s (Akyüz, 1993; Calvo, 1986, p. 515).

Domestic debt levels increased as well. Financial liberalization
does appear to have increased firms' access to loanable funds. Large
firms with links to banks and international contacts gained increased
access to cheap dollar-denominated debt, while small firms increased
their leverage through new access to high-cost debt denominated
in domestic currency (McKinnon, 1984: Calvo, 1986; Ramos, 1986a).
In this respect financial markets stubbornly refused to be reformed:
financial liberalization succeeded in resolving the fragmentation of
domestic financial markets only to displace it internationally. And,
now purged of 'political influences', financial markets nevertheless

continued to operate' inefficiently' in that private patronage and cronyism continued to influence credit allocation, especially dollar-denominated credit to members of large industrial conglomerates called grupos (Burkett and Dutt, 1991; Ffrench-Davis, 1993; Taylor, 1994).

Financial liberalization also failed to create functionally efficient financial systems in the sense of providing credit to long-term productive investment (Tobin, 1984). Rather, banks allocated credit to firms that assumed risky financial structures and engaged in short-term speculative activities. When these highly leveraged firms began to experience distress, the stage was set for widespread banking crises and economic collapse (Diaz-Alejandro, 1985; Akyüz, 1993).

When the collapse of the newly liberalized financial systems did occur in the mid-1980s, governments intervened in order to contain the negative externalities (Ramos, 1986a). Ironically, the end of the three neoliberal experiences was 'accompanied, if not caused, by the collapse of the very financial system they had created' (Ramos, 1986b, p. 2).

Revisionism, Round One: Sequencing Reform

In the wake of these difficulties, neoclassical economists began a self-critical assessment of the feasibility of the McKinnon–Shaw prescription (see McKinnon, 1989). They concluded that sudden liberalization was not viable. A consensus emerged that a 'second-best' strategy had to be found, one that was more attuned to the particular features of developing country economies. Neoclassical theorists (including McKinnon himself – see 1989, 1991), began to incorporate new developments in macroeconomic theory – which focused on the uniqueness of financial markets – into their *ex post* assessments of the neoliberal experiences. First, they came to see that very high real interest rates could exacerbate problems of moral hazard and adverse selection in lending, thereby inducing financial (and macroeconomic) instability (Balassa, 1990–1; Galbis, 1993; 1991; Sundararajan and Balino, 1991). Second, they recognized that conflicts might arise between different aspects of the reform programmes, with the effect of disrupting the real sector during financial liberalization (Sachs, 1988).

By the mid-1980s, neoclassical theory also reflected the insight that financial markets were unique in their ability to adjust instantaneously to changes in sentiments, information, etc. Goods markets, on the other hand, were seen to fall short of the textbook model, as they adjusted sluggishly from one equilibrium to another. The models of Edwards (1987, 1989), Frenkel (1983), and McKinnon (1989, 1991) (among others) reflect this insight through the incorporation of different adjustment parameters for the financial and goods markets. Thus, given these differences, financial markets could be reformed *in the same manner and in the same instance* as other markets. Instead, a broad-based programme of economic reform had to be sequenced. Successful reform of the real sector came to be seen as a prerequisite for financial reform: firewalls – in the form of temporary financial repression – had to be maintained during the first stage of economic liberalization in order to insulate the economy from financial disruptions.[8]

But this insight about divergent adjustment speeds produced another: namely, that *different aspects of reform programmes may work at cross-purposes*. This conflict has been termed the 'competition of instruments' (Sachs, 1988). For present purposes the most important competition of instruments relates to the relationship among capital inflows, changes in the real exchange rate, and current account conditions. The real currency appreciation generated by the opening of the capital account undermines the competitiveness of domestic goods, causing a deterioration of the current account.[9]

The second-best liberalization strategy requires that trade liberalization occur in the context of an appropriate degree of temporary financial repression (Edwards, 1987, 1989; World Bank, 1989; McKinnon, 1991; Fischer and Reisen, 1993). During a transition period following trade liberalization, the capital account is to be managed through the retention of capital controls (especially limiting inflows). Finally, the capital account is to be opened only after domestic financial markets have been liberalized (Edwards, 1987).[10]

Revisionism, Round Two: Reforming the Policy Environment

The financial liberalization prescription was modified further in the mid to late-1980s to take into account the policy environment in which liberalization is to occur (Frenkel, 1983; Khan and Zahler, 1985; Corbo and de Melo, 1987; Srivastava, 1987). This new focus is manifested in discussions of the appropriate macroeconomic conditions for liberalization. Of particular importance is the determination whether the liberalization programme is *credible and consistent*.

Unfortunately, the credibility and consistency of a liberalization programme is not easily assessed. At issue is the perceptions of the economic actors in the affected economy concerning the viability of the proposal (Srivastava, 1987; Edwards, 1989; Agenor and Taylor, 1992). An *in*credible or *in*consistent liberalization programme is one that the public believes is likely to be reversed. Such policies are likely to be sabotaged, as the public engages in behaviour (for example, capital flight) which undermines the success of the programme.[11]

The new preoccupation with credibility and consistency of the financial liberalization programme has certain affinities with the old 'financial repression as distortion' argument. But there is a new twist. Informed by New Classical economics, rational agents are now understood to take into account *all available* information when forming expectations about the future, *including the likelihood of policy reversal or collapse*. This current New Classical focus is apparent in the incorporation of a variable which serves as a proxy for policy credibility. In the face of in-credible policy, rational agents will fail to react to market signals in the manner prescribed by traditional neoclassical theory.

How could economic policy be developed in this new, complex environment, in which the success of policy depends critically on agents' perceptions of its viability? There seemed to be two choices: one could shade policy toward existing popular sentiments; or, one could implement 'correct' policy, one which respected the principles of neoclassical theory. The former option was ruled out of court on the simple grounds that incorrect policy could not possibly retain credibility in the wake of the disruptions that would inevitably attend it. The latter, on the other hand, would induce credibility as it proved itself uniquely capable of promoting development, even if it were unpopular in the short run. Hence, a correctly-specified policy would impel rational agents to act 'properly', at once achieving growth and the credibility necessary to sustain itself. On this account, financial liberalization could only be credibly implemented in an economy in which government budget deficits are closed, inflation is tamed, and in which exchange rates reflect economic fundamentals (Lal, 1987; McKinnon, 1991, ch. 3).

The Case for Stock Markets

Today, the most obvious sign of financial liberalization is the rapid promotion of stock markets in countries where they did not previously exist and their deepening in those countries where they predated liberalization efforts.[12]

Most neoclassical commentators have argued that the growth in stock markets has been an unmitigated benefit for developing and former socialist countries. Je Cho (1986) and Levine (1990) argue that stock markets are a co-requisite of successful financial liberalization. In these accounts, equity markets are seen to supplement the scant domestic finance available from banks, governments and corporate retained earnings (Drake, 1985; Je Cho, 1986; Levine, 1990, 1996; Mullin, 1993).

Je Cho (1986) and Levine (1990, 1996) also argue that stock market-based finance is superior to bank-based and government-based finance because of its risk sharing and liquidity attributes. In addition, stock market-based allocations are seen to have efficiency advantages in that the 'arms-length' nature of well-functioning stock markets precludes the rent seeking, moral hazard and informational problems that are inherent in bank-based and government-based allocations. The efficiency of stock market-based finance is also understood to translate into superior macroeconomic outcomes, namely, increased investment efficiency. The efficiency of this market is due in part to its liquidity and the related ability of share holders to influence corporate managers through the 'threat of continual auction,' thereby 'punishing' firms with higher borrowing costs where managers underperform (Manne, 1965).

From a neoclassical perspective, the increase in financial deepening associated with stock market activity should also decrease financial market volatility by increasing the numbers of both investors and tradeable shares, and by encouraging the increased production and dissemination of reliable information via the increased profit opportunities available to investors. Furthermore, even if stock trading does lead to an increase in volatility, the capital asset pricing model (Merton, 1980) suggests that increases in volatility would not impair macroeconomic performance provided that stock returns incorporate appropriate risk premia (that is, that markets are efficient) (Chou, Engle and Kane, 1992).

A final benefit of stock market promotion is that it is seen to integrate developing and former socialist countries into the international financial system (Mullin, 1993). Thus, the financial openness that is associated with foreign equity purchases enhances available investment finance and encourages international financial integration.[13]

Assessing the Neoclassical Case

The financial liberalization hypothesis has encountered substantial empirical difficulties, as noted above, and these difficulties spawned the revisionism we have seen. But it is not at all clear that the sequencing and credibility revisions overcome the kinds of empirical challenges that emerged in the wake of financial liberalization. For example, the evidence on the relationship between real interest and savings rates in developing countries is ambiguous at best (Gonzales Arrieta, 1988; Khatkhate, 1988; Warman and Thirlwall, 1994), and completely unsubstantiated at worst (Dornbusch and Reynoso, 1989; Akyüz, 1993; Burkett and Lotspeich, 1993). One study, by Shafik and Jalali (1991), finds that high interest rates have had a positive effect on growth in developed countries, but a negative effect on developing country growth. A second (Ostry and Reinhart, 1995) finds that high interest rates do not have a significant effect on household savings in low-income countries. A third, by Dornbusch and Reynoso (1989), concludes that the posited correlations between financial deepening and economic growth, between real interest rates and investment, and between real deposit rates and economic growth lack any empirical substantiation (see also Bienefeld, 1992).

Sequencing has not seemed to solve these problems. Chile liberalized finance only after having liberalized trade. But as previously discussed, the Chilean experience was hardly successful (see Lal, 1987). In this case, the problems associated with the competition of instruments was merely postponed until completion of the full liberalization programme. Reverse sequencing – in which financial liberalization precedes trade liberalization – has not, however, proven to be more robust. For example, Uruguay followed this path (over a short period of time), with results markedly similar to the Chilean experience. It is reasonable to enquire, then, whether the problem is not in the sequence but in the very nature of the liberalization programme.

Section 5.4 below will develop an alternative, post-Keynesian account which will identify the disruptive effects of financial liberalization. More immediately, we can take note of important new-Keynesian insights that might also shed some light on the difficulties that have attended financial liberalization.

The neoclassical case is predicated on the notion that the unregulated financial market represents the paradigmatic case of the perfectly and instantaneously adjusting market. The observed price in this market is therefore the equilibrium price: by definition, this must be the optimal price, regardless of its level. But new-Keynesian theory reaches a different conclusion – that because financial markets depart in essential ways from the Walrasian ideal, the market equilibrium price might not be optimal. Specifically, financial markets are seen to be characterized by unique imperfections associated with information and enforcement problems, and these problems are amplified at high equilibrium interest rates. For example, high interest rates exacerbate the problems of moral hazard and adverse selection, as 'good' borrowers are squeezed out of the market. High rates may therefore lead to a deterioration in the quality of the economy's aggregate investment portfolio, and may also contribute to borrower and bank distress and financial crisis (Rittenberg, 1990; Sundarajan and Balino, 1991; Bienefeld, 1992; Grabel, 1995a). The parallels between these predictions and actual events in the Southern Cone and the Philippines is indeed striking. To date these insights have been incorporated into neoclassical work on financial liberalization only in the form of cautionary notes regarding the need to prevent interest rates from rising too high, especially before a set of prudent domestic banking regulations have been implemented (see Balassa, 1990–1; Galbis, 1993; McKinnon, 1991). As with empirical difficulties, then, sequencing is offered as the means to handle this theoretical challenge. But if the new-Keynesian insights are correct, it is difficult to see how appropriate sequencing might resolve the matter: sequencing, after all, was predicated on the assumption that the financial market (unlike the goods market) approached the Walrasian ideal. The new-Keynesian perspective, in contrast, suggests that the instantaneous price adjustment in this market (which neoclassical celebrate) actually exacerbates the lender risk in the face of moral hazard and adverse selection. In the face of these imperfections, a second-best situation would seem to be one in which the financial market adjustments were actually *more sluggish*.

The credibility argument is likewise suspect. If one rejects the premise that expectations of agents are uniformly derived from the same economic model, then it becomes apparent that the effects of a financial liberalization programme are exceedingly difficult to predict. Acting on expectations formed under different models, economic agents will pursue behaviours that generate unpredictable macroeconomic outcomes (see Frydman and Phelps, 1983).

But things are more complicated still. Even were one to grant the strong New Classical presumption of rational expectations, the assumption that economic agents could assign the identical, correct probability distribution to the likelihood of policy failure is implausible in the case of a unique policy reform. The non-recurrent nature of financial liberalization affords no basis for applying past learning: hence, agents might be expected to form diverse and inconsistent subjective probability distributions regarding policy reversal or collapse (see Lucas, 1973; Agenor and Taylor, 1992). But this dispersion of expectations complicates greatly any evaluation of policy credibility, and hence, about a policy's likelihood of success. These complications are simply ignored in the credibility extension to the financial liberalization hypothesis.

Moreover, while a proposition which states that credible policies are more likely to succeed seems innocuous enough, it has a dark side, especially in the political context in which financial liberalization was introduced during the 1970s in the Southern Cone. In short, the thesis can be reduced to a simple set of propositions:

1. economic policy will garner credibility only to the degree that it is likely to survive;
2. an economic policy is likely to survive only to the degree that it attains its stated objectives;
3. an economic policy is likely to attain its stated objectives only to the degree that it reflects and operationalizes the *true* theory of market economies;
4. a policy reflects the true theory of market economies only to the degree that it is *neoclassical*.

The exclusionary, dissent-suppressing manoeuvre that has been undertaken here is captured in propositions three and four. Alternative economic theories are banned on the grounds that they could not possibly meet the unforgiving 'credibility' test, because they could not possibly be true. Hence, policy regimes founded upon them must collapse, with deleterious social and economic consequences.

Notice what is absent from this account: in the context of authoritarian rule in the target countries, the neoclassicals imputed credibility to policies based on their own, true theories, rather than on the collective will of the disenfranchised citizenry. In a deft manoeuvre, the neoclassicals installed themselves as the omniscient, benevolent despot, the theoretical counterpart to the very real despots whom they counselled, issuing decrees for the betterment of their subjects. Of dissent, the best that could be said is that it threatened to disrupt the credibility of the instituted policies (by undermining confidence in them), jeopardizing the entire 'liberal' policy regime. In both these respects – the theoretical and the political – the credibility thesis as developed in the literature bars the plurality of views and denies the value of dissent, both hallmarks of liberal democratic society.

5.3 THE NEOSTRUCTURALIST RESPONSE: AMBIGUITY ON MARKETS

While neoclassicals began to introduce the sequencing and credibility caveats to the financial liberalization prescription during the 1980s, dissent was simultaneously launched from outside this paradigm. The neostructuralist paradigm attempted to capitalize on the insights of the structuralists of the 1950s and 1960s, in order to challenge neoclassical theory's hold on development policy (Toye, 1987; Lustig, 1991; Sunkel, 1993).

Building Blocks of the Critique

Several assumptions of neostructuralist theory bear directly on its critique of the neoclassical theory of financial liberalization:

- as a consequence of markup pricing, increased interest rates and higher import costs are likely to lead to higher prices (and real wage reductions) and a lower level of economic activity;
- profit-receiving households allocate their assets among a portfolio of inflation hedges, bank deposits in the formal banking sector, and curb market deposits;[14]
- banks in the formal sector are subject to a fixed required-reserve ratio. Banks in the curb market, on the other hand, are not subject to government regulation. The neostructuralist theorists further assume that, but for those borrowers who are squeezed out of the formal market, borrowers and savers have access to the formal banking system and the curb market, and funds are shifted between these two markets;
- in the curb market the free market nominal interest rate adjusts perfectly to equate demand for and supply of credit.

The Curb Market

In the neostructuralist view, the incorporation of the curb market into evaluations of financial liberalization programmes cements the relevance of the paradigm as against neoclassical economic theory. But this aspect of neostructuralist theory remains aporiatic. Since the curb market is at the heart of the neostructuralist critique of financial liberalization, it warrants special attention.

Neostructuralist theory places great significance on the lack of state regulation of curb market institutions. The absence of state-imposed reserve requirements is assumed to imply a greater 'efficiency' of curb market institutions in terms of loan creation for a given deposit base as compared to formal financial institutions.[15] It is generally assumed by neostructuralist theorists that these banks lend out all of their deposits, providing 'one-for-one intermediation, whereas (formal sector) banks provide only partial intermediation' (van Wijnbergen, 1983a, pp. 438–9; see also Taylor, 1983, pp. 92, 100; van Wijnbergen, 1983b, p. 434; Buffie, 1984, p. 312).

Curb markets are also understood to be 'competitive and agile' (Taylor, 1983, p. 92) in responding to unmet demands for loanable funds, particularly in regard to the need for short-term credit (for example, in relation to the harvest cycle).[16] These latter attributes are seen to be manifested in the *allocational* efficiency (in the Walrasian sense) of curb market institutions. Curb market institutions are also seen to be *informationally* efficient, demonstrating an impressive degree of sophistication in lending practices. Finally, numerous studies of the curb market find that the relationship-based nature of lending in these markets, along with social and community pressures for repayment, accounts for the very low levels of loan defaults in this market (Rahman and Wahid, 1992; Otero and Rhyne, 1994). This suggests that the uniqueness of curb lending arrangements provides a means to overcome some of the problems that new-Keynesians argue are inherent in lending.

Financial Liberalization: the Verdict

Neostructuralist theory weighs in with a verdict on financial liberalization that is opposite to that reached by neoclassical theory. In the neostructuralist literature, the growth-impeding consequences of financial liberalization are accounted for in three ways (Arida, 1986).

Interest Rate Effects

The loan rate of interest increases in both formal and curb markets in tandem with financial liberalization.[17] This increase in the loan rate has both supply-side and demand-side effects. An increase in the loan rate has a cost-push effect on the price level. Financial market segmentation exacerbates these cost-push pressures (Foxley, 1983, p. 166) as firms in the curb market are assumed to face even higher capital costs. The consequences of this shock are amplified, in the neostructuralist view, by the highly debt-dependent nature of production in developing countries. An increase in borrowing costs also has important demand-side effects which contribute to the creation of a stagflationary spiral. Lower real wages and higher borrowing costs reduce aggregate demand, inducing firms to decrease their inventories and reduce production (Foxley, 1983, p. 169). Theoretically, the decline in aggregate demand might offset these inflationary pressures so that a new lower equilibrium level of output (at a higher price level) is reached. But the neostructuralist focus on supply rigidities and bottlenecks in developing countries yields the conclusion that the supply-side inflationary price effects of higher borrowing costs dominate the demand-side deflationary effects causing a stagflationary dynamic and a deteriorating distribution of income.

Hedge Effect

The success of the neoclassical policy prescription hinges on the substitution of hedge assets for bank deposits. In the neoclassical view, higher interest rates are the necessary and sufficient condition to bring about this reallocation of household assets. Neostructuralist theorists counter with the 'French peasant syndrome', arguing that risk-averse investors may fail to substitute hedge assets for bank deposits when deposit rates rise. This is particularly likely in countries where confidence in financial institutions may be lacking. If this substitution fails to obtain, financial liberalization will fail to stimulate an increase in savings, investment, and growth.

Curb Effect

The most important aspect of the neostructuralist case against financial liberalization turns on its assumptions involving portfolio reallocation and the curb market. Neostructuralist theorists expect the increase in formal sector deposit rates that stem from financial liberalization to induce a portfolio shift by households from curb market deposits to formal sector deposit accounts[18] (Taylor, 1983; van Wijnbergen, 1983a, 1983b; Buffie, 1984, p. 312). This shift, in turn, decreases the degree of financial intermediation for a given deposit base, because of the greater loan creation efficiency of curb lenders.

Of course higher interest rates may at the same time stimulate a broad-based portfolio reallocation, thereby drawing not only curb deposits but also hedge assets, domestic currency holdings, and foreign holdings into formal sector deposit accounts. While this possibility is recognized by Buffie (1984, p. 312) and van Wijnbergen (1983b. pp. 439–44), they argue that any increase in loanable funds that may derive from these reallocations is more than likely to the offset by the reduced intermediation offered by formal sector deposit accounts.

Financial liberalization, then, has two negative effects that contradict the neoclassical prescription:

1. the total supply of loanable funds is reduced (even in the long run) by the portfolio shift to formal sector deposit accounts;
2. the curb market lending rate increases as the deposit base in this market declines following financial liberalization.

The increase in the curb market rate follows from the neostructuralist assumption that the curb market rate adjusts perfectly to equilibrate the supply and demand for loanable funds. Thus, *as long as formal sector banks provide less intermediation than curb markets and the portfolio shift is as expected*, an increase in the curb market rate and decreases in the total supply of loanable funds and investment combine to touch-off a stagflationary spiral. In this sense, financial liberalization is equivalent to contractionary monetary policy (van Wijnbergen, 1983b; Buffie, 1984).

Assessing the Neostructuralist Critique

Although neostructuralist theory attempts to develop a theoretical analysis which is subversive of the neoclassical programme, it fails to develop a clearly articulated oppositional programme which, one expects, would involve alternative conceptualizations of both financial market efficiency and regulation. Its silence on the matter of alternative financial market organization, combined with theoretical conundrums (to be discussed), leaves this paradigm in an ambiguous position *vis-à-vis* neoclassical conclusions regarding the dynamism and allocational efficiency of market-mediated finance. Two factors undermine the neostructuralist case against financial liberalization. First, despite the analytical weight assigned to it, the hedge effect has not been empirically substantiated (Ghate, 1992, pp. 868–9). In the absence of the hedge effect, the credit-reducing aspects of the portfolio reallocation from curb to formal sector accounts may be offset by an increase in total savings following an increase in the deposit rate. Under these circumstances, the increase in total formal-sector saving may counteract the switch to formal-sector deposit accounts which are assumed to offer less financial intermediation. The neostructuralist argument may very well obtain in the short run, then, but may be contradicted by medium-run and long-run increases in total savings, especially as savers gain confidence in the liberalized formal banking sector (Buffie, 1984; see also Fry, 1995).

Second, the critical neostructuralist assumption regarding the efficiency advantages of the curb market – on which much else hinges – likewise has not been unambiguously substantiated. The evidence to date indicates heterogeneity across curb markets. Some empirical research supports the claim that curb lenders may self-impose substantial reserve requirements (Balassa, 1990–1, p. 62; Je Cho, 1990; Ghate, 1992, pp. 868–9; Kapur, 1992). Indeed, in order to maintain depositor confidence in the face of market volatility and in the absence of public deposit insurance, curb banks may self-impose reserve requirements that are as high, or higher, than formal sector banks (Je Cho, 1990, p. 479). If this is the case, the assumed portfolio reallocation stimulated by financial liberalization will not reduce the total supply of credit. But it is also conceivable that the self-imposed reserve requirement may be lower in the curb market, as Christensen (1993) suggests. Because curb lenders face a different clientele – one that has been squeezed out of the formal market by quantity rationing of credit – and because curb lenders do not give their depositors the freedom to withdraw deposits at any time (Christensen, 1993), it is plausible that their role as 'lender of last resort' may give them considerable latitude to operate with minimal reserves.

In any event, it is obvious that the curb market is not as homogeneous as many neostructuralist theorists seem to claim. At any given time, there are a variety of curb market institutions having varying degree of intermediation and required reserve ratios (Owen and Solis-Fallas, 1989; Ghate, 1992). In founding their *theoretical* attack on an *empirically* unsubstantiated characteristic of curb lending, the neostructuralist critique of financial liberalization loses much of its power.

The superiority of curb markets is also assumed to be manifested in their 'competitive and agile' adjustment to market conditions. This would imply, of course, that the curb market lending rate increases in the face of increases in the formal sector rates due to the siphoning of deposits from the former to the latter. Equilibrating the supply of loanable funds available to it with the demand it faces, curb lenders are presumed to raise lending rates when formal rates rise (Buffie, 1984; van Wijnbergen, 1983a; Taylor, 1983, ch. 5). But the empirical evidence on the relationship between formal and curb rates suggests that this relationship is tenuous, at best (Fry, 1995), and counter to the neostructuralist assumption, at worst (Callier, 1990; Ghate, 1992, pp. 866–7). For example, a study of curb markets in India finds that curb rates are unaffected by increases in formal lending rates (Timberg and Aiyar, 1984). But this empirical evidence ought not be surprising. For in the discussion of curb market dynamics following financial liberalization, the neostructuralist theorists have isolated only one side of the market, *the supply side*. Once we take account of the *decreased demand for credit* in the curb market following financial liberalization, we see immediately that the trend for curb market rates is *indeterminate*, depending on the relative magnitude of the shift in supply and demand, relative elasticities and so on. Hence, financial liberalization might induce rising, constant, or declining curb market rates – vitiating the necessity of the neostructuralist conclusion concerning stagflation.

In summary, the neostructuralist critique of financial liberalization is largely based on empirical generalizations that are nevertheless unsubstantiated. In addition, certain of its strictly theoretical criticisms are undeveloped and inconclusive. The theorization of the portfolio reallocation and the curb market serve particularly to frustrate the critique.

Stepping back from the specifics of the theory, we arrive at a far-reaching shortcoming of the neostructuralist critique of financial liberalization. Neostructuralist theory appears most incomplete in its failure to develop an alternative to market-mediated financial systems (embodied in a financial policy programme).[19] Here, the thrust of the neostructuralist critique of financial liberalization, embodied in its treatment of the curb market, appears to undermine its own opposition to neoclassical theory. Indeed, it is not clear how its apparent glorification of the unregulated curb market translate into alternative conceptions of financial market efficiency and financial policy. Out of this silence (generally), and, from the idealization of the curb market (in particular), one may infer a residual idealization of the free market that even its neoclassical antagonists would surely find comforting. As we have seen, many neostructuralist theorists write as *if* they hold up the *un*fettered, *un*regulated, thoroughly *un*-repressed curb market as the most efficient allocator of credit.[20]

What is at stake, then, between these two paradigms? In the end, both appear to hope for the developing countries' transition to mature market-mediated financial systems. For neoclassical theory, the ground can only be prepared for the reign of the market by the market itself. Intervening political measures, no matter their intention, distort development by sending the wrong signals to market participants. For neostructuralist theory, in contrast, conditions for free financial markets can only be prepared by a series of unspecified government policies designed to overcome rigidities, bottlenecks, and supply-side shortages. Its quarrel with neoclassical theory on this point has to do with the latter's failure to recognize how financial liberalization actually interferes with the operation of the curb market. This paradoxical commonalty is obscured only by the silences in the neostructuralist corpus.

To be fair, in the context of the broader neostructuralist paradigm this goal of generalizing the free market seems unlikely. But the underdevelopment of its critique of financial liberalization, coupled with its theoretical treatment of the curb market, is suggestive of fundamental ambiguities in the theoretical foundation. Such a foundation is a poor basis for critical theory and for the development of financial policy. For example, it is difficult to ascertain the relationship between Taylor's critique of financial liberalization with his Minskyian accounts of financial fragility (Taylor and O'Connell, 1985; Taylor, 1994, 1991). Moreover, the relationship between Ffrench-Davis (1993) – who develops a broadly defined neostructuralist case for state-centric 'development from within' – and the neostructuralist view of curb markets is by no means obvious. This ambiguity carries over to the neostructuralist treatment of stock market-based finance in developing countries. To date, the most prominent neostructuralist critics of financial liberalization have had little to say about the matter. And when they have, such as in Taylor (1991, 1994), the critique draws more explicitly on the work of Minsky and other post-Keynesians than on the central precepts of neostructuralist theory.

5.4   A POST-KEYNESIAN REJECTION OF MARKET-MEDIATED FINANCE

I have argued above that neoclassical theory and the neostructuralist response fail to develop a convincing set of arguments, respectively, for or against financial liberalization in developing countries. In the case of neoclassical theory, financial liberalization programmes – *now properly specified and implemented* – are assumed to have no significant or long-term deleterious consequences for these countries. This continued faith in the model seems particularly inappropriate in the wake of the low levels of productive investment, savings and growth, high levels of risky investments, and the financial crises and government bailouts of financial institutions that have attended financial liberalization experiments throughout the developing world.

The neostructuralist case against the neoclassical financial liberalization prescription, on the other hand, is undermined by theoretical underdevelopment and aporia, as well as by empirical indeterminacies. To their credit, neostructuralists have created space for criticisms of financial liberalization programmes in their recognition that macroeconomic instability and non-Walrasian equilibria may attend adjustment programmes. These latter insights, however, remain largely unexplored within the neostructuralist corpus, and (with few exceptions) have not served as a theoretical basis for their critique of financial liberalization. It is my intention to extend these and other insights in developing an alternative post-Keynesian understanding of financial liberalization.

Recently Post-Keynesian (and Kaleckian and Marxian) interpretations of financial liberalization experiences in developing countries have emerged (for example, Burkett, 1987; Dutt, 1990–1; Burkett and Dutt, 1991; Akyüz, 1993; Studdart, 1993). These accounts acknowledge that unproductive investment may be fuelled by financial liberalization (for example, Dutt, 1990–1, pp. 229–30). But this insight is under-exploited, as the focus of this work is instead on the effective demand and distributional problems that may attend financial liberalization. While these effective demand and real sector problems are no doubt important (and valid), this does not address the central financial concerns raised here. Hence, the following is intended to complement earlier post-Keynesian and Kaleckian treatments of financial liberalization.

A formal critique of financial liberalization must begin with a consideration of the potential obstacles to real sector development and macroeconomic stability posed by the attempt to create neoclassically-efficient liberalized financial systems. Specifically, these obstacles are the volume and composition of investment projects that are likely to be undertaken in the wake of financial liberalization and the concomitant creation of a fragile financial structure with attendant real sector effects. Rather than claiming that liberalization impedes growth *per se* (as do neostructuralists), I argue that financial liberalization can lead to a particular *kind* of development, that I have elsewhere termed 'speculation-led development' (Grabel, 1995a). Speculation-led development is characterized by a preponderance of risky investment practices, shaky financial structures, and ultimately by lower rates of real-sector growth than would prevail in the absence of liberalization. Thus, the creation of neoclassically-efficient financial systems – rather than the failure to do so – introduces the problem of speculation-led development. I argue further that stock market activity in developing and former socialist countries exacerbates speculation-led development.

Speculation-led Development

The deleterious macroeconomic effects of financial liberalization are an outcome of the pressures and incentives that are introduced by the changed regulatory and institutional environment of the financial sector. The mutually reinforcing effects of what are termed 'expectations-induced' and 'competition-coerced'[21] pressures contribute to the increased presence of short-term, high-risk speculative transactions in the economy and to the increased vulnerability to financial crisis.

Expectations-induced pressures to pursue speculative transactions obtain on both the demand and supply sides of financial markets. These stem from the availability of new types of instruments, markets, financing opportunities and projects that are introduced by the institutional innovations associated with financial liberalization. In the context of the boom-euphoric expectations that are likely to prevail following financial liberalization, these new projects are apt to be attractive to agents on both the demand and supply sides of financial markets.

Opportunities and Pressures to Speculate

Liberalized financial markets are especially prone to speculation and short-term trading of assets on secondary and tertiary markets (see Carter, 1991–2). Indeed, enhancing financial market liquidity and providing opportunities for greater risk sharing via the creation of new markets and instruments is one *raison d'être* for liberalization programmes. Investors are encouraged to part with capital by virtue of the apparent security afforded by the high degree of liquidity available in 'deep' financial markets (Keynes, 1964). Financial instruments afford the apparent protection of instantaneous withdrawal of funds by transforming illiquid real-sector investments in plant and equipment into financial claims that can trade hands as quickly as the institutional and technological structures permit. This liquidity also allows each investor to shuffle ownership among competing assets in response to changes in moods, rumours, and so on. The ability to 'churn' assets in this way, coupled with the ability to move out of all such instruments for money, provides a degree of apparent security to the financial investor that is not available to the industrial corporation that has undertaken long-term capital investment.

The liquidity of financial markets also amplifies the tendency for changes in market valuations. The creation of neoclassically-efficient financial markets – that is, the creation of markets in which financial asset prices rapidly reflect changes in market sentiment and information (whether it is accurate or not) – introduces opportunities for investors to capitalize on the very market volatility that is created by efficient financial markets. In such markets the rewards for successful financial trading can be immediate and large. The successful investor can realize substantial gains by anticipating (or even better, influencing) future sentiments of other market participants. Indeed, the proliferation of liquid financial instruments expands these opportunities, as they expand the possibilities for the churning of assets within financial portfolios. Every change of sentiment creates new opportunities to outguess the market, to buy the favoured instrument the day before other market participants reshuffle their assets.

A corollary of these opportunities, of course, is the diminution of the duration of financial 'commitments'. The relative independence of financial-asset values from underlying 'fundamentals' imparts an extreme variability to these values. Indeed, the successful financial investor need be little concerned with the long-term profitability of the firms whose equities she buys and sells (especially, of course, to the degree that new forms of instruments appear that bundle equities of diverse corporations, or that depend on future commodity valuations, and so on) (Keynes, 1964, ch. 12).

But these same attributes ensure that market participants will be driven to shorten their time horizons for defensive purposes as well. The same forces that reward the player who anticipates market behaviour penalizes severely the investor who lags behind, who acts only after a new mood or hunch has materialized in the market. The laggard is forcibly reminded that the apparent security which extreme liquidity provides for any individual investor to flee to money evaporates in the context of a general flight. The net effect may be to punish the investor who takes a long-term view. Thus, in efficient, volatile, financial markets a short-time horizon may be the most prudent one.

The dramatic changes heralded by financial liberalization, moreover, represent a regime shift of the sort that is likely to be associated with ruptures in the structure of conventional wisdom regarding investment risk.[22] Under such circumstances, market participants look out on an as yet unlived 'new era' which promises greater reward and lower risk. Thus, a more sanguine evaluation of speculative projects may be expectations-induced. In this manner, these projects can come to play a more important role in overall economic activity.

The preponderance of these speculative activities in the context of buoyant expectations about their profitability on the part of borrowers, lenders and investors has been a universally noted phenomenon in the Southern Cone, Philippine, Indonesian, Malaysian and Turkish financial liberalization experiments (see Diaz-Alejandro, 1985; Ramos, 1986a; Cho and Khatkhate, 1989; World Bank, 1989; Rittenberg, 1990; Sundararajan and Balino, 1991; Akyüz, 1993). These occurrences are reflected in run-ups in stock and real estate price indexes and the growth in Ponzi and secondary and tertiary-type investment activities during these experiences.

Competition-coerced Speculation

Combined with this expectations-induced move toward speculative projects, there is likely to be an element of competition-coerced profit-seeking among agents on the demand and supply sides of financial markets (following financial liberalization).

On the demand side, financial and erstwhile non-financial corporations, ranging (for example) from insurance to industrial manufacturing enterprises, may feel compelled to chase the higher returns apparently available through financial speculation, and they may come to divert resources from their primary activities to the financial arena. Such practices may be seen by corporate managers either as a substitute for the corporation's traditional economic activity, or indeed as a strategy designed to enhance the firm's financial position precisely to further its competitive position within its traditional sector. In either event, a critical manifestation of the new mood among market participants is increasing borrowing to finance short-term financial speculation. The net effect of these demand-side changes is a preponderance of speculative activities.

On the supply side of financial markets, lenders and investors are also likely to be affected by the increased competitive pressures unleashed by financial liberalization (Keynes, 1964; Minsky, 1986). A financial institution that does not validate these new speculative activities in the context of a boom may face slower growth of its capital base and a loss of market share. Financial institutions are compelled to finance investment projects and to reduce their reserve margins in ways that might be unacceptable in a less competitive climate. In this context, even formerly 'prudent' financial institutions may be impelled toward speculative financing. These institutions may also be driven to abandon financing of real-sector activities.[23]

These market pressures are also reflected *internally* in firms in what Crotty (1994) terms the 'asymmetric reward structure'. In the context of financial institutions, the asymmetric reward structure means that lenders/money managers are 'rewarded' for riding speculative waves and indeed are compelled to engage in these activities in order to cement their institutional positions. Additionally, implicit or explicit government bailouts of failed financial institutions may provide an additional incentive for adventurism by lenders (and even borrowers) during the boom.

In summary, the regime shift to financial liberalization is likely to induce increasing speculative activity. Thus, speculation-led development is a likely outcome of the 'success' of financial liberalization in constructing a liberalized, competitive and efficient financial system. This outcome is consistent with the actual experiences of developing countries with financial liberalization.

Consequences of Speculation-led Economic Development

There are several likely consequences of the speculation-led development that is induced by financial liberalization. The first is that the economy is forced to bear a greater degree of 'ambient' risk than it would in the absence of financial liberalization, as a result of the growth of speculative projects (cf Snowden, 1987; DeLong, Shleifer, Summers, and Waldmann [DSSW], 1989, p. 681). This may reduce the total volume of real-sector investment with concomitant multiplier effects on economic activity (cf Federer, 1993), while exerting upward pressure on interest rates in order to compensate lenders for increasing risk (DSSW, 1989, p. 687). This increase in the economy's ambient level of risk during developing country financial liberalization experiments in the 1970s and 1980s may be one factor accounting for the decline in overall investment in this period.

The second likely consequence of speculation-led development is that the economy becomes more susceptible to financial crises, with disruptive spillover effects in the real sector (see DSSW, 1989, p. 687). A variety of 'surprise' macroeconomic events (for example, a sudden rise in interest rates) can ultimately threaten the fragile financial structure, leading to bank distress and loan defaults (Wolfson, 1986). In this context, expectations regarding profitability may head south, and banks may cut back on lending accordingly, inaugurating a 'credit crunch'. It is in this manner that the real sector is forced to pay a high price for financial liberalization (Minsky, 1986). The wave of bank collapses and lending cutbacks that marked the end of most developing country financial liberalization experiments (especially in the Southern Cone) may be a case in point (see Sundararajan and Balino, 1991).

Third, the economy may be forced to bear an increase in what Bhagwati (1982) terms 'directly unproductive profit-seeking' (DUP) activity. Even if one concedes the neoclassical view that speculation is both privately profitable and price stabilizing, speculative activities may nevertheless be resource-wasting in the short run as long as real resources are expended on garnering returns from speculation (see Kemp and Sinn, 1990). If the social costs outweigh the private gains from speculation, then these activities may be conceptualized as DUPs (in Bhagwati's sense), since they do not directly increase the flow of new goods and services in the short run.[24] Contra neoclassical political economy, removing the government from financial markets *may induce new DUPs as private sector agents expend resources in seeking out profitable opportunities for speculative trading.* This rise in the proportion of DUP to non-DUP activity has been widely noted in the case of the actual developing country financial liberalization experiences (Diaz-Alejandro, 1985; Ramos, 1986a; Cho and Khatkhate, 1989).

The post-Keynesian recognition of the possibility of unemployed resources in an economy may lead to the conclusion that DUP activity – which promotes increased aggregate demand – is not altogether undesirable. But we should be mindful that a DUP-dependent regime creates economic interests that are not likely to disappear on cue with the attainment of full employment. Hence, the macroeconomy becomes more wasteful precisely as it tends towards full employment. Moreover, if we are concerned with the character of resource use as well as its level, as we should be, then we should seek regimes that minimize the role of DUPs in periods of under and full employment.

A fourth and final consequence is that credit and investment capital may be misallocated to the detriment of long-term economic growth. If expectations-induced and competition-coerced pressures lead to the allocation of an increasing share of finance to speculative activities, then long-term real sector investment may suffer. In this sense, finance may be misdirected, and the conditions for long-term economic growth in developing countries may be undermined.

Speculation-led Development and Stock Market Promotion

Perhaps no institutional innovation reflects the aim of creating neoclassically-efficient financial systems in developing countries more than the current trend of stock market promotion. From a post-Keynesian perspective it is clear that the sanguine claims of stock market proponents are misguided.

Against the claims of stock market proponents (for example, Drake, 1985; Je Cho, 1986; Levine, 1990, 1996), recent comparative studies have concluded that in countries with highly developed stock markets (such as the USA and UK), only a small proportion of new investment is financed by these markets.[25] Not only do stock markets fail to provide a significant volume of external finance for new investment, but the finance provided is relatively expensive (Stiglitz, 1992) and short-term.

The short-term nature of stock market-based finance has important implications for the character and time horizon of the investment undertaken.[26] When rapid portfolio turnover predominates in the absence of effective countervailing extra-market institutional mechanisms (see below), the threat of continuous auction compels managers to attend to the maximization of current market value of the expense of potentially rewarding long-term, high-cost investment strategies (Corbett and Mayer, 1991; Crotty and Goldstein, 1993).[27]

To the extent that such threats become manifest, such that these concerns enter into firms' decisions, the composition of aggregate economic activity may be decisively affected. Stock market-based finance in the context of a liberalized financial system may expose industrial enterprises to the volatility of highly liquid stock markets, and engender an excessive and detrimental preoccupation with short-term returns at the expense of long-term performance. At a minimum it should be recognized that the operation of highly liquid financial markets may aggravate a tension between short-run financial practices and forward-looking investment strategies, resulting in a shortening of the time horizon of the investment projects undertaken and the pursuit of seemingly more profitable speculative transactions as against investment.

From a post-Keynesian perspective, whether, and to what degree expanded stock markets are a boom or impediment to real-sector growth and stability in developing and former socialist countries also depends on the level of volatility they exhibit: markets with frequent and severe price swings might be much more apt to induce short-term speculative investment practices and might also be more likely to induce broader macroeconomic instability (see Grabel, 1995b). Volatility may be expected to result from the quickened pace of financial transactions which neoclassically-efficient, liquid stock markets allow. Moreover, volatility may be self-exacerbating: volatility forces investors to shorten their time horizons for both offensive (profit-seeking) and defensive (loss-minimizing) reasons, with the paradoxical effect of inducing increased volatility. The implies that an increase in market volatility may lead to reductions in real-sector investment activities (Keynes, 1964, ch. 12; Singh, 1993).

Increasing volatility might also have deleterious effects on the macroeconomy via increasing financial fragility. This could dampen overall economic activity, and in the event of an exogenous shock (such as an unexpected increase in the interest rate), could lead to forced asset sales and a cumulative debt-deflation. In sum, the success of stock markets (and of financial liberalization programmes, more generally) in introducing mechanisms of rapid asset price adjustment may introduce increased volatility into the economy and may, as a consequence, undermine macroeconomic stability and/or distort the nature of economic growth.

In keeping with the broader financial liberalization prescription, many developing and former socialist countries today are promoting stock markets as a means of securing capital inflows. But this success at attracting portfolio investment, and hence of successfully pursuing increased financial integration, comes at a high price – a price that is largely unacknowledged by stock market proponents.[28] External inflows of highly liquid, volatile portfolio investment represent an additional source of financial market volatility, introducing yet another means by which financial volatility may have negative spillover effects on the macroeconomy.

This 'increased risk potential' (Grabel, 1996b) stems from the combined effects of stock market liquidity and international financial integration. Liquidity and financial openness are preconditions for portfolio investment inflows, but, at the same time, these conditions provide investors with an international 'exit' option that, if exercised, can give rise to financial crisis and cross-border contagion. While these risks are endemic to portfolio investment in all countries, investors may be more prone to exit suddenly from developing and former socialist country financial markets given the greater perceived risk in such markets (associated, for example, with political and exchange-rate risks).

Not only is the risk potential of portfolio investment greater in developing and former socialist countries, but its realization is also more costly to the economy. In capital scarce countries, large, sudden withdrawals of portfolio investment may threaten the viability of domestic investment as available financing is reduced. Furthermore, under floating exchange rates, such a withdrawal of portfolio investment may trigger (or exacerbate) a nominal and real depreciation of the domestic currency in the likely event that the government does not have foreign exchange reserves sufficient to stabilize the currency value.[29] These circumstances are likely to threaten the stability of the macroeconomy, and may trigger a broad-ranging financial crisis (as recent Mexican experience suggests).[30] In the event that financial crisis does obtain, the macroeconomy and vulnerable segments of the citizenry ultimately bear the costs of the austerity measures generally taken in the wake of crisis (Taylor, 1991). In addition, Grabel (1996b) argues that a dependence on portfolio investment inflows may exacerbate already existing problems of 'constrained policy autonomy'. As with other forms of capital inflows, portfolio investment entails restrictions on host country autonomy, although its constraining effects are indirect. Countries that become dependent on portfolio investment inflows need to maintain policies that secure investor confidence and rentier rewards. Chief among these is deflationary macroeconomic policy. Foreign investors may be especially concerned that macroeconomic policy be contractionary in order to offset concerns about currency and inflation risks in developing countries. In a world in which even the poorest countries have open capital markets offering highly liquid investment opportunities, investors may 'discipline' what they view as errant (that is, pro-growth) policy-makers through portfolio reallocation.[31] This threat of flight constitutes a powerful *ex ante* constraint on macroeconomic policy.

In addition to the *ex ante* constraint on policy autonomy, there is the possibility of an ex post constraint as well. This may obtain if, in the advent of financial crises, the government is compelled to adopt measures aimed at reversing or stemming the outflow of portfolio investment. These measures would likely involve intensification of the policies initially pursued in efforts to market the economy as an attractive site for portfolio investment. Therefore, the constraints that obtain in the context of a crisis may exacerbate the pro-investor policy bias with detrimental effects on vulnerable groups (as recent Mexican experience again suggests). In the particular case of developing countries, an economic crisis is likely to mean that foreign governments or multilateral institutions are called upon to offer assistance. Such assistance introduces a further constraint on policy autonomy.

5.5 A POST-KEYNESIAN FINANCIAL REFORM AGENDA

The practical implications of the post-Keynesian case against financial liberalization programmes in developing and former socialist countries remain to be explored. At the broadest level, the post-Keynesian view concludes that efforts to enhance financial system efficiency in the neoclassical sense have a number of adverse effects. The macroeconomy is made more volatile and short-term speculative transactions are rendered more attractive than long-term investment activities. As a consequence, the vulnerability to financial crises is enhanced. The character of economic activity is distorted due to the growth in speculative transactions and the need to orient macroeconomic policy around investor rather than growth objectives. The most general *negative* policy implication of this work, then, is that financial reform projects in developing and former socialist countries should not aim to create neoclassically-efficient financial systems.

Financial reform efforts should be guided by developmental imperatives and other social objectives. In practice, this means that governments in developing and former socialist countries should slow or counteract the trend toward creating financial systems that are entirely market mediated. To the extent that fostering economic development is a goal of financial policy, reform efforts must be guided by a vision of creating a financial system that is above all functionally efficient, and not just one that creates opportunities for high-stakes gambling. Stated simply: finance should be placed in the service of productive investment (Callier and Mayer, 1989; Ffrench-Davis, 1993).

While identifying a specific financial policy programme for developing and former socialist countries is outside the scope of this chapter, I will identify three broad directions for financial policy reform that are consistent with the arguments made thus far.

Encouraging State-mediated Financial Intermediation

It is critical for post-Keynesians to reclaim – rhetorically and practically – the case for the developmental benefits of state-mediated financial flows. This may involve elevating the importance of both banks and governments in financial intermediation. The successful industrialization of continental European countries such as France, Germany and Switzerland and of Asian countries such as Japan, South Korea and Taiwan all involved a large degree of state influence over financial sector decision-making and, more generally, rested on state-imposed constraints over the autonomy of the financial sector.[32] And, despite the World Bank's recent revisionist analysis of the lessons of the East Asian successes, the consensus view on East Asian development confirms that state control over finance was central to the achievements of these developmental states (see Amsden, 1989; Hart-Landsberg, 1991; Chang, 1993). More specifically, ensuring that finance be harnessed to play developmental objectives would involve the creation of public development or industrial banks. A post-Keynesian financial reform agenda should focus on identifying the mandate and financing arrangements of these institutions. The mandate of these development banks should be to operate in a functionally efficient manner, that is to provide stable, long-term sources of finance to the types of investments that are critical to long-term economic development (such as infrastructure and manufacturing). These development banks should be the institutional counterpart of the industrial policies and public investment programmes that are critical components of economic development, especially for 'late development' as the Japanese and South Korean experiences suggest.[33] The successful operation of development banks would ensure that the objectives of industrial policy and public investment programmes are not frustrated by a lack of finance at attractive terms. Moreover, evidence from East Asia and continental Europe suggests that there is no prima facie reason why development banks can not be managed and regulated effectively, as has been established by numerous comparative finance studies.[34]

National governments and multilateral institutions should provide finance for development banks. Depending on particular institutional characteristics, in some cases it may be feasible to have the state own outright these development banks (as in South Korea). In others, state influence over the allocative decisions of these institutions may be sufficient (as in Japan). There is also a role for state direction or negotiation of some of the decisions of privately-owned development banks. This can occur through a variety of 'market-compatible' incentive programmes, including government loan guarantees and/or mechanisms to diffuse lending risk. The latter might entail, for example, government-sponsored private lending consortia as in Germany or Japan. In any event, comparative experience suggests that there are myriad ways in which states can intervene directly and indirectly in financial intermediation in order to ensure that finance serves productive aims.[35]

Dampening the Market-mediated Financial Sector

There are essentially two avenues by which the existent private, market-mediated financial sector could be made less problematic from the perspective of developmental objectives. Either avenue could be compatible with a financial system comprising both market- and state-mediated finance.

The first type of reform involves the creation of proscriptions on the reach, depth and behaviour of financial markets. For example, such measures might dampen the growth, liquidity and volatility of financial markets, while insulating the real economy from disruptions emanating in the financial sector. This could be accomplished by slowing the pace of financial innovation and the rate at which new types of secondary and tertiary markets are introduced. Mechanisms might also be designed to make the market-mediated component of the financial sector more sluggish, less volatile and hence *less efficient* in terms of asset price adjustments. Restrictions on portfolio churning, taxes on assets sales, and 'circuit breakers' designed to call a halt to trading during periods of high volatility might achieve this objective.

Alternatively, a second type of reform could be pursued that changes the institutional context (and attendant incentive structure) in which market-mediated finance operates. In particular, the objective of insulating real sector investment from the vagaries of volatile stock markets would be served through the proposal discussed above – the creation of strong development banks. In economies with development or, as they are often called, 'industrial' banks (like Japan, Germany, and South Korea), financial intermediation tends to take on a much longer time horizon than that found in systems lacking these institutions, like the USA and UK. Industrial banks serve as 'committed investors,' and lending officers in these banks exhibit far more patience than do financiers in the latter countries (Grabel, 1996a). Directly involved in corporate management and planning, these banks agree to provide funding for long-term investment projects that they expect will be mutually beneficial in the long run, if not immediately. Corporate managers can therefore afford to adopt longer time horizons.

The presence of these banks therefore has two immediate effects. Because they tend to extend loans over long periods, they serve to dampen volatility in financial markets. But more importantly, they insulate industrial corporations from financial volatility when it does occur. Together, these promote long time horizons on the part of lenders and investors, and thereby promote a degree of functional efficiency not found in systems lacking such institutions. It is especially noteworthy that in financial systems where industrial banks (or some type of state-mediated finance) operate successfully, stock markets do not exhibit the volatility and short-termism traditionally associated with their operation. Equity financing in such economies, such as Japan, Germany, and South Korea, tends also to be of a 'committed nature', in that majority shareholders – usually institutional investors and/or industrial banks themselves – tend to refrain from churning their stockholdings. This commitment on the part of majority stockholders is not primarily due to the existence of proscriptions on short-term trading, but rather to the fact that large stockholders are often the same institutions that have made long-term loans to the corporation. Even when other (minority) stockholders engage in active stock trading, industrial corporations remain buffered from financial turbulence. It must be emphasized, then, that stock markets *per se* are not functionally inefficient: it is the matrix of institutions and incentives that obtain in the broader financial system that determines whether or not stock markets (and liberalized finance) undermine functional efficiency.

Dampening Financial Openness[36]

The previous discussion of stock markets in developing and former socialist countries suggests that the combined effects of liquidity and financial openness render portfolio investment inflows a problematic panacea to the problem of capital scarcity. If portfolio investment is to be encouraged at all, policymakers would be advised to *manage* aggressively portfolio investment, even at the risk that such management will reduce the overall volume of inflows.

Management of portfolio investment itself may take a variety of forms. The most extreme measure would involve outright restrictions on openness in the form of stringent capital controls, especially aimed at outflows (see Crotty and Epstein, 1996). These measures might be in the spirit of Keynes' (1933) prescriptions. Given that any individual country today undertaking such measures would be placed at a relative disadvantage, such measures would have to be pursued on a regional or South–South basis (see, for example, Taylor, 1991).

The inevitability and immutability of openness should not be accepted. Multilateral organizations like the UN and the OECD are bucking the celebration of openness. They are today discussing the viability and desirability of dampening openness and the hyper-liquidity of capital markets (see Fischer and Reisen, 1993, UNDP, 1994). For example, a recent OECD sponsored study of financial openness makes a case for the 'late' removal of capital controls in developing countries (Fischer and Reisen, 1993). What precisely constitutes 'late' removal is a bit unclear, but the study presents the achievement of sound government finances and an appropriate institutional and regulatory structure for financial sector supervision as preconditions. Obviously, given these preconditions, many developing and former socialist countries today appear to be good candidates for capital controls.

The successful use of stringent capital controls by South Korea and Japan during their periods of rapid economic development is instructive in this regard. The consensus in the literature on East Asian development confirms that capital controls were an integral part of the achievements of these developmental states (for example, Amsden, 1989; Hart-Landsberg, 1993). During Japanese industri-alization, for example, there was an outright prohibition on foreign ownership of securities and equities. In South Korea, violations of prohibitions on overseas capital transfers were particularly strong (Amsden, 1989, p. 17). Alternatively, volume- or price-based re-strictions on purchases and sales of portfolio investment may be used to manage portfolio investment and to slow the pace of flight during crises. Similarly, the implementation of 'circuit breakers' would accomplish the same aim. A variety of measures aimed at dampen-ing financial market volatility and encouraging (foreign or all) in-vestors to lengthen their time horizons are currently in place in some developing countries (see *The Economist*, 4 August 1995). For example, in Colombia foreign investors are free to engage in (less-liquid) direct investment, but are precluded from purchasing debt instruments and are discouraged from purchasing corporate equity. In Chile, foreign portfolio investors are required to keep their cash in the country for at least one year.

It is also possible to use the tax system in order to dampen port-folio investment liquidity and to provide some compensation for the costs of liquidity. This uniform, global transaction or 'Tobin' tax has been taken up recently by the UN and several prominent development economists (Tobin, 1978; Felix, 1993; Singh, 1993; UNDP, 1994, p. 70).[37] Felix (1993), for example, proposes that the proceeds of such a globally imposed transactions tax of around 0.5–1 per cent could be collected by national authorities over residents within their jurisdiction. The proceeds of this tax would be transferred to a central fund controlled by the IMF or the World Bank and used for long-term relending to developing countries. In this regard, it is instructive to note that nearly all OECD countries today (excepting the USA) already have transaction taxes in place.[38] Moreover, as Felix (1993) points out, there are already a variety of measures in place globally or within the G7 countries that establish a framework for supranational policy or economic co-operation. These range from agreements to share tax information, to co-ordinate macroeconomic policy, and to impose uniform capital standards and bank regulation.

Finance and Development: Some Final Remarks

This chapter has developed a post-Keynesian account of the problems associated with the extension of neoclassically-efficient, liberalized financial systems in developing and former socialist countries. It has attempted to demonstrate that this approach offers a more coherent explanation of the effects of financial liberalization than those offered by the revisionist neoclassical and neostructuralist perspectives.

These three perspectives embrace different notions of efficiency, as we have seen. For neoclassical theory, the creation of an efficient financial system presupposes mechanisms of rapid price adjustment and arms-length financial intermediation. It has been shown, however, that these reforms are apt to distort economic development, giving rise to speculation-led development. Neostructuralist theory is ambivalent with respect to the meaning of financial sector efficiency, but tends towards a focus on the level of deposit-creation for a given deposit base. In contrast, this paper adopts the criterion of functional efficiency as the chief criterion against which financial reform projects should be adjudicated.

In keeping with the latter criterion, the paper has advanced a variety of policy reforms. All of the policy measures outlined here are costly in some respect, to be sure. For example, portfolio investment inflows may be discouraged by measures aimed at reducing market liquidity or trading activity. Similarly, introducing or revitalizing development banks may cause political problems as powerful multilateral institutions and financial sector actors are likely to oppose state encroachment into finance. But if the arguments presented here are correct, these costs may be minimal when weighed against the costs of pursuing further financial liberalization.

Notes

1. Reactions to this paper by Philip Arestis and Malcolm Sawyer greatly improved the work. The careful comments on an earlier version of the paper by Paul Burkett, James Crotty, George DeMartino, Gerald Epstein, Alan Gilbert, Robert Pollin, J. Mohan Rao and Don Richards are also very much appreciated. Michael Herrmann provided excellent research assistance.
2. Note that the term neostructuralist will be used throughout to refer to the work both of structuralist (for example, Taylor, 1983, 1991) and neo-structuralist theorists (for example, Buffie, 1984). There are no important conceptual differences between these two approaches in regards to the theory of financial liberalization.
3. These two points are developed briefly in Grabel (1994).
4. A related literature on the relationship between the level of financial development and various macroeconomic indicators continues to be tested extensively as well (Gerschenkron, 1962; Goldsmith, 1969; Schumpeter, 1977). For a heterodox treatment of this issue, see Arestis and Demetriades (1994). For an orthodox treatment, see King and Levine (1993).
5. See Akyütz and Held (1993), Fischer and Reisen (1993), Galbis (1993), Haggard, Lee and Maxfield (1993), Ramos (1986a) and Sundararajan and Balino (1991).
6. Note that McKinnon (1973, ch. 6) makes passing reference to the problem of lending at very high interest rates (as early as 1973), but he does not address this issue clearly in his early work. I thank Paul Burkett for this point.
7. Note that others provided more optimistic interpretations of the experiment. These observers assert that financial liberalization led to higher savings, financial deepening, higher levels of financial intermediation, and an improved efficiency of investment (Balassa, 1990–1). These cases overlook the significant foreign debt component of private savings, and the role of increased currency substitution or 'dollarization' of Southern Cone economies in measures of financial deepening.
8. Southern Cone countries did in fact sequence the liberalization of their financial and goods markets in various ways. But these theorists now argued that the process had nevertheless been too abrupt and premature to overcome these adjustment problems (McKinnon, 1991).
9. This problem is termed the Dutch-disease effect.
10. See Lal (1987) for an opposing view.
11. See Bruno (1993), Calvo (1986) and essays in Williamson (1994).

12. Mullin (1993) is an excellent survey of these markets. See also Levine (1996), Littler and Maalouf (1996) and the annual issue of the International Finance Corporation's emerging stock markets factbook.
13. In section 5.4 I respond critically from a Post-Keynesian perspective to the neoclassical case for stock market promotion. I argue that the introduction or deepening of these markets exacerbates the problems that arise from liberalized finance.
14. Given its informal character, the size of the curb market is difficult to assess. Some investigations have suggested that in some countries (or regions) the curb market may supply as much funds as the formal banking system. Empirical estimates of the magnitude of the curb market are provided in Callier (1990), Tang (1995), Timberg and Aiyar (1984) and World Bank (1989, ch. 8). Christensen (1993) and Ghate (1992) review the recent empirical research on curb markets.
15. Note that the assumption of a zero reserve requirement is widely held in the neostructuralist literature. The greater loan-creation efficiency of curb lenders would be retained even if the assumption were weakened, such that curb lenders self imposed a reserve requirement, provided that it was lower than that imposed on formal institutions. A recent study of curb lenders by Christensen (1993) finds that their self-imposed reserve requirements are indeed lower than those faced by formal lenders. Both the strong and the weak forms of the reserve requirement assumption have been questioned recently in the literature (see below).
16. There is an extensive literature that focuses on exploring the niche filled by curb lenders in developing countries. For example, research by Callier (1990) and Christensen (1993) finds that curb lenders play an important role in providing credit to disenfranchised borrowers (and do so with minimum operating costs and an impressive degree of efficiency). But they argue that these institutions do not have sufficient resources to finance significant amounts of investment. By contrast, other studies of curb lenders have found that in some countries (such as Taiwan) a large proportion of overall investment is financed by curb lenders (Otero and Ryhne, 1994; Tang, 1995).
17. The curb market adjustment mechanism requires some explanation (see below).
18. van Wijnbergen writes that the 'results obtained by McKinnon . . . depend crucially on one hidden assumption on asset market structure, an assumption that is never stated explicitly: all these authors assume that the portfolio shift into time deposits is coming out of an "unproductive" asset like gold, cash . . . This seems an overly drastic simplification of the financial structure of LDCs' (1983b, p. 434). van Wijnbergen argues that by failing to 'take into account curb market loans which provide more rather than less intermediation than the banking system,' neoclassical theorists are able to assume that the portfolio reallocation following financial liberalization unambiguously results in an increase in the total supply of loanable funds and therefore an increase in economic activity (pp. 434, 440).

19. An important exception is Ffrench-Davis (1993) who does develop some general views on alternative neostructuralist-inspired macroeconomic policies.
20. Note that Je Cho (1990) advances the argument that the neostructuralist treatment of the curb market implies that this theoretical project does not in any fundamental way depart from that of neoclassical theory. In his view, the neostructuralist opposition to financial liberalization is then a false opposition. This argument is *not* being made here.
21. The term competition-coerced is borrowed from Crotty (1993).
22. This point is explicit in the work of the previously cited post-Keynesians.
23. In the Southern Cone financial liberalization experiments an additional factor leading to the validation of borrowers' adventurism was the existence of *grupos* (see Burkett and Dutt, 1991).
24. This is especially the case when the majority of financial trading is in the secondary rather than the new issues market. Whether the increased income that may emanate from DUP activity in the short run eventually results in higher levels of productive activity is unclear. Under a financial liberalization regime it is not at all evident that the increased income flowing from DUPs will be expended on non-DUP (that is, productive) activities such as manufacturing.
25. For example, see Akyüz (1993), Corbett (1990), Cox (1986), Goldstein (1995), Pollin (1996), Stiglitz (1992) and Zysman (1983). For an extensive discussion, see Grabel (1996a).
26. The following two paragraphs draw heavily on Grabel (1996a).
27. Note that in the context of the preponderance of long-term financial commitments by equity owners this threat of auction might very well commit managers to long-term goals including, for example, the maximization of future income streams and technological innovation.
28. The following arguments are developed in Grabel (1996b). See also Singh (1993).
29. Of course flight may both cause real currency depreciations and be triggered by real currency depreciations (or expectations thereof) (see for example Taylor, 1994).
30. See Wolfson (1986) Eichengreen and Portes (1987) and Krugman (1991) on the transmission mechanisms of financial crises. See also Taylor's (1994) generalization of Minsky (1986).
31. Keynes wrote presciently in 1933 of the constraining effect on domestic policies posed by the threat of capital flight. See Crotty's (1983) discussion of Keynes' views on this matter.
32. See the studies cited in n. 24, and Amsden (1989), Gerschenkron (1962), and Goldsmith (1969). See also Burkett and Hart-Lansberg (1996) for an excellent critical discussion of what they identify as the overenthusiastic embrace of Japan's financial system by liberals and leftists today.
33. See Pollin (1993, 1996) for a discussion of public credit allocation programmes in the USA and in other advanced capitalist countries.
34. Callier and Mayer (1989) and Lesser (1991) make a related point. They argue that past government failures do not prove market superiority.

35. Grabel (1996a) surveys some of these mechanisms.
36. The arguments below draw on Grabel (1996b).
37. Summers and Summers (1989) and Baker, Pollin and Schaberg (1994) make a case for the implementation of such a tax in the USA.
38. Hakkio (1994) and Summers and Summers (1989) survey the particulars of transaction taxes in OECD countries.

References

Agenor, P.-R. and M. Taylor (1992) 'Testing for credibility effects', *IMF Staff Papers*, 39(3): 545–71.

Akyüz, Y. (1993) 'Financial liberalization: key issues', *UNCTAD Report*, pp. 8–10.

Akyüz, Y. and G. Held (eds) (1993) *Finance and the Real Economy* (Chile: ECLA).

Amsden, A. (1989) *Asia's Next Giant* (New York: Oxford University Press).

Arestis, P. and P. Demetriades (1995) *Finance and Growth: Schumpeter Might be 'Wrong'*, University of East London, Department of Economics, mimeo.

Arida, P. (1986) 'Macroeconomic issues for Latin America', *Journal of Development Economics*, 22: 171–208.

Baker, D., R. Pollin and M. Schaberg (1994) 'Taxing the Big Casino', *The Nation*, 9 May, pp. 622–4.

Balassa, B. (1990–1) 'Financial liberalization in developing countries', *Studies in Comparative International Development*, 25(4): 56–70.

Bhagwati, J. (1982) 'Directly unproductive profit-seeking activities', *Journal of Political Economy*, 90(5): 998–1002.

Bienefeld, M. (1992) 'Financial deregulation: disarming the nation state', *Studies in Political Economy*, 37: 31–58.

Bruno, M. (1993) *Crisis, Stabilization, and Economic Reform* (Oxford: Clarendon).

Buffie, E. (1984) 'Financial repression, the new structuralists, and stabilization policy in semi-industrialized economies', *Journal of Development Economics*, 14: 305–22.

Burkett, P. (1987) 'Financial "repression" and financial "liberalization" in the Third World: a contribution to the critique of neoclassical development theory', *Review of Radical Political Economics*, 19: 1–21.

Burkett, P. and A. Dutt (1991) 'Interest rate policy, effective demand, and growth in LDCs', *International Review of Applied Economics*, 5(2): 127–53.

Burkett, P. and M. Hart-Lansberg (1996) 'The use and abuse of Japan as a progressive model', in L. Panitch (ed.) *Socialist Register: Are There Alternatives?* (London: Merlin) pp. 62–92.

Burkett, P. and R. Lotspeich (1993) 'Review essay: the order of economic liberalization: financial control in the transition to a market economy (R. McKinnon)', *Comparative Economic Studies*, 35(1): 59–85.

Callier, P. (1990) 'Informal finance: rotating saving and credit association – an interpretation', *Kyklos*, 43(2): 273–76.

Callier, P. and C. Mayer (1989) 'The assessment: financial liberalization, financial systems, and economic growth', *Oxford Review of Economic Policy*, **5**(4): 1–12.

Calvo, G. (1986) 'Fractured liberalism: Argentina under Martinez de Hoz', *Economic Development and Cultural Change*, **34**(3): 511–34.

Carter, M. (1991–2) 'Uncertainty, liquidity and speculation: a Keynesian perspective on financial innovation in debt markets', *Journal of Post Keynesian Economics*, **14**(2): 169–82.

Chang, H-J (1993) 'The political economy of industrial policy in Korea', *Cambridge Journal of Economics*, **17**: 131–57.

Cho, Y.J. and D. Khatkhate (1989) 'Lessons of financial liberalization in Asia: a comparative study', *World Bank Discussion Paper*, no. 50.

Chou, R.Y., R.F. Engle, A. Kane (1992) 'Measuring risk aversion from excess returns on a stock index', *Journal of Econometrics*, **52**: 201–25.

Christensen, G. (1993) 'The limits to informal financial intermediation', *World Development*, **21**(5): 721–31.

Corbett, J. (1990) 'Policy issues in the design of banking', *European Economy*, **43**: 205–15.

Corbett, J. and C. Mayer (1991) 'Financial reform in Eastern Europe', *Oxford Review of Economic Policy*, **7**(4): 57–75.

Corbo, V. and J. de Melo (1987) 'Lessons from the southern cone policy reforms', *World Bank Research Observer*, **2**(2): 111–43.

Corbo, V., J. de Melo and J. Tybout (1986) 'What went wrong with the recent reforms in the Southern Cone', *Economic Development and Cultural Change*, **34**(3): 607–40.

Cox, A. (1986) *State, Finance and Industry* (New York: St Martin's).

Crotty, J. (1983) 'On Keynes and capital flight', *Journal of Economic Literature*, **21**: 59–65.

Crotty, J. (1993) 'Rethinking Marxian investment theory: Keynes–Minsky instability, competitive regime shifts, and coerced investment', *Review of Radical Political Economics*, **25**(1): 1–26.

Crotty, J. (1994) 'Are Keynesian uncertainty and macropolicy compatible? Conventional decision making, institutional structures, and conditional stability in macromodels', in G. Dymski and R. Pollin (eds) *New Perspectives in Monetary Macroeconomics: Explorations in the Tradition of Hyman P. Minsky* (Ann Arbor: University of Michigan Press) pp. 105–42.

Crotty, J. and Epstein, G. (1996) 'Capital controls for a new social contract', in L. Panitch (ed.) *Socialist Register: Are there Alternatives?* (London: Merlin Press) pp. 118–49.

Crotty, J. and D. Goldstein (1993) 'Do US financial markets allocate credit efficiently? The case of corporate restructuring in the 1980s', in G. Dymski, G. Epstein and R. Pollin (eds) *Transforming the US Financial System* (Armonk, NY: M.E. Sharpe) pp. 253–86.

De Long, J., A. Shleifer, L. Summers and R. Waldmann (DSSW) (1989) 'The size and incidence of the losses from noise trading', *Journal of Finance*, **44**(3): 681–96.

de Melo, J. and J. Tybout (1986) 'The effects of financial liberalization on savings and investment in Uruguay', *Economic Development and Cultural Change*, **34**(3): 561–88.

Diaz-Alejandro, C. (1985) 'Good-bye financial repression, hello financial crash', *Journal of Development Economics*, **19**: 1–24.

Dornbusch, R. and A. Reynoso (1989) 'Financial factors in economic development', *American Economic Association*, **79**(2): 204–9.

Drake, P. (1985) 'Some reflections on problems affecting securities markets in less developed countries', *Savings and Development*, **9**(1): 5–14.

Dutt, A. (1990–1) 'Interest rate policy in LDCs: a post-Keynesian view', *Journal of Post Keynesian Economics*, **13**(2): 210–32.

Economist, The (1995) 'The Tequila hangover', 8 April, pp. 65–6.

Edwards, S. (1987) 'Sequencing economic liberalization in developing Countries', *Finance and Development*, pp. 26–9.

Edwards, S. (1989) 'On the sequencing of structural reforms', *OECD Department of Economics and Statistics Working Paper*, no. 70.

Eichengreen, B. and R. Portes (1987) 'The anatomy of financial crises', in R. Portes and A. Swoboda (eds), *Threats to International Financial Stability* (Cambridge University Press) pp. 10–66.

Federer, P. (1993) 'The impact of uncertainty on aggregate investment spending: an empirical analysis', *Journal of Money, Credit and Banking*, **25**(1): 30–45.

Felix, D. (1993) 'Developing countries and joint action to curb international financial volatility', *UNCTAD Bulletin*, **21**: 7–9.

Ffrench-Davis, R. (1993) 'Capital formation and the macroeconomic framework: a neostructuralist approach', in O. Sunkel (ed.) *Development from Within* (Boulder, Colo.: Lynne Rienner) pp. 151–84.

Fischer, B. and H. Reisen (1993) *Liberalising Capital Flows in Developing Countries: Pitfalls and Prerequisites* (Paris: OECD).

Foxley, A. (1983) *Latin American Experiments in Neo-conservative Economics* (Berkeley: University of California Press).

Frenkel, J. (1983) 'Panel discussion on the southern cone', *International Monetary Fund Staff Papers*, **30**(1): 164–84.

Fry, M. (1995) *Money, Interest, and Banking in Economic Development* (Baltimore: Johns Hopkins University Press).

Frydman, R. and E. Phelps (eds) (1983) *Individual Forecasting and aggregate outcomes: rational expectations* (NY: CUNY Press).

Galbis, V. (1993) 'High real interest rates under financial liberalization: is there a problem?', *IMF Working Paper*, no. 7.

Gerschenkron, A. (1962) *Economic Backwardness in Historical Perspective* (Cambridge, Mass.: Harvard University Press).

Ghate, P. (1992) 'Interaction between the formal and informal financial sectors', *World Development*, **20**(6): 859–72.

Goldsmith, R. (1969) *Financial Structure and Development* (New Haven, Conn.: Yale University Press).

Goldstein, D. (1995) *Financial Structure and Corporate Behavior in Japan and the US: Insulation Versus Integration with Speculative Pressures*, Allegheny College, Department of Economics, mimeo.

Gonzales Arrieta, G. (1988) 'Interest rates, savings, and growth in LDCs: an assessment of recent empirical research', *World Development*, **16**(5): 589–605.

Grabel, I. (1994) 'The political economy of theories of "optimal" financial repression: a critique', *Review of Radical Political Economics*, **26**(3): 47–55.

Grabel, I. (1995a) 'Speculation-led economic development: a post-Keynesian interpretation of financial liberalization programmes in the Third World', *International Review of Applied Economics*, **9**(2): 127–49.

Grabel, I. (1995b) 'Assessing the impact of financial liberalisation on stock market volatility in selected developing countries', *Journal of Development Studies*, **31**(6): 903–17.

Grabel, I. (1996a) 'Savings, investment and functional efficiency: a comparative examination of national financial complexes', in R. Pollin (ed.) *The Macroeconomics of Finance, Saving, and Investment* (Ann Arbor: University of Michigan Press).

Grabel, I. (1996b) 'Marketing the Third World: The Contradictions of Portfolio Investment in the Global Economy', *World Development*, **24**(11): 1761–76.

Haggard, S., C. Lee and S. Maxfield (eds) (1993) *The Politics of Finance in Developing Countries* (Ithaca, NY: Cornell University Press).

Hakkio, C. (1994) 'Should we throw sand in the gears of financial markets?', *Federal Reserve Bank of Kansas City Economic Review*, pp. 17–29.

Hart-Lansberg, M. (1993) *The Rush to Development* (New York: Monthly Review Press).

Je Cho, Y. (1986) 'Inefficiencies from financial liberalization in the absence of well-functioning equity markets', *Journal of Money, Credit and Banking*, **18**(2): 192–9.

Je Cho, Y. (1990) 'McKinnon–Shaw versus the neostructuralists on financial liberalization: a conceptual note', *World Development*, **18**(3): 477–80.

Kapur, B. (1992) 'Formal and informal financial markets, and the neostructuralist critique of the financial liberalization strategy in less developed countries' *Journal of Development Economics*, **38**: 63–77.

Kemp, M. and H. Sinn (1990) 'A simple model of useless speculation', *NBER Working Paper*, no. 3513.

Keynes, J.M. (1933) 'National self-sufficiency', *Yale Review*, pp. 233–46.

Keynes, J.M. (1964) *The General Theory of Employment, Interest, and Money* (New York: Harcourt Brace Jovanovich).

Khan, M.S. and R. Zahler (1985) 'Trade and financial liberalization given external shocks and inconsistent domestic policies', *International Monetary Fund Staff Papers*, **32**: 22–55.

Khatkhate, D. (1988) 'Assessing the impact of interest rates in less developed countries', *World Development*, **16**(5): 577–88.

King, R. and R. Levine (1993) 'Finance and growth: Schumpeter might be right', *Quarterly Journal of Economics*: 717–37.

Krugman, P. (1991) 'International aspects of financial crises', in M. Feldstein (ed.) *The Risk of Economic Crisis* (University of Chicago Press) pp. 85–109.

Lal, D. (1987) 'The political economy of economic liberalization', *World Bank Economic Review*, **1**(2): 273–99.

Lazonick, W. (1991) *Business Organization and the Myth of the Market Economy* (New York: Cambridge University Press).

Lesser, B. (1991) 'When the government fails, will the market do better? The privatization/market liberalization movement in developing coun-

tries', *Canadian Journal of Development Studies*, **12**(1): 159–72.
Levine, R. (1990) 'Stock markets, growth, and policy', *International Finance Discussion Papers*, Federal Reserve Bank, no. 374.
Levine, R. (1996) 'Stock markets: a spur to growth', *Finance and Development*, **33**(1): 7–10.
Littler, G. and A. Maalouf (1996) 'Emerging stock markets in 1995', *Finance and Development*, **33**(1): 27–9.
Lucas, R., Jr (1973) 'Some international evidence on output–inflation tradeoffs', *American Economic Review*, **63**: 326–34.
Lustig, N. (1991) 'From structuralism to neostructuralism: the search for a heterodox paradigm', in P. Meller (ed.) *The Latin American Development Debate* (Boulder, Colo.: Westview) pp. 27–41.
Manne, H. (1965) 'Mergers and the market for corporate control', *Journal of Political Economy*, **73**: 693–706.
Merton, R. (1980) 'On estimating the expected return on the market: an exploratory investigation', *Journal of Financial Economics*, **8**: 323–61.
McKinnon, R. (1973) *Money and Capital in Economic Development* (Washington, DC: The Brookings Institution).
McKinnon, R. (1984) 'The international capital market and economic liberalization in LDCs', *Developing Economies*, **22**(4): 476–81.
McKinnon, R. (1988) *Financial Liberalization and Economic Development: A Reassessment of Interest-rate Policies in Asia and Latin America* (International Center for Economic Growth).
McKinnon, R. (1989) 'Macroeconomic instability and moral hazard in banking in a liberalizing economy', in P. Brock, M. Connolly and C. Gonzalez-Vega (eds) *Latin American Debt and Adjustment* (New York: Praeger) pp. 99–111.
McKinnon, R. (1991) *The Order of Economic Liberalization: Financial Control in the Transition to a Market Economy* (Baltimore: Johns Hopkins University Press).
Minsky, H. (1986) *Stabilizing an Unstable Economy* (New Haven, Conn.: Yale University).
Mullin, J. (1993) 'Emerging equity markets in the global economy', *Federal Reserve Bank of New York Quarterly Review*: 54–83.
Ostry, J. and C. Reinhart (1995) 'Saving and the real interest rate in developing countries', *Finance and Development*: 16–8.
Otero, M. and E. Rhyne (eds) (1994) *The New World of Microenterprise Finance* (Hartford, Conn.: Kumarian Press).
Owen, P.D. and O. Solis-Fallas (1989) 'Unorganized money markets and "unproductive"' assets in the new structuralist critique of financial liberalization', *Journal of Development Economics*, **31**: 341–55.
Pollin, R. (1993) 'Public credit allocation through the Federal Reserve: why it is needed; how it should be done', in G. Dymski, G. Epstein and R. Pollin (eds) *Transforming the US Financial System: Equity and Efficiency for the 21st Century*, Economic Policy Institute Series (Armonk, NY: Sharpe).
Pollin, R. (1996) 'Financial structures and egalitarian economic policy', *International Papers in Political Economy*, **2**(3).

Rahman, A. and A.N.M. Wahid (1992) 'The Grameen Bank and the changing patron–client relationship in Bangladesh', *Journal of Contemporary Asia*, **22**(3): 303–21.

Ramos, J. (1986a) *Neoconservative Economics in the Southern Cone of Latin America, 1973–1983* (Baltimore: Johns Hopkins University Press).

Ramos, J. (1986b) 'Rise and fall of capital markets in the southern cone', *Helen Kellogg Institute for International Studies Working Paper*, no. 81, University of Notre Dame.

Rittenberg, L. (1990) 'Investment spending and interest rate policy: the case of financial liberalization in Turkey', *Journal of Development Studies*: 150–67.

Rybczynski, T. (1984) 'Industrial finance systems in Europe, US and Japan', *Journal of Economic Behavior and Organization*, **5**: 275–86.

Sachs, J. (1988) 'Conditionality, debt relief and the developing countries' debt crisis', in J. Sachs (ed.) *Developing Country Debt and Economic Performance* (University of Chicago Press) pp. 225–98.

Schumpeter, J. (1977) *The Theory of Economic Development* (Cambridge, Mass.: Harvard University Press).

Shafik, N. and J. Jalali (1991) 'Are high real interest rates bad for world economic growth?', *World Bank Working Paper*, no. 669, Department of Policy, Research and External Affairs.

Shaw, E. (1973) *Financial Deepening in Economic Development* (New York: Oxford University Press).

Singh, A. (1993) 'The stock market and economic development: should developing countries encourage stock markets?', *UNCTAD Review*, **4**: 1–28.

Snowden, P. (1987) 'Financial market liberalisation in LDCs', *Journal of Development Studies*, **24**(1): 83–93.

Srivastava, P. (1987) 'Credibility in trade liberalization', Yale University, Department of Economics, mimeo.

Stiglitz, J. (1992) 'Banks versus markets as mechanisms for allocating and coordinating investment', in J. Roumasset and S. Barr (eds) *The Economics of Cooperation* (Boulder Colo.: Westview) pp. 15–38.

Studdart, R. (1993) 'Financial repression and economic development: towards a post-Keynesian alternative', *Review of Political Economy*, **5**(3): 277–98.

Summers, L. and V. Summers (1989) 'When financial markets work too well: a cautious case for a securities transactions tax', *Journal of Financial Services Research*, **3**: 261–86.

Sundararajan, V. and T. Balino (eds) (1991) *Banking Crises: Cases and Issues* (Washington, DC: IMF).

Sunkel, O. (1993) *Development from Within* (Boulder, Colo.: Lynne Rienner).

Tang, S-Y. (1995) 'Informal credit markets and economic development in Taiwan', *World Development*, **23**(5): 845–55.

Taylor, L. (1983) *Structuralist Macroeconomics: Applicable Models for the Third World* (New York: Basic Books).

Taylor, L. (1991) *Income Distribution, Inflation, and Growth: Lectures on Structuralist Macroeconomic Theory* (Cambridge Mass.: MIT Press).

Taylor, L. (1994) 'Financial fragility: is an etiology at hand?', in G. Dymski and R. Pollin (eds) *New Perspectives in Monetary Macroeconomics* (Ann Arbor: University of Michigan Press).

Taylor, L. and S. O'Connell (1985) 'A Minsky crisis', *Quarterly Journal of Economics*, **100**: 871–86.

Timberg, T. and C. Aiyar (1984) 'Informal credit markets in India', *Economic Development and Cultural Change*, **33**(1): 43–60.

Tobin, J. (1978) 'A proposal for international monetary reform', *Eastern Economic Journal*, **4**(3–4): 153–59.

Tobin, J. (1984) 'On the efficiency of the financial system', *Lloyd's Bank Review*, **153**: 1–15.

Toye, J. (1987) *Dilemmas of Development* (Oxford: Blackwell).

United Nations Development Programme (UNDP) (1994) *Human Development Report* (Oxford University Press).

van Wijnbergen S. (1983a) 'Credit policy, inflation and growth in a financially repressed economy', *Journal of Development Economics*, **13**(1): 45–65.

van Wijnbergen, S. (1983b) 'Interest rate management in LDCs', *Journal of Monetary Economics*, **12**(3): 433–52.

Warman, F. and A. Thirlwall (1994) 'Interest rates, saving, investment and growth in Mexico 1960–90: tests of the financial liberalisation hypothesis', *Journal of Development Studies*, **30**(3): 629–49.

Wickrama, K. and P. Keith (1994) 'Savings and credit: women's informal groups as models for change in developing countries', *Journal of Developing Areas*, **28**: 365–78.

Williamson, J. (ed.) (1994) *The Political Economy of Policy Reform* (Washington, DC: Institute for International Economics).

Wolfson, M. (1986) *Financial Crises* (Armonk, NY: Sharpe).

World Bank (1989) *World Bank Development Report 1989* (New York: Oxford University Press).

Zysman, J. (1983) *Government, Markets and Growth: Financial Systems and the Politics of Industrial Change* (Ithaca, NY: Cornell University Press).

6 The Tobin Financial Transactions Tax: Its Potential and Feasibility

Philip Arestis and Malcolm Sawyer

6.1 INTRODUCTION

There has been considerable interest in the idea of a tax levied on financial transactions, particularly on those involving foreign exchange dealings. The root of the argument is that many financial market transactions are purely speculative and as such they merely reallocate the ownership of existing financial assets without any beneficial impact on the productive economy. Indeed volatility of prices thereby generated may have adverse effects on the real economy. If these transactions are costly, they are socially wasteful. It was this type of argument which led Keynes (1936) to conclude that 'it is usually agreed that casinos should, in the public interest, be inaccessible and expensive. And perhaps the same is true of stock exchanges' (p. 159). In terms of currency markets, it led Tobin (for example, 1978) to propose the taxation of foreign exchange transactions, and a fiscal intervention now normally labelled as the Tobin tax.[1]

The origins of the Tobin tax idea can be traced to Keynes's assertion (1980, ch. 36) in the *Treatise on Money* that it may be necessary to tax foreign lending to contain speculative capital movements. In 1936, Keynes wrote that '[t]he introduction of a substantial government transfer tax on all transactions might prove the most serviceable reform available, with a view to mitigating the predominance of speculation over enterprise in the United States' (Keynes, 1936, p. 160) though that was more related to domestic financial transactions. In his 1972 Janeway lecture at Princeton, Tobin (1974, see also 1966, 1978, and Eichengreen, Tobin and Wyplosz, 1995) specifically proposed a tax on foreign exchange transactions as a way of limiting speculation, enhancing the efficacy of macroeconomic policy in the process and raising some tax revenue as a by-product. Following the Stock Market crashes of 1987, Summers and Summers (1989) updated the argument and proposed new taxes on securities transactions (see also Stiglitz, 1989). Harcourt (1995) and Kelly (1993, 1994) have advanced variants of a tax on foreign exchange dealings: this concern has emerged in view of the severe speculative attacks on the European Exchange Rate Mechanism (ERM) (see also Neuburger and Sawyer, 1990, p. 116). A recent proposal along Tobin's line of argument is Spahn's (1995) suggestion of a two-tier system. This would impose additionally a penal tax on transaction outside a specified band. For example, the penal rate could be imposed on the difference between the exchange rate in the transaction and the specified outer limit of the band.

Some official interest in a transactions tax has been expressed by United Nations Development Programme (1994) and UNCTAD (1995), who have seen its possibilities for raising large amounts of money which could be used to finance development. Tobin suggests that 'the revenue potential is immense, over $1.5 trillion a year for the 0.5% tax' (in UNDP, 1994, p. 70). It can also be noted that in the wake of the 1994 Mexican peso crisis, even the IMF endorsed, albeit cautiously, limited reliance on transactions taxes and restrictions on selected international financial transactions (Folkerts-Landau and Ito, 1995).

The purpose of this chapter is to evaluate the proposals for a tax on foreign exchange dealings. We assume that levying such a tax on a national basis would not be feasible and do not discuss that possibility further. We initially assume that a tax could be levied on a co-ordinated international basis in a workable manner and this enables us to discuss the merits and demerits of the tax. In the last main section of the chapter we discuss the feasibility of such a tax.

6.2 RATIONALES FOR A TRANSACTIONS TAX

Three rather different (but not mutually exclusive) sets of reasoning have been advanced in support of a transactions tax (which we will use as shorthand for a tax on foreign exchange dealings). The first is that there is a sense in which the volume of foreign exchange transactions are excessive, being many times greater than the volume required to finance trade. It is, of course, the case that an appropriate level of foreign exchange transactions would be several times the volume of international trade to allow for the financing of both direct and portfolio investment, to allow for a degree of financial mobility in pursuit of higher rates of return which serves to bring about a degree of equalization of returns and to permit some risk shifting and spreading; but there is little reason to think that the factor of 60 (see p. 253 below) would be the appropriate one. This volume of transactions absorbs resources to effect the transactions but more significantly is seen to have an adverse effect on the world economy. In a world of floating exchange rates, this large volume of transactions is often viewed as generating volatility in exchange rates with consequent detrimental effects on real economies. Any attempts at fixed exchange rates are made much more difficult by the volume of transactions. This is reflected in:

> Modest uncertainty about whether national monetary authorities are inclined to make use of their theoretical independence can lead to significant financial market volatility. If currencies are floating, they can fluctuate widely. If the authorities attempt to peg them, the costs of doing so, measured by reserve losses or interest-rate increases, can be extremely high. Even a government otherwise prepared to maintain a pegged exchange rate may be unwilling or unable to do so when attacked by the markets and forced to raise interest rates to astronomical heights. (Eichengreen, Tobin and Wyplosz, 1995, p. 162)

Harcourt (1995) argues that

> if we want exchange rates to reflect real economic forces – trading prospects, real investment opportunities – we need greatly to reduce speculation and thereby its effects on the determination of exchange rates in both the short and longer term. For neither in the short term nor on average over longer periods do exchange rates at the moment reflect these economic activities. This is especially so if we accept that there is no underlying set of long-term equilibrium exchange rates, reflecting a long-term equilibrium of an interrelated system but, rather, changing structures which reflect the appreciation and depreciation of individual rates because of the underlying differences in the growth rates of productivity and national products. (p. 34)

A transactions tax should change the balance of factors influencing the exchange rate, away from short term expectations towards longer-run and more trade-orientated factors.

This rationale for the transactions tax requires that, under a floating exchange rate regime, there is excessive volatility of exchange rates (where excessive is taken to imply detrimental) and that reducing the volume of transactions would reduce volatility. The more usual proposition is that a thin market will tend to exhibit volatility whereas a thick market will not. The rationale for the transactions tax appears to be based on almost the opposite view (or at least over the range of interest, an increase in the volume of transactions, 'thickness' of the market, increases volatility). Since issues of whether speculation is stabilizing and indeed what is meant by speculation are involved here as well, we have an extensive discussion of these issues in section 6.3.

The second rationale for a transactions tax is simply its tax raising potential. Tobin (1978) suggested this possibility as a by-product of a transactions tax, not as the main aim of his proposal. The United Nations Development Programme (1994) says that a

> logical source of funds for a global response to global threats is a set of fees on globally important transactions or polluting emissions. . . . One is a tax on the international movements of speculative capital suggested by James Tobin . . . Tobin suggests a tax rate of 0.5% on such transactions, but even a tax of 0.05% during 1995–2000 could raise $150 billion a year. Such a tax would be largely invisible and totally non-discriminatory. (p. 9)

These tax receipts could be used for worldwide public investment.

This may be linked with the view that the financial sector is relatively undertaxed in the sense that financial transactions do not usually bear general sales or value added taxes nor are they usually subject to specific taxes in the way in which, for example, tobacco and alcohol are. Table 6.1 reports for a range of countries the proportion of tax revenue arising from taxes on financial and capital transactions, and these include taxes on the buying and selling of equity. It can be seen from the table that on average such taxes account for 1.3 per cent of tax revenue. It is worth pointing out here that most industrialized countries do, in fact, have transaction taxes (Campbell and Froot, 1994, summarized in Frankel, 1996)

The third rationale concerns the possibility of enhancing the

Table 6.1 Proportion of total tax revenue accounted for by taxes on financial and capital transactions, 1994 (%)

Australia	4.34
Austria	0.70
Belgium	1.86
Canada	0.00
Denmark	0.88
Finland	0.88
France	1.13
Germany	0.57
Greece	2.22
Ireland	1.57
Italy	2.29
Japan	2.13
Netherlands	1.17
New Zealand	0.51
Norway	0.33
Portugal	0.11
Spain	2.54
Sweden	0.68
Switzerland	2.12
Turkey	1.80
UK	0.80
USA	0.14
Average	1.31

Source: Calculated from OECD (1995).

autonomy of national economic policy, and reducing the constraints on such policy imposed by the financial markets. This runs counter to the widely held view that since financial markets 'know best' (and since exchange rates and stock market prices reflect 'fundamentals') they exert a healthy discipline on central banks and governments. Adverse capital movements is the usual example cited to support this view. These should be read as a sober judgement that macroeconomic policies are unsound, and as such they should be abandoned. A further argument in this context is that a transactions tax can potentially tackle these problems more flexibly than financial controls – especially quantitative exchange controls which are normally viewed as unduly rigid. A related argument is that a transactions tax by reducing foreign exchange rate volatility increases the independence of policy-makers. The famous 'impossible trinity' may be invoked to make this point. This is that out of the three attributes of financial openness, currency stability and monetary independence, a country can only have two. Thus, for a country seeking currency stability, a transactions tax might help to restore some measure of monetary independence, and widen the scope in, for example, the determination of domestic interest rates.

Reasons for Interest in Tobin Tax

The reasons for the increased interest recently in the Tobin tax proposals are threefold. The first is the growing volume of foreign exchange trading. The volume of foreign exchange transactions worldwide reached $1300 billions a day in 1995 (with the corresponding figure in the early 1970s being $18 billion), equivalent to $312 trillion in a year of 240 business days (Tobin, 1996, p. xvi). By comparison, the annual global turnover in equity markets in 1995 was $21 trillion, the annual global trade in goods and services was $5 trillion, and total reserves of central banks around $1.5 trillion at the end of 1995. The second reason is that a transactions tax is now seen as important not merely by policy-makers and others concerned with foreign exchange market volatility, but by those who attach significance to public financing of world development.

The third reason is an increasing realization that foreign exchange markets do not operate in as an efficient manner as portrayed in, for example, the rational expectations literature. It is recognized that foreign exchange markets suffer from asymmetric information and herd behaviour, moral hazard when participants are too big or powerful to fail, and also from the possibility of multiple equilibria. An important implication of all of these is persistent misalignments and unstable exchange rate regimes. Asymmetric information and herd behaviour imply that incompletely informed investors suffer bouts of optimism and pessimism. Indeed foreign exchange market speculators watch other speculators rather than 'fundamentals'. Frankel (1996) reports the results of surveys of speculators' expectations which clearly suggest that forecasts are dominated by 'technical models' which reflect the type of behaviour just alluded to. Swings in sentiment not obviously associated with the arrival of economic or political news occur frequently in the foreign exchange markets (Kindleberger, 1978; Eichengreen and Lindert, 1989; Eichengreen, 1991). Moral hazard in the banking system can produce instabilities in the foreign exchange markets (Felix and Sau, 1996). This can happen when regulators are unwilling or unable to allow domestic banks to fail. Under these circumstances, domestic banks would have the incentive to borrow abroad in order to lend domestically, leading to exchange rate swings under a flexible exchange rate system, and pressures on the rate in a fixed exchange rate system. Multiple equilibria become an additional source of exchange rate volatility: not only does the exchange rate exhibit wide fluctuations when the 'fundamentals' change, but it can move from one equilibrium to another even when the 'fundamentals' remain unchanged.

6.3   VOLATILITY AND SPECULATION

In this section, our main concern is flexible exchange rate systems. Although, in some respects, many of the arguments discussed apply equally to an adjustable exchange rate one (or as at present a mixed mode regime). Obviously in a flexible exchange rate regime, speculation may increase the volatility of both the nominal and the real rate of exchange, whereas in the adjustable exchange rate system there is considerable stability in the nominal exchange rate with occasional changes with speculation placing pressure on the authorities to change the rate at times. Tobin (1996) argues that the transactions tax 'could be helpful in either regime – fixed or floating or hybrids like floating bands' (p. xiv).

The term 'volatility' suggests an instability on a short-term basis, for example, variance of price or price change measured on a daily basis. It can, of course, be the case that there is considerable volatility on this basis and the market be deemed efficient (in the sense that there is a lack of correlation between daily price movements).[2] But this volatility may be inconvenient for those involved in international trade because of the uncertainty which it engenders, though the use of forward contracts can reduce the uncertainty. Volatility which involved minor fluctuations around the 'fundamental' equilibrium exchange rate would be little more than a nuisance. The aspect of exchange rate movements since the early 1970s which is of more significance is the year (or longer) to year volatility which has generated substantial periods when exchange rates are substantially over-valued or under-valued. This volatility cannot be escaped through the use of forward contracts (which generally do not extend more than 12 months into the future), and has a much more significant impact on international trade.

There can be little doubt that the era of flexible exchange rates since 1971 has been associated with a considerable degree of volatility of exchange rates. Table 6.2 provides some crude indicators of the extent of volatility of the sterling relative to the DM, and of the dollar relative to the yen since 1980, based on monthly averages. It can be seen that on average the standard deviation relative to the mean of the sterling/DM rate was 3.9 per cent, and the ratio of the maximum to minimum during a year varied from 5 per cent (in 1991 the only full year for which sterling was a member of the ERM) and 22 per cent. There is also considerable variation in the month to month changes with an average standard deviation of 2.33 per cent. Comparable figures for the dollar: yen rate are 5.2 per cent for the standard deviation relative to the mean, a ratio of maximum to minimum up to 30 per cent and a standard deviation of monthly changes of 2.83 per cent. These figures suggest significant volatility within a year, as well as suggesting considerable variation in the real value of the exchange rates.

Mussa (1986) calculates the changes in the logarithm of the ratio of price levels in the case of the nominal exchange rate and of the real exchange rate. He concludes that under floating exchange rates, 'there is a strong correlation between short-term movements in the real exchange rate and short-term movements in the nominal exchange rate' (p. 131). Further 'short-term changes in nominal exchange rates and in real exchange rates show substantial persistence during sub-periods when the nominal exchange rate in floating' (p. 132). He makes many cross-currency comparisons, and not surprisingly there is a wide variation in the degree of variability in bilateral exchange rates. Variances of up to 25 per cent per quarter are found, implying a standard deviation of 5 per cent per quarter. This would of course mean that in approximately one third of quarters the rate of change deviated by more than 5 per cent from the average. Further evidence is provided in Rose (1994) (cited by Eichengreen *et al.*, 1995). Rogoff (1996) poses what he terms the purchasing power parity puzzle, which is

> How can one reconcile the enormous short-term volatility of real exchange rates with the extremely slow rate at which shocks appear to damp out? . . . Consensus estimates for the rate at which PPP deviations damp . . . suggest a half-life of three to five years, seemingly too long to be explained by nominal rigidities. (pp. 647–8)

Table 6.2 Indicators of volatility

Sterling/Mark

Year	Standard deviation/ Mean	Standard deviation of % monthly changes	Maximum	Minimum	Ratio maximum/ minimum	Annual average nominal	Annual average real*
1980	0.0556	3.40	4.672	3.945	1.18	4.271	3.086
1981	0.0598	3.27	5.051	4.159	1.21	4.557	3.523
1982	0.0357	2.43	4.348	3.837	1.13	4.218	3.357
1983	0.0376	3.30	4.052	3.589	1.13	3.887	3.156
1984	0.0216	1.51	3.949	3.641	1.08	3.775	3.136
1985	0.0393	3.22	3.984	3.555	1.12	3.788	3.258
1986	0.0756	3.17	3.442	2.840	1.21	3.160	2.721
1987	0.0243	1.32	2.996	2.766	1.08	2.934	2.607
1988	0.0259	1.90	3.221	2.967	1.09	3.135	2.909
1989	0.0547	2.49	3.284	2.726	1.20	3.053	2.962
1990	0.0246	1.77	2.969	2.749	1.08	2.881	2.881
1991	0.0133	1.04	2.980	2.836	1.05	2.923	2.996
1992	0.0799	3.21	2.936	2.410	1.22	2.733	2.798
1993	0.0276	2.08	2.576	2.343	1.10	2.482	2.546
1994	0.0194	1.31	2.567	2.413	1.06	2.474	2.539
1995	0.0274	1.83	2.409	2.214	1.09	2.261	2.324
Average	0.0389	2.33			1.13		

Dollar/Yen

Year	Standard deviation/ Mean	Standard deviation of % monthly changes	Maximum	Minimum	Ratio of maximum/ minimum	Annual average nominal	Annual average real*
1980	0.0674	3.66	251.7	209.1	1.20	226.7	169.7
1981	0.0486	2.17	233.7	202.0	1.16	220.5	175.1
1982	0.0561	4.12	271.4	224.6	1.21	249.1	206.6
1983	0.0158	1.64	244.3	232.9	1.05	237.5	202.1
1984	0.0355	2.02	247.9	224.9	1.10	237.0	206.2
1985	0.0861	2.98	260.2	202.8	1.28	238.5	211.6
1986	0.0829	3.41	200.1	154.0	1.30	168.5	150.7
1987	0.0524	3.06	154.5	128.6	1.20	144.6	133.5
1988	0.0302	2.67	134.4	123.2	1.09	128.2	122.4
1989	0.0509	2.09	145.1	127.2	1.14	137.9	135.3
1990	0.0682	3.62	158.5	129.1	1.23	144.8	144.8
1991	0.0301	2.32	139.8	128.1	1.09	134.7	138.4
1992	0.0306	2.16	133.5	121.0	1.10	126.7	130.7
1993	0.0587	2.35	125.0	103.8	1.20	111.2	116.7
1994	0.0408	2.06	111.3	97.5	1.14	102.1	109.5
1995	0.0778	4.90	101.9	83.8	1.22	94.0	103.8
Average	0.0520	2.83			1.17		

* based on GDP (GNP for Japan) deflators.
Source: Own calculations from *International Financial Statistics*, various issues.

In the context of the transactions tax, two specific questions arise: firstly, is volatility harmful? and secondly, would such a tax reduce volatility? We now address the first question and return to the second after some discussion of the theory of speculation. The possible costs of volatility are relatively well known even if they are difficult to quantify and are subject to some debate. Volatility engenders a degree of price uncertainty, making effective decision-making more difficult. The price (currency) uncertainty may lead firms to be reluctant to engage in international trade and thereby reduce the volume of international trade. Others (for example, Krugman, 1989a, 1989b) suggest that uncertainty over exchange rates generates incentives for firms to postpone investment in export (or import substitution) capacity that would be difficult to reverse. In the context of exchange volatility, there may be asymmetric responses to the upward and downward movements of the exchange rate. An over-valued exchange rate reduces export demand, leading to a decline in the domestic tradable goods sector and a reduction of capacity (or a failure to invest) in that sector, and this may not be fully compensated by the stimulus of export demand coming from an under-valued exchange rate in terms of the opening of new capacity.

The effect of volatility on policy-makers can be a further concern in so far as volatility generates uncertainty and deflationary responses. If, say, a fall in the exchange rate (arising from the volatility of the exchange rate and unconnected with real variables) generates a deflationary response (for example, increase domestic interest rates) there are detrimental effects on the domestic economy. This may, of course, be offset by a reflationary response to a rising exchange rate, and if the policy responses are symmetrical there would appear to be no net damage. Even so, there may still be some harm in so far as sudden and frequent changes in exchange rate movements generate changes in the economic policy stance, and thereby a more uncertain economic environment. However, Frankel (1996), drawing on the survey of Goldstein (1995) argues that 'Most studies have concluded that short-term volatility has little effect on trade.' But a study by Frankel and Wei (1995) on bilateral trade 'shows statistically significant effects of bilateral volatility in the 1960s and 1970s' (Frankel, 1996, p. 52). Similarly Isard (1995) concludes that 'empirical studies have failed to uncover statistical evidence that exchange rate variability has had much of a depressing effect on international trade volumes' (p. 196). However, we can note the conclusions of Gagnon (1993) based on a theoretical approach that

> under a very extreme combination of assumptions, the breakdown of Bretton Woods is estimated to reduce the level of trade by about 3 per cent. This effect is shown to be too small to detect statistically. A further increase in exchange rate variability would lower the volume of trade by a statistically significant 9 per cent, but this latter scenario requires a degree of exchange rate variability much larger than has been observed historically. (p. 287)

Two broader issues arise here. The first is how are financial markets to be modelled, particularly with regard to speculation? We discuss this immediately below in terms of two competing traditions. Second, what is the nature of the relationship between the real sector and the financial sector? Specifically, is there some form of classical dichotomy whereby we can separate the real and the monetary, or is there some important feedbacks from the financial to the real whereby volatility of financial markets would have a real effect? Here we can note the idea of talking of 'fundamentals' is highly suggestive of a separation between real and monetary, with the 'fundamentals' relating to the real side of the economy. But, it may well be the case that there is no classical dichotomy so that there is an intimate link between the real and the financial: specifically that the effects which the financial system has on prices (levels and changes in) feed through into effects on decisions in the real sector, notably over investment and employment.

It is clear that there are (at least) two distinct traditions in the analysis of competitive markets. The first, which can be associated initially with Friedman (1953), suggests that speculation would be stabilizing in a competitive foreign exchange market. Speculation is the act of buying or selling seeking to benefit from price movements, rather than to finance international trade, or to acquire interest bearing assets. The mechanism is clear: when price is above equilibrium, speculators believe that the price will fall, and consequently sell now to gain from the currently high price: their actions help the price to fall, and the price to move more quickly to equilibrium. The assumption of rational expectations held by market participants will merely serve to reinforce the conclusions. Speculation is akin to arbitrage in that it involves buying low and selling high, albeit across time rather than across space. This model of speculation clearly rests on the market participants having (on average) an accurate measure of the equilibrium and speculators in the real world behaving as the model would require them to. But that may not be the case, and the market participants may not expect the price to fall when the price is above equilibrium – indeed they may expect the price to move even higher in which case prices tend to go up rather than down, thereby destabilizing the price process. Clearly, under rational expectations, applied to a competitive market which behaves according to a Walrasian adjustment mechanism, this cannot happen – speculators know the equilibrium price so that when price is above the equilibrium price, price should only fall, not increase.

The second tradition begins with Keynes (1936, ch. 12) who emphasized the role of expectations, conventions and perceptions of the views of others ('we devote our intelligences to anticipating what average opinion expects the average opinion to be', p. 156), the instability which arose from speculation and the suggestion that long term commitment should be encouraged. In this second approach, market operators are more concerned with the rate of change of price than with the price level. This has variously been described as, for example, 'noise' trading and trading motivated by price dynamics. The signal contained within a particular price may include the rate of change (and higher orders) of price, and a price above the 'equilibrium' may not signal a price fall. This can be interpreted in terms of signal attraction, which is the information contained within a specific price. A price may be seen as high or low (relative to equilibrium) and/or may be interpreted as rising or falling (and/or involving higher derivatives). In the first tradition above, which is based on an essentially static analysis (prices are high or low rather than rising or falling), a high price signals a lower price, whereas in the second tradition a price may be high and rising and signal further rises.

The key issue is to 'whether market prices are based on economic fundamentals or bubbles, fads and herd behaviour' (Sayer, 1992). Clearly, if it is the former then the financial markets may perform a useful service by providing early signals of long-term economic developments. However, even if the actions of the financial markets are based on bubbles, fads etc. they may nevertheless influence the economic 'fundamentals'. If the fad raises interest rates, investment may be thereby affected and hence the 'fundamentals' of the economy change. Similarly, a falling exchange rate would stimulate domestic inflation which would raise the fundamental value of the nominal exchange rate.

In the context of equities, the 'fundamentals' may be clear-cut, namely the discounted expected future dividends even though that raises the questions of the relevant discount rate and how the expectations on future dividends are formed and measured. The 'fundamentals' for the foreign exchange rate are not so clear. Clearly reference can be made to the purchasing power parity exchange rate or the fundamental equilibrium exchange rate. The difficulties surrounding the measurement of these notions are well-known, but of particular significance here is the fact that these exchange rates are often calculated as substantially different.[3] It can further be noted that a model such as that of 'over-shooting' (for example, Dornbusch, 1976) with rapid price adjustment in the financial markets combined with sluggish price adjustment in the product and labour markets can generate volatility in the real exchange rate. In such models there is a sense in which the fundamentals do not change (for example, the purchasing power real exchange rate) but the actual exchange rate does. However, the movement in the exchange rate (within the model) does not come through de-stabilizing speculation on future movements of the exchange rate. There can be hysteresis effects through which the equilibrium exchange rate becomes path-dependent (Krugman, 1989b).

There is now an extensive literature which indicates that financial market prices can be over-valued or under-valued for substantial periods of time (and casual observation of the movements in the exchange rates in the past 25 years, reflected to some degree in Table 6.2, would be supportive of that view), and in that sense suffer from medium-term volatility. The work of Shiller (1981, 1984, 1989 and 1990) has strongly suggested that there is excessive volatility in the stock and bond markets. Further, there are theoretical literatures, surveyed by Camerer (1989) for example, which show that behaviour which could be termed as rational or 'near rational' at the level of the individual can generate 'bubbles'.[4] Indeed, bubbles can be an intertemporal manifestation of markets having 'multiple' equilibria. Under these circumstances bubbles 'need never break' (Stiglitz, 1990, p. 14). Also under the assumptions of uncertainty and of investors being short-lived and risk averse, again 'bubbles need not be completely eliminated' (Shleifer and Summers, 1990). Even if there are some risk-averse and some risk-loving speculators, to the extent to which they have limited access to capital, they are likely to have only a limited impact on markets – a result which is consistent with the Stiglitz and Weiss (1981) analysis of capital markets under asymmetric information.[5] In a world of uncertainty where knowledge of the economic fundamentals is given to few, it is perhaps inevitable that asset prices will fluctuate and follow fads and fashions. It is also relevant to ask whether the adoption of policies of reflation of demand (especially if pursued by a left-of-centre government) would set off adverse reactions in the financial markets. These reactions may be individually rational in the sense that if most individuals believe that others believe that such a reflection would be harmful and mark down prices, then doing so themselves may be rational. There is no need to evoke conspiracy theories but rather that if there are sufficient perceptions that others think that some policy or event will lead to a deterioration in 'fundamentals', whether or not it would actually do so, then the exchange rate falls and interest rates rise. Expectations and beliefs are important driving forces behind price movements in financial markets, and expectations have a self-fulfilling element to them. Expectations that the price of a particular currency is going to fall set up forces which lead to a fall in that currency's price.

Most economists today believe 'foreign exchange markets behave more like the unstable and irrational asset markets described by Keynes than the efficient markets described by modern finance theory' (Krugman, 1989a). Isard (1995), in particular, has argued that 'few [economists] still believe that the behavior of

> flexible exchange rates can be accurately described by a model based on the hypothesis that market participants are both fully rational and completely informed about the structure of the model and the behavior of relevant macroeconomic fundamentals. (p. 182)

From the first tradition identified above, it can be concluded that the greater the volume of speculation the quicker would be the movement to equilibrium, and that any volatility of the exchange rate would be a consequence of movements of that equilibrium position. It could, though, be noted that according to the rational expectations and efficient markets literatures a rapid movement of price to its equilibrium value does not need substantial trading volume. The efficient market hypothesis appears to rule out volatility other than which arises from changes in 'fundamentals' with the market price incorporating all (publicly) available information including presumably knowledge on those 'fundamentals'. From the second tradition, in contrast, we would conclude that a greater volume of speculation would exacerbate volatility in that, when prices were generally believed to be rising, this would increase the demand for the currency, thereby exacerbating the rise in price. Hence the demand for a particular currency could be positively related to the rate of change of the value of that currency. A simple model which combines these two traditions on speculation can be readily outlined. In a floating exchange rate regime, on any day assume that the exchange rate adjusts to balance demand and supply on that day, that is, $d = m$ where d is the ratio of demand for domestic currency to the demand for foreign currency, and m the ratio of stock of domestic currency to the stock of foreign currency. Take s as the logarithm of the exchange rate (expressed in terms of units of domestic currency per unit of foreign currency). The relative demand for currency is taken as composed of four elements:

1. a trade related element (for simplicity we will ignore any lags) as a function of the level of the exchange rate: that is, $d_1(s)$ with the derivative of d_1 being positive (assuming Marshall–Lerner conditions are fulfilled);
2. stabilizing speculation under which the demand for currency depends on its current value relative to a view of the underlying 'equilibrium' rate (s^*), that is, $d_2(s - s^*)$ with the derivative of d_2 positive. We allow s^* to differ from the underlying equilibrium rate which would be the rate $s^\wedge$ as in $m = d_1(s^\wedge)$;
3. 'noise trading' or destabilizing speculation where the demand for the currency is related to the rate of change of the exchange rate on the basis of extrapolative expectations, that is, $d_3(s - s(-1))$. The derivative of d_3 is negative since when s is declining, the value of the domestic currency is rising, thereby increasing demand;
4. a random element which is the underlying source of fluctuations: the random term is labelled u below.

Then we have

$$d_1(s) + d_2(s - s^*) + d_3(s - s(-1)) + u = m$$

Linearise

$$a_1 s + b_1 + a_2(s - s^*) - a_3(s - s(-1)) = m - u$$
$$(a_1 + a_2 + a_3) s = m - b_1 - a_2 s^* - a_3 s(-1) - u$$

$s^\wedge$ would be given by $a_1 s^\wedge + b_1 = m$ $s = (m - b_1)/a_1$.
Then

$$(a_1 + a_2 - a_3) (s - s^\wedge) = a_2(s^* - s^\wedge) - a_3 (s(-1) - s^\wedge) - u$$
$$(a_1 + a_2 - a_3)^2 \operatorname{var} s = a_2^2 (s^* - s^\wedge)^2 + a_3^2 \operatorname{var} s(-1) + \operatorname{var} u$$

with the mean of $s(-1)$ equal to s.
Hence

$$((a_1 + a_2 - a_3)^2 - a_3^2)) \operatorname{var} s = a_2^2 (s^* - s^\wedge)^2 + \operatorname{var} u.$$

Clearly the variance of the exchange rate depends on the 'mistakes' of the stabilizing speculators over the equilibrium rate and the underlying random process. The values of a_1, a_2, a_3 depend on the elasticity of each of the first three components of demand and the relative weights to be assigned to each component. The first derivative of var s with respect to a_3 is positive. Hence, as may be expected, an increase in the relative importance of the 'noise trading' would increase the variance of the exchange rate.

Since it is clearly the case that a transactions tax has a much greater impact on short-term dealing than on long-term dealing (as illustrated below), such a tax could be expected to reduce short-term dealing, and hence reduce 'noise trading' and volatility. Figures from the BIS survey (as reported in Felix, 1996) suggest that around 80 per cent of foreign exchange turnover involves a round-trip of less than 7 days, and Felix and Sau (1996) (p. 248) make an estimate of 8.67 days as the weighted average duration. The transactions tax would particularly affect short-term deals, though we cannot associate short-term deals with necessarily generating volatility. Further, there may be links between short-term volatility and longer-term misalignments. For example, it is argued that 'evidence shows that a reduction of speculation in more normal times will less than the number of incidents of larger-scale speculative instability' (Griffiths-Jones, 1996, p. 144)

If speculation were stabilizing (which would hence result in prices displaying little more volatility than would be explained by movements in 'fundamentals'), then the first rationale for the transactions tax would fall. If we proceed on the basis that financial markets in general and the exchange markets in particular display a greater volatility that can be explained by reference to 'fundamentals', then the first rationale given above becomes an important component of the argument for a transactions tax.

One method of testing the information efficiency of a market has been to investigate the relationship between price changes in successive periods (which in the case of commodity, equity and exchange markets is often taken to be a day or less). The presumption is that if there is no significant correlation then 'news' is rapidly incorporated into the price. This would stand in some contrast to the 'rational bubbles' literature where there would be some presumption towards correlation from period to period. Data covering the period 1980–92 involving daily changes in the sterling–DM exchange rate, reveal some small correlation between daily changes in the exchange rate. Monthly data for the same period show more of a bubble effect in the dollar–yen exchange rate changes than is the case for the sterling–DM exchange rate changes, which is perhaps not surprising in that there were various official attempts to stabilize the sterling–DM but not the dollar–yen rate.

6.4   TAX RAISING POWERS

The tax raising potential of a transactions tax is considerable, to say the least. The most widely cited figures on turnover on the foreign exchange markets are summarized in Table 6.3. In April 1992, the gross daily turnover was estimated at over $1.3 trillion, which comes down to around $1.08 trillion when local double-counting is eliminated. This represented a growth of 50 per cent in three years. For April 1995, the figure had grown again by nearly 50 per cent to $1.57 trillion. After adjustments for cross-border double-counting and for gaps in data, the net daily turnover was estimated at $880 billion in 1992 and $1.25 trillion in 1995. The latter figure generates, on the basis of 240 business days, an annual turnover of $300 trillion. World trade for 1995 is a little over $5 trillion[6] suggesting a multiple of financial transactions relative to world trade of around 60.

The estimation of potential tax yield would clearly require estimates of the price-elasticity of the volume of foreign exchange transactions,

Table 6.3 Countries with the largest volume of trading in foreign
currency, 1992 and 1995[a]

I. Foreign exchange turnover

	Daily average foreign exchange turnover 1992 (US$bn)	% share	Daily average foreign exchange turnover 1995 (US$bn)	% share
UK	290.5	27	464.5	30
USA	166.9	16	244.4	16
Japan	120.2	11	161.3	10
Singapore	73.6	7	105.4	7
Switzerland	65.5	6	86.5	5
Hong Kong	60.3	6	90.2	6
Germany	55.0	5	76.2	5
France	33.3	3	58.0	4
Australia	29.0	3	39.5	3
All others	181.9		246.2	
Total of above	1076.2		1572.2	

II. Market segments, April 1992[b]

Market segment	Gross turnover (US$bn)	share %
Total	1353.7	100
of which:		
Spot market	659.5	49
Forwards	626.4	46
of which		
Outright	77.6	6
Swaps	547.1	40
Futures	9.5	1
Options	51.6	4

Notes:
[a] Net of local double-counting, but not adjusted for cross-border double-counting.
[b] Gross of both local and cross-border double-counting. Totals do not sum because of incomplete reporting of market segment breakdowns. The number of countries reporting disaggregated data varies from component to component: total 21, spot 20, outright forwards and swaps 12, futures 12, and options 17.
No adjustment for double-counting in futures and exchange-traded options.

Source: (Part I) BIS estimates as reported in Felix (1996);
(Part II) BIS (1993) Table IV, as reported in Mendez (1996).

and of the degree of tax avoidance and evasion which could be expected to be involved with some shift to untaxed transactions (for example, to countries which do not impose the tax) and also to non-reporting of transactions which should be subject to tax. The proportional significance of a transactions tax will vary greatly between different types of purchaser. For the tourist buying foreign exchange with a buy-sell spread of say 7 per cent and a transaction fee of 2 per cent, a 0.5 per cent tax would be of little significance. For the long term investor, a 0.5 per cent tax (1 per cent on a round trip transaction) represents an annualized cost of 0.1 per cent over 10 years. In contrast, for the short-term such a tax represents nearly 4000 per cent per annum on a one-day shift, and for those transacting large volumes the buy-sell spread and the current transactions costs are likely to be small. Mendez (1996) suggests a spread of 10 basis points for the publicly quoted markets and 3 to 4 basis points on the interbank market (basis point being one digit in the fourth decimal place of a foreign exchange price quotation). We would assume that the vast bulk of foreign exchange transactions fall into the latter rather than the former categories, and hence a transactions tax would have a substantial impact. If we take the 'price' of a round trip foreign exchange transaction to be the spread, then the imposition of a 0.5 per cent tax (equal to 1 per cent on the round trip) would amount to a very substantial price increase: on the basis of a 0.1 per cent spread, a tenfold increase. We would assume that the vast bulk of foreign exchange transactions fall into the latter rather than the former categories, and hence a transactions tax would have a substantial impact. At one extreme, the tax may have little effect on the volume of transactions but would have an enormous tax yield. The 1992 figures of $300 billion daily turnover in the UK would yield on the basis of a 0.5 per cent tax on transactions in the UK and unchanged volume would yield around £1 billion per day, and £240 billion per annum which is comparable to the total tax yield (cf. Kelly 1994, p. 230).

But the tax may have considerable effect on the volume of transactions, and obviously the tax yield is much reduced. In this case the tax would have achieved its objective of reducing the volume of transactions, with (it would be hoped) the benefit of reduced volatility. It would, though, seem quite possible that a 0.5 per cent tax could reduce financial flows to say one-tenth of their present volume (a unit elasticity in face of a ten-fold increase in the cost as indicated above) which still put the world-wide yield at $150 billion (in 1995). However a realization of the relative size of say a 0.5 per cent tax and the spreads has led to suggestions of a tax more of the order of 0.1 per cent. As indicated below, there are possible adverse effects of a transactions tax on the volume of international trade. These costs have to be weighed against the costs imposed by the taxes which could be replaced by the transactions tax.

D'Orville and Najman (1995) estimated the revenue from a transactions tax for 1992 at $140.1 billions for a tax of 0.25 per cent and $56.32 billions for a 0.1 per cent tax (as reported in Frankel, 1996, p. 60). However, Frankel (1996) argues that they have made a major mistake in these calculations:

> They have assumed, incorrectly, that only a portion of transactions carried out through foreign exchange brokers would be subject to the tax – about one-third of the total. The mistake probably arose from assuming that the term 'brokers' applies to all foreign exchange dealers or traders. In reality, the other two-thirds of transactions are handled directly by foreign exchange dealers at private banks, who would be subject to a Tobin tax every bit as much as brokers (p. 60).

D'Orville and Najman estimate a fall in volume of 20 per cent as a result of the imposition of a transactions tax.

Frankel (1996) suggests that an elasticity of 0.32 for transactions initiated by financial customers 'might not be a bad guess' (p. 62), but with no change in orders from exporters and importers. With an assumed doubling of transaction costs through the imposition of a 0.1 per cent tax, he suggests a fall in transactions from $376 billion to $346 billion per diem for transactions by financial customers. Further, it is assumed that the customer-to-transaction ratio rises from the current 0.31 to 0.5. The new volume of transactions would be $346/0.5 billion per diem (that is, $629 billion) which provides an annual revenue of $166 billion. Felix and Sau (1996) provide a range of estimates though starting with an assumption of considerable higher transaction costs (0.5 per cent and 1 per cent are used): their central estimates range between $205.5 billion and $267.6 billion for a 0.25 per cent tax in 1995.

We may conclude that revenue of the order of $200 billion could be generated through a modest transactions tax.

6.5   RESOURCE EFFECTS

A reduction of say half in the volume of foreign exchange transactions would also result in some significant resource savings. Frankel (1996, p. 61) suggests 'a typical transaction cost for foreign exchange might be 0.1 per cent' though much smaller for interdealer trading. As has been seen, Felix and Sau (1996) use the much higher figures of 0.5 per cent and 1.0 per cent for the transaction costs in their estimates of the yield from a transactions tax. But they also report that 'the quoted bid-ask spreads on trades of major currencies in the "wholesale" foreign exchange market over the electronic network are usually less than 0.1%. . . . The spreads are doubled for "retail" trades (less than $5 million) and can rise to more than 1.0% for small retail transactions' (p. 231). However, other figures on the bid-ask spread are much lower (noting that transaction costs are broader than the bid-ask spread). Kenen (1996) states that 'spreads in the wholesale market are well below 10 basis points [i.e. 0.1 per cent] for the major currencies' (p. 110). Hartmann (1996, Table IV.1) reports Reuters spreads for a wide range of bilateral exchange rates. For some of the major currencies, the quoted spreads reported are around 5 basis points (for example, US dollar–DM is 4.5, for Yen–US dollar 5.7 and US dollar–pound 4.6), though it is thought that traded spreads are smaller by a factor of two to three.

On the basis of the estimates given above on the volume of transactions, a figure of 0.05 per cent for transaction costs would suggest a total costs of $150 billion per annum (in 1995). This may suggest that if a transactions tax halved the volume of transactions, and assuming that the transaction costs reflect resource costs, then annual savings of the order of $75 billion (£15 billion) could be involved (that is, more than 6 per cent of UK GDP, and nearly 0.4 per cent of OECD GDP). This figure may be an over estimate if there are economies of scale in foreign exchange transactions and to the extent that the foreign exchange transactions which are reduced are concentrated amongst those which attract lower transaction costs (for example, in wholesale market).

Any resource saving has to be placed alongside the associated reduction in foreign exchange transactions. What are the gains from, say, a volume of foreign exchange transactions 60 times the volume of world trade to a volume, say, 20 or 30 times? Insofar as foreign exchange dealing (for speculative purposes) is a zero sum game, undertaken because of different expectations on interest rate and exchange rate movements, then a lower volume of transactions does not entail any costs (though there would be a redistribution of benefits and costs). It is argued that arbitrage through foreign exchange dealings brings about an equalization of interest rates (adjusted for expected exchange rate movements), and that a 'thicker' market would encourage a speedier return to equilibrium and to such an equalization of interest rates across countries. Assuming that such equalization brings a benefit, even then we do not know what volume of transactions would be required to bring it about. Indeed the theory of efficient markets would suggest that very few, if any, transactions would be required for any such equalization. Thus, if the foreign exchange market has elements which could be seen as efficient (with respect to use of information), then the current volumes of transactions would not be required in order for the exchange rate to be in line with 'fundamentals'. Trading in currencies does not occur for that reason alone (or indeed, no one would play the equivalent of the disinterested Walrasian auctioneer bringing the market into equilibrium), in order to establish the optimal amount of trading it would be necessary to establish the extent of foreign exchange required for international trade, direct and portfolio investment.

6.6 INCIDENCE AND DISTORTIONARY EFFECTS OF TRANSACTIONS TAX

The final incidence of the transactions tax is significant for at least three reasons:

- the extent to which the tax falls upon those involved in international trade or in long-term foreign investment will determine the degree to which the transactions tax reduces international trade and investment;
- the incidence of the tax will influence the impact on the level of aggregate demand;
- the distributional effects of the tax will clearly depend on the final incidence of that tax.

We would anticipate that the incidence of part of a transactions tax would be on the purchasers and on the suppliers of internationally traded goods and on those undertaking foreign investment. It could then be expected that there would be some diminution of trade and overseas investment, as discussed below. However, it could be expected that for those who are operating in foreign exchange markets for gain based on price movements, then the incidence of the tax could not be shifted on to others: for the obvious question is on to whom would they be able to shift the tax?

One common argument raised against the transactions tax relates to its possible distortionary effects. The argument is straightforward with a tax which leads in a competitive market to an equilibrium being established which involves lower quantity and fewer resources being allocated to that particular market. As Eichengreen and Wyplosz (1996) remark 'most economists are instinctively sceptical about taxing international financial transactions as a way to enhance the operation of the international monetary system. Holders of the union card are taught to prize the efficiency of the market and to regard intervention through taxation and controls as welfare reducing' (p. 15).

For the proposed transactions tax there are three points to be made in connection with this argument. First, as suggested above, the financial sector may be relatively lightly taxed, and the 'products' of the financial sector are generally not subject to either general sales or value added taxes nor to specific excise taxes and the like. This would mean that the imposition of a transactions tax may, in effect, be removing some distortions rather than imposing them. To the extent to which that view is accepted, then the introduction of a transactions tax would help to reduce the distortionary effect of the tax system.

Second, the distortionary nature of a tax arises from some potentially beneficial trades not taking place that would have otherwise happened. This leads us back to the question raised above, namely are there gains from the current volume of exchange transactions which would not arise with a substantially smaller volume? Some further doubt is cast on the distortionary argument by the observation that whilst the two parties to a foreign exchange trade may believe that they will gain from the trade (through a favourable price movement), both cannot do so in the outturn.

Third, the analysis of distortions is an equilibrium one and it is equilibrium trades which are discouraged. But there is a sense in which much of the trading in currency markets is disequilibrium trading in terms of seeking to take advantage of price changes.

Thus the conventional analysis of distortions does not apply to this situation, and if it is argued that the amount of 'noise trading' is excessive, then a tax is beneficial rather than distortionary.

6.7 TRADE EFFECTS

Holtham (1995) argues that proposals for a transactions tax 'could inhibit international financial investment or trade finance' (p. 237). The imposition of a transactions tax in itself would add to the costs of conducting international trade, and the likelihood is that trade would thereby be diminished. We could first note that the proposals of Harcourt (1995) would seek to exempt foreign exchange deals which were for these purposes:

> The taxation authorities would require that the turnovers of the foreign exchange dealers who pay tax in their countries be classified into three broad categories: foreign exchange bought and sold for purposes of trade (and consumption, for example, tourism) and for long-term investment either in securities or directly. (In so far as traders were concerned with the sale or purchase of commodities, spot or future, a case would have to be made by the tax-payers that these were to help production, or that they were legitimate sales, rather than for speculation.) This would leave a residual third category which would be mainly accounted for by speculative activities. Then the proportions of each category in total turnovers would be used to assess the total taxation paid on the profits of the dealers. There would be a much higher rate for the third category than for the first two, so that the larger was the amount of speculation which was financed by foreign exchange purchases or sales, the greater would be the taxation on the profits of the dealers. (Harcourt, 1995, p. 35)

We would though doubt the practicality of such exemptions. Any attempt to distinguish between transactions which come under speculation and non-speculative transactions as required for the differential tax treatment as suggested by Harcourt, will prove difficult in its implementation and in practice will prove impossible to enforce.

Goodhart (1996) argues that multiple exchanges take place through the banking sector as one bank seeks to balance its books through exchanges with other banks. This may be described as the 'hot potato' syndrome. The argument can then be put that a transactions tax would mean that each of the multiple transactions would be subject to tax, which in turn would in effect be passed back to the original customer: 'no one knows what the multiple involved in rebalancing inter-bank transactions actually is, and also that the sharply widening spread would make the market thinner, more expensive and at any rate in the very short run more volatile than now' (Goodhart, 1996, p. 93). The question is that since 'no one knows' what the multiple might be, it is rather difficult to assess the extent of the implications of Goodhart's remarks. Be that as it may, we would make three points on this. First, this provides the institutional detail which lies behind the volume of transactions being a large multiple of transactions required for trade and investment purposes. It would be surprising if something akin to the 'hot potato' syndrome did not apply given what we know about the volume of transactions. Second, each exchange transaction in the chain is subject to some transaction costs. Thus there are resource costs involved at present which would be reduced by a transactions tax. If, for example, the transactions tax doubled the transaction costs, then the effects would be much as we have already calculated. Third, a bank faced with a transactions tax is likely to reduce the extent to which it re-arranges its portfolio in terms of different currencies.

Davidson (1996) argues that a 0.5 per cent transactions tax would, in effect, represent a much larger tax on trade than would be immediately apparent. Davidson argues that

> a Tobin tax will stop speculation on expected relatively small movement in the exchange rate (similar to the differential encountered by arbitrageurs). The tax tends to have an equal or even significantly larger impact on stemming real international trade.... The Tobin tax creates additional permanent private costs (in excess of social costs) on real international trade (p. 8).

He argues that 'there is a rule of thumb that suggests that ... there are five normal hedging trade transactions in every final goods trade compared to two for every speculative flow in international finance' (pp. 11–12). Hence a transactions tax of 0.5 per cent would, in effect, involve a 2.5 per cent tax on trade. Assuming that the tax was fully passed onto consumers, it is clear that there could be a substantial impact on the volume of international trade. However, we would note that many have advocated a rather lower rate of taxation, that the multiple of 5 to 1 may be doubtful and some of the tax may be absorbed by producers rather than passed on to consumers.

Unfortunately Davidson does not cite any evidence for his figure of 5:1, and it is not clear whether it is five exchange transactions (of varying size) which precede final sale of goods or many transactions amounting to five times the value of the goods exchanged. It could be expected that in either case those involved in trade would seek to economise on exchange transactions in the face of a transactions tax. It can also be noted that much of international trade (of the order of 30 to 40 per cent) takes the form of shipment of goods (usually semi-finished) from one branch of a transnational corporation to another. Most of that trade can be financed by book-keeping entries rather than conversion of one currency into another. As such it would not bear a transactions tax.

Some back of the envelope calculations suggest that the direct effect on trade of a transactions tax would be less than 1 per cent. Even if a 0.1 per cent tax was effectively a 0.5 per cent tax, as Davidson would suggest, then only part would be borne by the consumers. The proportion of the tax borne by consumers (and hence that also borne by producers) depends on the relative elasticities of demand for traded goods and of supply of those goods. Assuming the elasticities are roughly equal, so that half of the tax is borne by consumers, and with a relatively high elasticity of demand for traded goods of 4, the direct effect on international trade would be 1 per cent. A high elasticity suggests that traded and non-traded goods are readily substituted for one another, and the welfare loss to consumer is minor.

In evaluating the overall balance of effects of a transactions tax on international trade, due consideration would need to be given to the effects of reduced volume of exchange transactions, of reduced volatility, enhanced independence of national economic policies and the probable stimulus to world-wide aggregate demand. These latter factors would stimulate international trade, and the overall net effect of a transactions tax on international trade cannot be readily predicted.

Holtham (1995) further argues that 'given the existence of a J-curve in the response of the current account to exchange rate changes, any exchange rate driven wholly or largely by the current account (the situation in the absence of capital flows), is subject to unstable oscillations. Some speculative capital flows are necessary for stability'

(p. 237). In the extreme case where the only foreign exchange dealings which occurred were those related to trade, then this argument may hold. At present, the general calculations is that the foreign exchange flows are of the order of 60 times those which would be necessary for financing international trade, from which we would infer that even after the imposition of a transactions tax foreign exchange flows would remain significantly in excess of those required to finance trade (perhaps of the order of 30 times).

6.8 DEVALUATIONS

A number of authors (for example, Davidson, 1996) have made the point that a transactions tax would have been virtually powerless to have inhibited movement out of the Mexican peso in late 1994. Kenen (1995) invokes the work of Eichengreen and Wyplosz (1993) when he argues that they 'have shown that a small transactions tax will not much affect the return on a long-term investment, but they have not shown that it can offset the gain expected from betting on a near-term devaluation' (p. 189). Eichengreen, Tobin and Wyplosz (1995) readily concede that point when they write that the transactions tax 'could not protect patent mis-valuations in exchange parities; speculators' gain from betting on inevitable near-term realignments would far exceed the tax costs' (p. 165). Eichengreen (1996) makes the same point as Davidson when he argues that there may be occasions when speculators may not be deterred by a Tobin tax. He notes that investors speculating on a 15 per cent devaluation would hardly be discouraged by a transactions tax of even 1 per cent. Eichengreen and Wyplosz (1996) argue, however, that in a crisis, the transaction tax could slow down the depletion of foreign exchange reserves and thus give the authorities some breathing space to negotiate orderly realignments.

The lessons from the peso crisis are not straightforward, basing our discussion here on Sachs *et al.* (1996). On the other hand, they argue that 'fundamentals cannot fully account for the December crisis' (p. 15) and 'the Mexican currency crisis, unlike many others in Latin America, was not the result of irresponsible fiscal behaviour' (p. 16). While this may support the general view underlying the Tobin tax proposal, namely that exchange rates are not driven by 'fundamentals', it may also support Davidson's contention that even a 1 per cent transactions tax is not going to be enough to inhibit movement out of a currency when there is the prospect of a large devaluation. But, on the other hand, Sachs *et al.* argue that 'the peso was somewhat overvalued and the current account deficit too large for comfort' and hence there was some requirement for a devaluation. López (1996) notes that 'in spite of the evidence of an increasing external imbalance, the economic crisis of December 1994 took almost everyone by surprise. Very few expected a serious disintegration of an economic strategy with such a good press' (p. 2) and that 'many students of the Mexican economy pointed out repeatedly, prior to the crisis, that the peso was becoming grossly overvalued and alerted the authorities to the dangers involved' (p. 24).

Throughout 1994, Tesobonos (short-term government bonds paid in pesos but indexed to the US dollar) increased from 6 per cent of the value of Mexican government debt in February 1994 to 50 per cent by the end of 1994 (IMF, 1995a). This vast increase of Tesobonos enabled Mexico to finance a current account deficit equivalent to 8 per cent of GDP. As their maturity date approached, however, speculation against the Mexican currency developed. The Mexican peso crisis could be read as the correction of a serious misalignment, and advocates of a transactions tax would not wish the re-alignment to occur (though they may regret that it had to come about through a crisis). But, equally, it could be argued that until December 1994, the financial markets had accepted an overvalued currency (on the criteria of the trade deficit).

We would not wish to argue that a transactions tax could or should prevent a change in the price of a currency in the context of severe misalignment. However, we would make two points. First, for a given set of expectations about the timing and extent of a devaluation, the presence of a transactions tax would tend to reduce the volume of transactions. Clearly those who would be close to the margin of being engaged in the sale of the currency concerned may be dissuaded from doing so by the transaction tax. It could also be noted that a flight from the currency under pressure would at least raise some tax. Second, the argument is applied to those cases where devaluation appears 'inevitable' and where there is a widely recognized serious misalignment. In retrospect, sterling's devaluation in September 1992 on its departure from the ERM looks 'inevitable' after a 'serious misalignment'.

What would be seen as the serious misalignment of currency values have arisen in the recent past in two quite distinct ways, namely within a flexible exchange rate regime and within a fixed exchange rate regime. There can be little doubt that the value of sterling was substantially over-valued in the early 1980s whilst the dollar was substantially over-valued in the mid-1980s. In both cases, the over-valuation arose under a flexible exchange rate regime, and is one aspect of the medium-term volatility of flexible exchange rates. If the transactions tax operated to successfully reduce the volatility of exchange rates, then an element of over-valuation would be removed.

The case with fixed exchange rates is, of course, rather different for then the over-valuation has arisen as a consequence of government decisions whether active (that is, in determining the rate at which a currency joins a fixed exchange rate club) or passive (that is, not devaluing in the face of relative price movements). It could be noted though that the over-valuation of sterling within the ERM came about through an over-valuation of sterling prior to entry into the ERM during an era of flexible exchange rates (though, of course, sterling had been shadowing the DM in the late 1980s). Almost by definition one would not wish to prevent or inhibit the rectification of mis-alignment: but are financial markets selective in only putting pressure on currencies with serious misaligned values? moreover, what is the role of financial markets in generating mis-aligned exchange rates?

6.9   FEASIBILITY ISSUES

Universality

Most advocates of a transactions tax recognize that it would have to be 'universal and uniform: it would have to apply to all jurisdictions, and the rate would have to be equalised across markets' (Eichengreen, Tobin and Wyplosz, 1995, p. 165). The tax

> would be an internationally agreed uniform tax, administered by each government over its own jurisdiction. Britain, for example, would be responsible for taxing all inter-currency transactions in Eurocurrency banks and brokers located in London, even when sterling was not involved. The tax proceeds could appropriately be paid into the IMF or World Bank. (Tobin, 1978, pp. 158)

While it is recognized that the tax could not be implemented in one country, the question does arise as to whether it would have to be universal in order to be effective. As Table 6.3 indicates, at present nine countries account for 84 per cent of foreign exchange transactions. A tax introduced in those nine countries plus a few others might be sufficient to provide a workable tax regime since, at least initially, this tax would capture the bulk of foreign exchange transactions. There may be ways of avoiding a shift of transactions to 'tax havens'. One possibility is to consider the transfer of funds to or from such location as taxable transactions at penalty rates. Thus the movement of say £1 million in sterling from the UK (assumed to be applying the tax) to a 'tax haven' (not applying the tax) would be subject to tax at a multiple of the transaction tax. Another possibility would be to tax at the site where the deal is made rather than at the site where the transactions occurs. Tobin (1996) considers both these possibilities as ways forward and maintains that the danger of transfers of funds to tax-free countries is vastly exaggerated. These are low-cost sites for financial dealing around the world which, however, do not seem to have driven activity away from the main financial centres such as London, New York and Tokyo. The imposition of a transactions tax would probably not affect them substantially either.

The widely recognized requirement that any transactions tax on foreign exchange dealing would have to be virtually universal may well be the most important practical obstacle to the implementation of a transactions tax. It would clearly require the co-operation of all countries with significant foreign exchange dealings within their borders (and, one might add, those with the potential to develop foreign exchange dealing centres), although there would be incentives (comparable to any cartel) for countries to apply a lower tax rate within their jurisdiction. One partial solution to this runs as follows: 'Enforcement of the universal tax would depend principally on major banks and on the jurisdictions that regulate them. The surveillance of national regulatory authorities could be the responsibility of a multilateral agency like the Bank of International Settlements or the International Monetary Fund' (Eichengreen, Tobin and Wyplosz, 1995, p. 165). We would suggest that given the IMF's considerable expertise in international financial markets it should be in a good position to undertake such a task. Furthermore, in view of the IMF's central objectives of the promotion of international monetary co-operation, to maintain exchange rate stability, and orderly exchange arrangements amongst its members, objectives which the Tobin transactions tax shares, strengthens the argument substantially that the IMF should play a central role in its implementation.

Defining the Currency Transaction

Garber and Taylor (1995) start from the view that 'a well-known feature of financial markets [is] that attempts to regulate them are frequently thwarted as market participants formulate sophisticated ways of avoiding the regulation' (Garber and Taylor, 1995, p. 173). They, then, argue that there are problems in defining the nature of the transactions to be taxed.

> The overall effect on gross volume, however, depends on how a foreign exchange transaction is defined by the regulators. If foreign exchange is defined as an exchange of one bank deposit for another in a different currency, gross trading in these claims will be effectively eliminated in favour of T-bill swaps in currencies with liquid (same day) T-bill markets. The swapped T-bills will be immediately sold for deposits. The foreign exchange market will shift to this form, no tax will be paid, and position taking will be unaffected. (p. 179)

Our view here would be that the appropriate definition of the transaction would be any transaction which involved the exchange of a financial asset denominated in one currency for a financial asset denominated in another currency. This was Tobin's initial suggestion when he wrote that

> the tax would apply to all purchases of financial instruments denominated in another currency – from currency and coin to equity securities. It would have to apply, I think, to all payments in one currency for goods, services, and real assets sold by a resident of another currency area. I don't intend to add even a small barrier to trade. But I see off-hand no other way to prevent financial transactions disguised as trade (Tobin, 1978, p. 159).

Other authors have made similar suggestions: for example the transactions to which the tax should apply 'include not only spot and forward transactions and foreign-exchange swaps (which combine the two) but also other contracts involving the obligation or right to exchange currencies at a future date. Thus the tax should cover spot transactions, outright forwards, foreign-exchange swaps, futures and options' (Akyüz and Cornford, 1995, p. 190). They acknowledge that if

> a tax on foreign exchange transactions were imposed, new instruments or contracts would be likely to be devised or existing ones to be adjusted with the objective of evading the tax or reducing the amounts paid. It would be difficult to design the tax in such a way that it contained safeguards against all such eventualities. A more reasonable approach would be to accept the need for alternation in the tax's design if the new or adjusted instruments seriously threaten its effectiveness. (p. 191)

Our discussion would lead us to occur with the following sentiments.

> While the implementation of the tax may appear complex, it is not any more complicated, probably much less so, than the detailed provisions of many existing taxes.... Indeed if the standards of what is feasible employed here had been used before imposing income tax or VAT they would never have been introduced! The dominant feature in the introduction of new taxation has always been the political will rather than administrative feasibility. (Grieve Smith, 1997)

Introduction of Tax

There can be little doubt that the introduction of a transactions tax would be a major economic and political development but at the same time it would have to be introduced on a 'big bang' basis for otherwise foreign exchange dealings would quickly move to those countries which were not applying the tax.

There can also be little doubt that a transactions tax would have a significant impact on world-wide aggregate demand. At this point we can do little more than speculate on the likely effects. Besides the obvious point that the aggregate demand effects will depend on the use to which the tax revenue is put and which, if any, other taxes are abolished. However, it is quite reasonable to think that a transactions tax would be levied on those with a low propensity to spend, and the redistribution would be towards those with a much higher propensity to spend. Hence aggregate demand may well increase. This would be added to by the effect of the enhanced capability of national governments to pursue economic policies which stimulate a higher level of demand. Below we discuss the uses of the revenue from a transactions tax, which again would add to aggregate demand.

To the extent to which the tax revenue does not lead (at the national and/or international level) to increased government expenditure, there would obviously be some reduction in budget deficits. Although we would not ourselves subscribe to this position, some would argue that the reduction in budget deficits would lead to a reduction in interest rates with some stimulus to investment.

Use of Revenue for a Transactions Tax

The application of an international tax would also raise questions of the allocation of the proceeds of the tax. A number of proposals have been put forward on the way to distribute the tax proceeds. To the extent that it is the IMF or World Bank who are the intermediate recipients, a further proposal may be to enhance the lending capabilities of these institutions especially to the third world counties which could embrace development and anti-pollution projects. Kaul and Langmore (1996) focus on three: the 'Agenda 21' action programme emanating from the 1992 UN Conference on Environment and Development which would cost $125 billion per annum in terms of external concessional financing alone; a poverty eradication programme as formulated at the World Summit for Social Development, 1995 at an additional external cost of $40 billion per annum; infrastructure and other needs which according to World Bank estimates would involve external concessional funding of around $20 billion per annum. These total $185 billion per annum, which is the same order of magnitude as many of the estimates of the revenue from the transactions tax as discussed above.

The workings of the tax could be reinforced by making the administration of a transactions tax to be a condition of membership of the IMF and the BIS though that may not be sufficient to prevent the growth of off-shore dealing since a small country would have so little to gain from membership of the IMF as compared with the potential revenue for the location of off-shore financial markets (though if the off-shore locations are competing on the basis of low or no tax, there is the question of how much revenue would be generated). It can also be asked whether the tax could be levied on the participants based on their location rather than on the basis of the location of the transaction. Thus a UK bank (for this purpose being one which is regulated by the Bank of England) would be subject to a tax on its foreign exchange transactions, wherever they are made.

Political Realities

The possible obstacles at a political level to the introduction of a transactions tax are well summarized in the following:

> The institution of a [transactions] tax would be vigorously opposed by many as an interference in the market mechanism, one that would make it more inefficient and dampen capital investment. It could be argued that volatility is not a result of speculation but rather of balance-of-payments problems and uncoordinated national monetary policies, and that so-called speculators actually include companies changing currencies to protect themselves against losses from a depreciation of their currency holdings. It could also be asserted that the market is now too large for any single private or public party to sway, and that the activities of speculators actually contribute to the liquidity of the market. In view of the above, it is probable that the proposed tax, in political and practical terms, would be a 'non-starter'. (Mendez, 1996, p. 500)

The practical aspects have been discussed above, but there are clear political obstacles to the introduction of a transactions tax.[7] Two obstacles stand out: namely the international co-ordination which would be required, and the political power of the financial sector.

There is widespread agreement that the tax would have to be implemented on a co-ordinated international basis: 'The Tobin tax would be introduced through an international agreement, giving it its global characteristic. But revenue collection would be a national responsibility. Tax yields would accrue on a country-by-country basis, raising the question of how much revenue each country would be likely to collect' (Kaul and Langmore, 1996, p. 257). It may not be necessary for there to be full agreement over the tax rate, though there would be strong pressures towards a degree of uniformity (and probably a requirement for a minimum rate to avoid competitive undercutting of the tax rate between countries). It is clear that there would be very considerable differences in the amount of tax collected in each country. Based on the current composition of foreign exchange dealings (cf. Table 6.3), the UK would collect near to 30 per cent of the total, USA 15.5 per cent, Japan 10 per cent, Singapore 6.6 per cent and Hong Kong 5.7 per cent. Part of the international agreement could clearly be that a proportion of the tax collected is paid over to an international body and/or used for agreed development and environmental purposes (in one way this would be comparable to the collection of value added tax in EU member countries with the equivalent of 1 per cent of turnover being handed on to the European Commission). Kaul and Langmore (1996, pp. 260–1) point out that a modest transactions tax would have a large impact on the national budgets in a few countries (notably the UK, the USA and Japan) if the tax revenue collected within the country were largely or wholly retained by that country (and in the case of the UK would be sufficient to eliminate the current deficit). Kaul and Langmore (1996, pp. 266–7) make some suggestions on how the revenues might be shared (for example, the percentage of tax raised by a country retained would vary between 80 and 100 per cent, depending on their level of income). The obvious difficulty which arises here is obtaining international agreement over the introduction and the rate of the tax when the revenue from the tax would be so unequally distributed across countries (and to the extent to which countries fear that their financial centres would be reduced in size, the costs also unequally distributed). Further, a substantial retention of revenue at the national level obviously reduces the funds available for international development and environmental purposes.

We would also expect that the economic and political influence of the financial markets would also be much reduced (indeed the imposition of such a tax would be a clear signal that the influence of the financial sector was in decline). The point should be made, though, that the high yield of UK securities transactions tax (imposed on the transfer of legal ownership of UK shares), known as stamp duty with £830 million yield in 1993, has been maintained for a number of years in one of the most sophisticated financial markets. It has not obviously met with any serious opposition from the sophisticated financial market nor have there been cries of tax evasion in a market where players are most likely to find mechanisms to evade such a tax.

6.10 CONCLUSIONS

We would suggest that the Tobin transactions tax is a feasible tax for raising substantial sums of taxation. It would substantially reduce the volume of currency transactions, with significant resource savings and the hope that it would diminish the volatility of exchange markets. Its introduction would face formidable political problems and its implementation would need to be carefully arranged. In this sense, we should conclude by suggesting that the Tobin tax by itself cannot perform miracles. It would seem more appropriate to use the tax as one of several policy instruments that could be deployed to discourage speculation or unsustainable short-term capital flows.

Notes

1. Bencivenga, Smith and Starr (1996) develop a formal model and show the conditions under which the Tobin tax would be justified.
2. A (weakly) efficient market is regarded as one in which public information is rapidly absorbed into the price. A test for such efficiency is whether there is a significant relationship between changes in price in consecutive periods of time.
3. For example, Wadhwani (1996) reports a purchasing power parity for sterling of 2.75 DM, a fundamental equilibrium exchange rate of 2.50 DM and a productivity-adjusted measure of purchasing power parity of 2.65 DM at a time when the actual exchange rate was around 2.30 DM.
4. There are many formal definitions of what a 'bubble' is, and an example of the variety can be found in the *Journal of Economic Perspectives*, **4** (2). In the same issue, though, Stiglitz (1990) offers an intuitive definition which suggests that 'if the reason the price is high today is *only* because investors believe that the selling price will be high tomorrow – when "fundamental" factors do not seem to justify such a price – then a bubble exists. At least in the short run, the high price of an asset is merited, because it yields a return (capital gain plus dividend) equal to that on alternative assets' (p. 13).
5. Testing for the presence of a bubble is not an easy task. The main difficulty appears to be how to separate bubble movements for those where the underlying 'fundamental' model is misspecified. The 1990 Symposium on 'bubbles' in the *Journal of Economic Perspectives* is a good example of attempts to tackle problems of this kind by reference to indirect evidence.
6. The figures are $ 5239.4 billion for exports but only $ 5124.3 billion for imports (Source: *International Financial Statistics*, June 1996).
7. It was widely reported at the time that the Canadian government gave verbal support for a Tobin tax at the 1995 Halifax summit.

References

Akyüz, Y. and A. Cornford (1995) 'International capital movements: some proposals for reform' in J. Michie and J. Grieve Smith (eds) *Managing the Global Economy* (Oxford University Press).

Bank for International Settlements (1993) *Central Bank Survey of Foreign Exchange Market Activity in April 1992* (Basle: BIS Monetary and Economic Department).

Bencivenga, V.R., B.D. Smith and R.M. Starr (1996) 'Equity markets, transactions costs and capital accumulation: an illustration', *World Bank Economic Review*, 4(2): 241–65.

Camerer, C. (1989) 'Bubbles and fads in asset prices', *Journal of Economic Surveys*, 3: 3–43.

Campbell, J.Y. and K. Froot (1994) 'International experiences with security transaction taxes', in J. Frankel (ed.) *The Internationalization of Equity Markets* (University of Chicago Press).

Davidson, P. (1996) 'Are grains of sand in the wheels of international finance sufficient to do the job when boulders are often required?', mimeo, University of Tennessee, Knoxville, June 1996, forthcoming in S. Dow and J. Hillard (eds) *Keynes, Knowledge and Uncertainty* (Aldershot: Edward Elgar).

De Grauwe, P. (1991) 'Towards European monetary union without the EMS', *Economic Policy*, 18.

Dornbusch, R. (1976) 'Expectations and exchange rate dynamics', *Journal of Political Economy*, 84.

Dornbusch, R. (1990), 'Exchange rate economics', in D.T. Llewelyn and C. Milner (eds) *Current Issues in International Monetary Economics* (London: Macmillan).

D'Orville, H. and D. Najman (1995) *Towards a New Multilateralism: Funding Global Priorities* (New York: United Nations).

Eichengreen, B. (1991) 'Trends and cycles in foreign lending', in H. Siebert (ed.) *Capital Flows in the World Economy* (Tübingen: Mohr).

Eichengreen, B. (1996) 'The Tobin tax: what have we learned?', in M.U. Haq, I. Kaul and I. Grunberg (eds) *The Tobin Tax: Coping with Financial Volatility* (Oxford University Press).

Eichengreen, B. and P. Lindert (eds) (1989) *The International Debt Crisis in Historical Perspective* (Cambridge, Mass.: MIT Press).

Eichengreen, B., J. Tobin and G. Wyplosz (1995) 'Two cases for sand in the wheels of international finance', *Economic Journal*, 105: 162–72.

Eichengreen, B. and C. Wyplosz (1993) 'The unstable EMS', *Brookings Papers on Economic Activity*, 1: 51–145.

Eichengreen, B. and C. Wyplosz (1996) 'Taxing international financial transactions to enhance the operation of the international monetary system', in M.U. Haq, I. Kaul and I. Grunberg (eds) *The Tobin Tax: Coping with Financial Volatility* (Oxford University Press).

Felix, D. (1996) Statistical appendix to M.U. Haq, I. Kaul and I. Grunberg (eds) *The Tobin Tax: Coping with Financial Volatility* (Oxford University Press).

Felix, D. and R. Sau (1996) 'On the revenue potential and phasing in of the Tobin tax', in M.U. Haq, I. Kaul and I. Grunberg (eds) *The Tobin Tax: Coping with Financial Volatility* (Oxford University Press).

Folkerts-Landau, D. and T. Ito (1995) *International Capital Markets: Developments, Prospects and Policy Issues* (Washington DC: International Monetary Fund).

Frankel, J. (1996) 'How well do foreign exchange markets work: might a Tobin tax help?', in M.U. Haq, I. Kaul and I. Grunberg (eds) *The Tobin Tax: Coping with Financial Volatility* (Oxford University Press).

Frankel, J. and S-J. Wei (1995) 'Regionalization of world trade and currencies: economics and politics', in J. Frankel (ed.) *The Regionalization of the World Economy* (University of Chicago Press).

Friedman, M. (1953) 'The case for flexible exchange rates', in *Essays in Positive Economics* (University of Chicago Press).

Gagnon, J.E. (1993), 'Exchange rate variability and the level of international trade', *Journal of International Economics*, 34: 269–87.

Garber, P. and M.P. Taylor (1995), 'Sands in the wheels of foreign exchange markets: a sceptical note', *Economic Journal*, 105: 173–80.

Goldstein, M. (1995) *The Exchange Rate System and the IMF: A Modest Agenda*, Policy Analyses in International Economics no. 39 (Washington, DC: Institute for International Economics).

Goodhart, C.A. (1996), 'Discussant to Professor J. Tobin', *Economic Systems with Journal of International and Comparative Economics*, 20: 91–5.

Grieve Smith, J. (1997) 'Exchange rate instability and the Tobin tax: review article', *Cambridge Journal of Economics*, 21(6) November: 745–52.

Griffiths-Jones, S. (1996) 'Institutional arrangements for a tax on international currency transactions', in M.U. Haq, I. Kaul and I. Grunberg (eds) *The Tobin Tax: Coping with Financial Volatility* (Oxford University Press).

Haq, M.U., I. Kaul and I. Grunberg (eds) (1996) *The Tobin Tax: Coping with Financial Volatility* (Oxford University Press).

Harcourt, G.C. (1995), 'A "modest proposal" for taming speculators and putting the world on course to prosperity', in G.C. Harcourt, *Capitalism, Socialism and Post-Keynesianism* (Aldershot: Edward Elgar) ch. 3 (originally published in *Economic and Political Weekly* 29(28): 2490–92, September 1994).

Hartmann, P. (1996) 'Do Reuters spreads reflect currencies' differences in global trading volumes?', London School of Economics, mimeo.

Holtham, G. (1995) 'Managing the exchange rate system', in J. Michie and J. Grieve Smith (eds) *Managing the Global Economy* (Oxford University Press).

International Monetary Fund (IMF) (1995a) *International Capital Markets: Developments, Prospects and Policy Issues* (Washington, DC: IMF).

International Monetary Fund (IMF) (1995b) *World Economic Outlook*, May (Washington, DC: IMF).

Isard, P. (1995) *Exchange Rate Economics* (Cambridge University Press).

Kaul, I. and J. Langmore (1996) 'Potential uses of the revenue from a Tobin tax', in M.U. Haq, I. Kaul and I. Grunberg (eds) *The Tobin Tax: Coping with Financial Volatility* (Oxford University Press).

Kelly, R. (1993), 'Taxing the speculator: the route to Forex stability', Fabian Discussion Paper, no. 15.

Kelly, R. (1994) 'A framework for European exchange rates in the 1990s', in J. Michie and J. Grieve-Smith (eds) *Unemployment in Europe* (London: Academic).

Kenen, P.B. (1995), 'Capital controls, the EMS and EMU', *Economic Journal*, **105**: 181–92.

Kenen, P.B. (1996) 'The feasibility of taxing foreign exchange transactions', in M.U. Haq, I. Kaul and I. Grunberg (eds) *The Tobin Tax: Coping with Financial Volatility* (Oxford University Press).

Keynes, J.M. (1936) *The General Theory of Employment, Interest and Money* (London: Macmillan).

Keynes, J.M. (1980), *The Collected Writings of John Maynard Keynes*, vol. VI, *A Treatise on Money*: 2, 'The Applied Theory of Money' (London: Macmillan).

Kindleberger, C. (1978) *Monies, Panics and Crashes* (New York: Norton).

Kirman, A. (1995) 'The behaviour of the foreign exchange market', *Bank of England Quarterly Bulletin*, **35**(3): 286–93.

Krugman, P. (1989a) 'The case for stabilizing exchange rates', *Oxford Review of Economic Policy*, **5**.

Krugman, P. (1989b) *Exchange Rate Instability* (Cambridge, Mass.: MIT Press).

López, J. (1996) 'Mexico's crisis: alternative explanations', mimeo.

Mendez, R.P. (1996) 'Harnessing the global foreign currency market: proposal for a foreign currency exchange (FXE)', *Review of International Policy Economy*, **3**: 498–12.

Mussa, M. (1986) 'Nominal exchange rate regimes and the behavior of real exchange rates: evidence and implications', *Carnegie–Rochester Conference Series on Public Policy*, **25**: 117–214.

Neuburger, H. and M. Sawyer (1990) 'Macroeconomic policies and inflation' in K. Cowling and R. Sugden (eds) *A New Economic Policy for Britain: Essays on the Development of Industry* (Manchester University Press).

OECD (Organization for Economic Co-operation and Development) (1995) *Revenue Statistics 1995* (Paris: OECD).

Rogoff, K. (1996) 'The purchasing power parity puzzle', *Journal of Economic Literature*, **34**(2): 647–68.

Rose, A. (1994) 'Are exchange rates macroeconomic phenomena?', *Federal Reserve Bank of San Francisco Review*, **1**: 19–30.

Sachs, J., A. Tornell and A. Velasco (1996) 'The collapse of the Mexican peso: what have we learned?', *Economic Policy*, **22** (April).

Sayer, S. (1992) 'The city, power and economic policy in Britain', *International Review of Applied Economics*, **6**.

Shiller, R.J. (1981) 'Do stock prices move too much to be justified by subsequent changes in dividends', *American Economic Review*, **71**:421–35.

Shiller, R.J. (1984) 'Stock prices and social dynamics', *Brookings Papers on Economic Activity*, **2**: 457–98.

Shiller, R.J. (1989) *Market Volatility* (Cambridge, Mass.: MIT Press).

Shiller, R.J. (1990) 'Speculative prices and popular models', *Journal of Economic Perspectives*, **4**(2): 55–66.

Shleifer, A. and L. Summers (1990), 'The noise trader approach to finance', *Journal of Economic Perspectives*, 4(2): 19–33.

Spahn, P.B. (1995) *International Financial Flows and Transactions Taxes: Surveys and Options* (Washington, DC: International Monetary Fund).

Stiglitz, J. (1989) 'Using tax policy to curb speculative short-term trading', *Journal of Financial Services Research*, 3: 101–15.

Stiglitz, J. (1990) 'Symposium on bubbles', *Journal of Economic Perspectives*, 4(2): 13–17.

Stiglitz, J. and A. Weiss (1981) 'Credit rationing in markets with imperfect information', *American Economic Review*, 71 (June): 393–410.

Summers, L. and V.P. Summers (1989) 'When financial markets work too well: a cautious case for a securities transactions tax', *Journal of Financial Services Research*, 3: 163–88.

Tobin, J. (1966) 'Adjustment responsibilities of surplus and deficit countries', in W. Fellner, F. Machlup and R. Triffin (eds) *Maintaining and Restoring Balance in International Payments* (Princeton University Press).

Tobin, J. (1974) 'The new economics one decade older', The Eliot Janeway Lectures on Historical Economics in Honour of Joseph Schumpeter, 1972 (Princeton University Press).

Tobin, J. (1978) 'A proposal for international monetary reform', *Eastern Economic Journal*, 4(3–4): 153–9 (reprinted in J. Tobin, *Essays in Economics: Theory and Policy* (Cambridge, Mass.: MIT Press)).

Tobin, J. (1994a) 'Speculators' tax', *New Economy*, 1(2) (an earlier version appeared in *Greek Economic Review*, March 1993).

Tobin, J. (1994b) 'A tax on international currency transactions', in United Nations, *Human Development Report, 1994* (New York: United Nations).

Tobin, J. (1996), 'Prologue', in M.U. Haq, I. Kaul and I. Grunberg (eds) *The Tobin Tax: Coping with Financial Volatility* (Oxford University Press).

United Nations Conference on Trade and Development (UNCTAD) (1995) *Trade and Development Report, 1995* (New York and Geneva: United Nations).

UNDP (United Nations Development Programme) (1994) *Human Development Report 1994* (New York and Oxford: Oxford University Press).

Wadhwani, S. (1996) 'Sterling work for Labour', *New Economy*, 3(3).

Index